PAPER VOICES

PAPER VOICES

The Popular Press and Social Change
1935–1965

by

A. C. H. SMITH

with
Elizabeth Immirzi
and
Trevor Blackwell

With an Introduction by
Stuart Hall

ROWMAN AND LITTLEFIELD
TOTOWA, NEW JERSEY

First published in the United States 1975
by Rowman and Littlefield, Totowa, N.J.

Library of Congress Cataloging in Publication Data

Smith, Anthony Charles H.
    Paper voices.

    Bibliography: p.
    Includes index.
        1.   Daily express, London.   2. Daily mirror, London.
I.   Immirzi, Elizabeth, joint author.   II.   Blackwell,
Trevor, joint author.   III.   Title.
PN5129.L7D277   1975   072'.1   74-28146
ISBN 0-87471-568-7

Printed in Great Britain by
Cox & Wyman Ltd,
London, Fakenham and Reading

CONTENTS

The readers of the penny newspaper clearly find in it something that satisfies their reading needs. They find a brightly coloured kaleidoscopic picture of the world day by day. They find exciting incidents at home and abroad; they find pathos and tragedy mixed with sentiment and comedy; they find personal gossip about the great and notorious and about people in the news who are neither great nor notorious but have caught the popular imagination for the moment; they find well-produced photographs of people and places. Great affairs of national or international importance may not always get the space and the dispassionate treatment that is their due, but they are not neglected, nor are serious features lacking, even if the lighter predominate.

Report of the Royal Commission on the Press, 1948.

You see, the main mistake people make concerning the freedom of the press is to think that it is a right belonging to journalists. But this is a fallacy. It's a right belonging to the reader of the newspaper. It is the people working in offices, the people working in factories, who have a right to know what's happening, a right to draw their own conclusions. As a direct consequence of this, obviously, journalists should be allowed to express themselves freely. But that's only because they have to inform the people constantly. And the best way to do so is to let the people talk to the people.

Jean-Paul Sartre, interview with Nina Sutton,
The Guardian, 10 March 1973.

PREFACE

This study was financed by the Joseph Rowntree Memorial Trust, and undertaken at the Centre for Contemporary Cultural Studies, University of Birmingham, by Elizabeth Immirzi, Trevor Blackwell and myself. Our research report, *The Popular Press and Social Change, 1935–1965*, was published in a limited edition by the Centre in 1970. For the account now published as *Paper Voices* I have drawn most of my material from the earlier, collaborative project.

Professor Richard Hoggart, then Director of the Centre, and Stuart Hall, then Deputy Director, were closely associated with all stages of the research. Particular contributions to the study written by Stuart Hall and by Alan Shuttleworth have been acknowledged where they appear in the text.

The project was assisted by the criticism and advice of Professor Rolf Myersohn, Professor Douglas Johnson and Jay G. Blumler, by the typing of Joan Goode, and the secretarial help of Felicity Reeve.

The research would not have been possible without copyright clearance from the *Daily Express* and *Daily Mirror* for photocopying of files held at the British Museum Newspaper Library, Colindale; nor could the study have been published without their permission to quote extensively from their pages. To each request, both newspapers readily gave their agreement.

A.C.H.S

ᴀ*

I

INTRODUCTION[1]

THE project had two main purposes: to examine how the popular press interprets social change to its readers; and to explore and develop methods of close analysis as a contribution to the general field of cultural studies.

*   *   *

Our starting-point was the assumption that at all times, but especially in periods of rapid social change, the press performs a significant role as a social educator. By its consistent reporting and comment about people and events, the press reflects changing patterns of life in a society. More significantly, by its selectivity, emphasis, treatment and presentation, the press interprets that process of social change. What interested us most was this active process of interpretation.

The daily newspaper is governed by the rhythm of day-to-day events. The paper must appear fresh every day, giving dramatic coverage to urgent events. In this highly competitive field, the survival of a newspaper depends, to some degree, on its being first in the field with the 'fullest' possible coverage, with reports and comment which are later and newer than those contained in any of its rivals. Yesterday's news is stale, unless a new development has taken place, or a new angle can be found to give the item another lease of life. Even the best news stories have only a brief half-life in the daily press. The emphasis, then, is on immediacy, topicality, the dramatic, which give the daily newspaper its characteristic aspect of radical discontinuity. News stories break and disappear with indecent speed: one story is dropped between editions, or downgraded in importance, to give space to another.

But the air of immediacy is deceptive. Newspapers do not come absolutely fresh and open to news. They are already in a complex relationship with a body of regular readers. There is already in existence a strong, continuous practice which, by traditions and routines, defines what constitutes 'news', how to get it, how it should be presented, which is the hottest story. Individual items fit in with the longer preoccupations of a newspaper, and these

1 The Introduction is drawn from a longer one written by Stuart Hall for the research report published by the University of Birmingham, 1970.

preoccupations differ from one paper to another: a *Guardian* scoop is not necessarily the same as a scoop for the *Mirror* or the *Express*. As well as the immediate response to the news-gathering process, any newspaper must have a sense of the continuing areas of interest in the society it serves: a news item therefore takes its place and significance in an existing structure of awareness which frames events, changing at a slower pace than the sweep of events across the headlines suggests.

The crucial question, then, seemed to be this: when dealing with so complex a process as historical and social change, what already available stock of meanings was brought to bear by the newspaper so as to make that process intelligible to its readers? Are there core-values in a newspaper which provide its staff and its readers with a coherent, if not consistent, scheme of interpretation? Do these core-meanings change over time? And, if so, in response to what events?

Our first task was to select the papers for close study. We decided to take the 'popular' rather than the 'quality' press as the main focus. From this point of view, the *Mirror* and the *Express* virtually chose themselves. The time-scale for the project, from the Second World War to the mid-1960s, was the period in which these two papers established an unchallenged command over the daily newspaper reading public in terms of circulation. Within the field of mass circulation newspaper publishing, the *Express* and the *Mirror* provided us with striking contrasts, distinctive personalities and styles. They occupy opposed positions in the party-political spectrum. Each has a circulation spread through the social pyramid, though the *Mirror* has a massive readership in the CD categories which the *Express* does not match, and the *Express* has a spread throughout the class structure which no other daily newspaper commands. On political grounds alone, the *Sketch* might have seemed a more obvious match for the *Mirror*: but the gap between the two in terms of circulation was too wide. On the same grounds, neither the *Herald*, nor its successor, the *Sun*, nor the *Mail*, nor, before its decease, the *News Chronicle* could be considered a true match for the *Express*.

The time-scale for the project also presented us with few problems. Our project could not attempt a sustained chronological account of three decades; yet, for purposes of comparison, we wanted a period long and varied enough to enable us to test the response of the press to historical change *in depth*. The period from the war to the mid-1960s was a dramatic one in recent English social history—from slump and depression into the crisis of the war, to 'affluence' in the '50s and the 'permissive society' of the '60s. In addition, the period was punctuated by crucial mid-decade elections, in 1945, 1955 and 1964.

Since a close study of all live issues in that period was not possible, we had to choose lines of methodical enquiry, cuts into live material, which, though not exhaustive, were central enough to permit general conclusions to be drawn from them. The first was political, based on a selection of the newspapers from the middle years of each decade, focusing especially on the handling of politics under the pressure of a General Election. The intention was not simply to document the known political bias of each newspaper, but to try to get behind the overt political attitudes and reach underlying assumptions, in each newspaper, about the political process. What changes in popular political consciousness did each seem to assume in its readership? What were the changing ways in which newspapers spoke to their readers about politics? How did they seek to wield political influence?

Our second theme was more social in emphasis. It centred on the treatment in the press of changing 'styles of life' in society at large. Here, we took as our starting point the familiar contrast between 'then' and 'now' with reference to the spread of 'affluence' in the post-war period. We knew that 'affluence' was a controversial subject—that it had provided for British society a convenient, perhaps too neat and compressed, image for a complex process of social change. At the same time, we found it convenient to take this image, to start with, at its face value. Using 'affluence' as our way of cutting into the material, then, what picture of social change in the period emerged from our study of the two newspapers? How did the press interpret and define social change? What competing models of society were mediated by the press?

The political theme touched newspapers at the point where they intersected directly with public affairs. It enabled us to look at the more manifest purposes of the press—the coverage of events and personalities, the images of political parties, the whole business of electioneering, the expression and shaping of public opinion. In our second theme we hoped to catch the newspapers responding to subtle changes in public consciousness and in the culture. Elections tend to make shapes for themselves, somewhat independently of the press and media. But affluence needed to be shaped—by the press and the media, and in public debate—in order to be understood at all. Here, we tried to catch the press *responding* to new, complicated social forces, 'working harder' to represent them in swift, commanding images or myths, moving with the culture—often piecemeal, unconvincingly.

What we found does not yield a comprehensive picture of the

popular press in three decades of social change. But it does seem to us to clarify the nature of the relationship between the press and society. Our intention, broadly speaking, was to enable us, and later researchers, to pose the essential questions about this relationship in fuller, more complex and refined terms than is possible within the available clichés of influence, bias and effect.

*　　*　　*

Berelson, one of the fathers of content analysis in the social-science sense of the term, once observed that the crucial question is to know when, and when not, to count. The observation is eminently wise—though clearly it can be adapted to support quite different strategies. Those who believe that evidence is not hard until it is quantifiable will assent to Berelson's dictum—and count wherever possible: those who have an intrinsic sense that the type of evidence required is not quantifiable, will invoke Berelson's motto at every turn. The problem cannot be solved in this way.

In this study, we have tried to count and quantify where, and *only* where, it seemed relevant and economic to do so. When the distribution of content, or the relative weight of editorial attention and emphasis was in question; or where (as in the war years) restrictions on newsprint made the paper's choice of whether, say, to carry heavy correspondence columns or not a significant one; or where we wanted to know how much political coverage of the 1945 General Election turned out to be devoted to Churchill's country-wide tours —it seemed appropriate to summarise the findings in very simple quantifiable terms. But no strict classification scheme was devised and no objective content categories established for the purpose of a massive inventory of the newspapers. The type of evidence which would support or disprove the initial hypotheses of the study seemed to us not graspable in these terms.

Content analysis is at its strongest where *manifest content* is being analysed, and where the verifiability of any proposition with respect to content has to be supported by 'objective' criteria. Berelson himself has remarked that:

> content analysis is ordinarily limited to the manifest content of the communication and is not normally done directly in terms of latent intention which the content may express . . . Strictly speaking, content analysis proceeds in terms of what-is-said, and not in terms of why-the-content-is-like-that . . .[2]

2 Bernard Berelson, *Content Analysis in Communications Research*, Free Press, Glencoe, 1952.

Literary-critical, linguistic and stylistic methods of analysis are, by contrast, more useful in penetrating the latent meanings of a text, and they preserve something of the complexity of language and connotation which has to be sacrificed in content analysis in order to achieve high validation.

Both methods are based on a long preliminary soak, a submission by the analyst to the mass of his material: where they differ is that content analysis uses this process of soaking oneself to define the categories and build a code (based on an intuitive sense of where the main clusters occur), whereas literary, stylistic and linguistic analysis uses the preliminary reading to select representative examples which can be more intensively analysed. The error is to assume that because content analysis uses precise criteria for coding evidence it is therefore objective in the literal sense of the term: and because literary/linguistic analysis steers clear of code-building it is merely intuitive and unreliable. Literary/linguistic types of analysis also employ evidence: they point, in detail, to the text on which an interpretation of latent meaning is based; they indicate more briefly the fuller supporting or contextual evidence which lies to hand; they take into account material which modifies or disproves the hypotheses which are emerging; and they *should* (they do not always) indicate in detail why one rather than another reading of the material seems to the analyst the most plausible way of understanding it. Content analysis assumes repetition—the pile-up of material under one of the categories—to be the most useful indicator of significance.

Literary/linguistic and stylistic analysis also employs recurrence as one critical dimension of significance, though these recurring patterns may not be expressed in quantifiable terms. The analyst learns to 'hear' the same underlying appeals, the same 'notes', being sounded again and again in different passages and contexts. These recurring patterns are taken as pointers to latent meanings from which inferences as to the source can be drawn. But the literary/linguistic analyst has another string to his bow: namely, strategies for noting and taking account of emphasis. Position, placing, treatment, tone, stylistic intensification, striking imagery, etc., are all ways of registering emphasis. The really significant item may not be the one which continually recurs, but the one which stands out as an exception from the general pattern—but which is *also* given, in its exceptional context, the greatest weight.

The analysis of language and rhetoric, of style and presentation, was therefore chosen as the main method of the study in preference to more 'objective' approaches. In part, we wanted to examine how far these traditional methods of criticism could be adapted to the

study of social meanings in a popular medium. But the more forceful considerations related to the angle from which we approached
our material. The intention throughout has been to adopt procedures
which would enable us to get behind the broad distribution of
manifest content to the latent, implicit patterns and emphases. We
wanted to bring to light, not the direct and explicit political or
social appeals the newspapers made, but the structures of meanings
and the configurations of feeling on which this public rhetoric is
based. We wanted to know what image of the readers the newspaper
was taking for granted when it assumed it could write *in that way*
about politics and society. We wanted to know what image of the
society supported the particular treatment given to any set of topics.
We wanted to know how such assumptions came to be formed—in
response to what historical and social circumstances: and how,
through time, they were changed or adapted. What concerned us
was, precisely, the question given the lesser prominence in Berelson's
paradigm: 'why-the-content-is-like-that'. Our purpose was, where
possible, to uncover the unnoticed, perhaps unconscious, social framework of reference which *shaped* the manifest content of a newspaper
over relatively long periods of time.

Our strategy, therefore, reversed the traditional emphases of mass
communications research. Such studies, typically, concentrate on
the inventory of daily content, on overt appeals, opinions and
biases, treating underlying meaning-structures 'as, essentially, the
residues of long habitual practice. Our study was based on the
initial hypothesis that, once such implicit patterns were brought to
light, we would see that they exerted a shaping force over the treatment, on any particular day, of the events and personalities in the
news. We suggest that, alongside any day's 'news', there is a continuous and evolving *definition of what constitutes news* at any significant
historical moment. Naturally, such an analysis must begin with
manifest content and rhetoric, but it must find ways of moving
through and beyond that to the social foundations of the rhetoric:
an investigation, as Umberto Eco describes it, 'into the reciprocal
relations of a rhetoric and an ideology (both seen as "cultural"
phenomena and so limited by historical and social implications)'.[3]

We adopted the practice of giving as much of the evidence in its
own terms as we could manage: so that the reader can see for himself
how a particular interpretation has been arrived at, and also check
the reading offered against the material and offer counter-inter-
pretations where they seem appropriate. This accounts, in part, for

3 Umberto Eco, 'Rhetoric and Ideology in Eugene Sue's "Les Mys-
tères de Paris"', in *International Social Science Journal*, vol. XIX, No. 4 1967.

what may seem the over-insistent documentation of the study, the length of the quotations offered, and the fullness of the supporting evidence, since the texts studied will not be readily available to most readers.

Newspapers represent the 'marketable commodities' in an industrial and technical complex which is highly capitalized, and competitive. A full study of the press must take into account, at one end of the spectrum, the technical and social organization of the newspaper industry; and, at the other end, the readers who buy, read, use and discard 'the product'. The flow of news, from news-gatherers to readers, is a highly organized and institutionalized social process: a process of 'cultural production and consumption'.

Our study, deliberately, concentrates on only *one* aspect of this exchange—though we ourselves would argue that the study is not completed until the social product has been set back within, and interpreted in the light of, its structural position in this process of cultural production. We began with the least studied element—the contents and forms of the press, treated as privileged modes of communication in their own right. Here a necessary distinction must be drawn. It was not the purpose of this study to rank or judge the style of the *Express* or *Mirror* in literary terms. While certain evaluations could not be avoided, 'qualitative measures' were used, not—as is traditional in the literary-critical approach—to enforce a critical judgement, but to establish and support a reading of the material in terms of its social and historical meaning. Both kinds of approach are evaluative, but they point in different directions. It did not seem to us any longer right to retain, separate from the study of meaning, a reserved area for the analysis of literary/aesthetic values *per se*. Our intention here was to integrate the study of style, language, expression and rhetoric directly into the study of social meaning itself.

On the one hand, against the main weight of sociological practice, we approached the newspaper as a structure of meanings, rather than as a channel for the transmission and reception of news. Our study, therefore, treated newspapers as *texts*: literary and visual constructs, employing symbolic means, shaped by rules, conventions and traditions intrinsic to the use of language in its widest sense. On the other hand, we isolated this 'moment' in the analysis expressly in order to make, from the heart of the linguistic/stylistic analysis of the text, social and historical inferences and interpretations.

Newspapers are not simply noisy channels which connect one end of an information exchange with another. They employ verbal,

visual and typographic means for 'making events and people in the
news signify' for their readers. Every newspaper is a structure of
meanings in linguistic and visual form. It is a *discourse*. All newspapers
have distinctive rhetorics, ways of organizing the elements into a
coherent whole, styles of presentation. These represent so many ways
of reducing the formlessness of events to that socially-shaped,
historically-contingent product we call 'news'—for potentially,
every event on any day in the whole world is 'news'. The patterns of
meanings imposed on events, the logics of arrangement and presentation, are not given in the raw material: even when events have
a meaning of their own, those meanings are modified, and sometimes
transformed, when they enter an already formed discourse or
linguistic 'space'. Each style—whether of an individual writer or a
newspaper—is a system of meaningful choices, and these choices are
'epistemic': they are clues to the epistemology of those who produce
and employ them. Raymond Williams has made the connections
between structure, audience and style quite precise:

> What would happen, for example, if *The Times* or the *Guardian*
> headlined their correspondence columns 'You Write' or
> 'You're Telling Us'? It is a simple enough check: we know
> whether we have written and told them or not. But 'you'
> within a real community of interest is still specific, and the
> impersonality of 'Reader's Letters' is then a form of politeness.
> 'You' in the modern popular paper, on the other hand, means
> everyone who is not us: we who are writing the paper for 'you'
> out there. There are often blurred edges, but the line between
> those papers which assume quite different relationships—
> readers seen as consumers, as a market or potential market—
> is not too difficult to draw, and is usually directly visible in
> layout and style.[4]

Newspapers employ a variety of ways of distributing 'the news'
throughout their pages. They construct the news within the grid of
existing 'common-sense' categories. Over time, these categories
become convenient ways of pigeon-holing the data and generate
distinctive idioms of their own. By situating an event within one or
another of these categories, a newspaper signifies to its readers where
it considers the event to 'belong', in what context it is to be understood. The traditional newspaper categories—front-page news story,
feature, woman's page, gossip, sport, leader column—represent on-

4 Raymond Williams, 'Radical and/or Respectable', in *The Press We
Deserve*, ed. Boston, Routledge & Kegan Paul, 1970.

going schemes of interpretation. They are intended to awaken in the reader contexts of awareness,[5] appropriate referential associations. These are the habitual and inherited 'native schemes of classification' of the press as a discourse in our culture. Thus some items clearly 'belong' to the sports page: and if a sports item appears on a news page, it is because the newspaper has judged (and expects its readers to agree) that one context has prevailed over another. The banning of South Africa by the International Lawn Tennis Association is a hard news (front page) item, and could lead on to feature and leader column treatment (middle pages), though its *topic* is specifically sport (back pages), because its *political* context has been *judged more significant* than its sport context. Newspaper categories are, by now, so traditional and routine that we have to take our distance from them in order to bring to light, reflexively, what their 'meaning' is, and how they function as codes of signification. The process of sedimentation[6]—meaningful categories becoming so routine that they seem the natural way of making up newspapers— is a common phenomenon throughout the field of mass communications. Only when new categories arise—the *Mirror*'s Mirrorscope feature, the *Observer*'s Business Section, the *Sunday Times*'s Insight features, the *Guardian*'s Women's Page or the Colour Supplements— do we become aware that something more than a simple journalistic innovation or change in format is taking place. New categories suggest major shifts in the direction of a newspaper's appeal, changes in readership, or an assumed shift in the *pattern* of readers' interests and attention, and thus, indirectly, in cultural assumptions—those taken-for-granted, 'seen but unnoticed background features and expectancies' by means of which people share a collective world of cultural meanings.

A newspaper can also emphasize or depress individual items on a scale of significance by their positioning on a page, or by employing the whole repertoire of typographical distinctions: headlining, underlining, bold use of types, strapline elaborations, attention-getting captions, with or without illustration, and so on. Part of the folklore of newspaper layout is that there are consistent patterns in the ways newspapers are read—e.g. hardly ever from front to back in a steady progress: and in the way individual pages are read—

5 The phrase 'contexts of awareness' is borrowed on analogy from its use by B. Glaser and A. Strauss, *Awareness of Dying*, Weidenfeld & Nicolson, 1966.

6 The process of 'sedimentation' in language and social interaction is developed by A. Schutz, 'The Dimensions of the Social World', in *Collected Papers*, vol. 2, Nijhoff, 1964. It is elaborated in P. Berger and T. Luckmann, *The Social Construction of Reality*, Doubleday, 1966.

top left first, bottom left last. Focus of attention (and thus of significance) can be used by a newspaper as another way of ordering the news, either by working within these perceptual patterns, or by deliberately breaking them: using typographical devices to *guide* the reader's attention from the most crucial to the least crucial item on a page.

Newspapers not only employ classifying schemes. They develop special rhetorics. Some of these operate broadly across the whole spectrum of the national press. In general—whatever the paper— women's pages will be lighter in treatment, chattier; editorials are weighty, resonant, offering evaluative judgements, seeking to wield influence with readers or in high places; features are more personal, informative, analytic. Each of these available rhetorics carries powerful social connotations—e.g. politics is 'hard stuff' where 'tough decisions' are made and about which newspapers have 'views'; women are less interested in politics—there is some such thing as the 'feminine interest' with a typically 'feminine' range of topics; features enable us to make sense of the rapid march of wars, disasters and decisions across the front page; sport is entertainment, time out from politics *and* women, masculine and competitive, full of thrills and the unexpected; and so on. These are complex *social registers*. Indeed, the informal topics of news—as indeed of other themes in social life—appear to generate distinctive 'fields of association', semantic, lexical and linguistic 'sub-worlds', which define and circumscribe particular areas of experience. Our public language is in part built up out of these semantic and rhetorical clusters, and we inhabit such social registers both in our everyday speech and in our public communications.

Within those generally available rhetorics, *each* newspaper makes a selection of rhetorics appropriate to its *persona*; and these come to characterize the newspaper as a distinctive entity. Since, in our society, class, social position and education constitute a complex matrix, the individual styles of a newspaper represent a registration in language of the assumed social world of its readers: for example, the elaborated linguistic constructions and punctilious syntax of the 'quality' press, as compared with the restricted codes, truncated syntax and vivid vocabulary of the 'populars'. Even newspapers which, broadly speaking, occupy the same end of the spectrum will develop distinctive rhetorics and styles—compare, for example, the two quite distinctive types of demotic speech employed by the *Express* and the *Mirror*. Such 'epistemic choices' characterize the discourse of particular newspapers over relatively long periods of time. They nourish the image and personality of the newspaper.

This analysis could be extended. But perhaps enough has been said to establish the point that newspapers employ verbal, rhetorical, visual and presentational means as a structure of complex *codes* for giving 'the news' significance. Such codes, the way they orchestrate the day's news, constitute the heart, the matrix, of a newspaper as a 'structured totality'. It is only when we learn to interpret the codes, and the social meanings on which they are founded, that we are in a position to grasp the newspaper as a cultural product. This is not to deny that newspapers are also channels for the exchange of information between the producers and consumers of 'news'. But it leads us to insist that the two types of analysis cannot be collapsed into one. Cultural studies requires us to *work back* to the social and historical process *through* the necessary mediations of form and appearance, format, rhetoric and style.

We have spoken of the *persona* or personality of a newspaper. Newspapers are not, of course, 'persons': but, without pushing the parallel to absurd lengths, each does maintain through time something like a collective identity. Just as our sense of the identity of a person depends to a great extent upon his appearance, style of being-in-the-world, how he presents himself, in the same way the collective identity of a newspaper rests not simply on *what* is said (the predominant number of *items* in all newspapers on the same day being largely determined by events outside their control) but on *how* what is said is presented, coded, shaped, within a set of signifying meaning-structures. Gregory Stone observes that 'By appearing, the person announces his identity, shows his value, expresses his mood or proposes his attitude ... whenever we clothe ourselves, we dress "towards" or address some audience whose validating responses are essential to the establishment of our self.' He adds:

> Appearance, then, is that phase of the social transaction which establishes identifications of the participants. As such it may be distinguished from discourse, which we conceptualize as the text of the transaction—*what* the parties were discussing. Appearance and discourse are two distinct dimensions of the social transaction. The former seems the more basic.[7]

Newspapers, then, do not merely report the news: they 'make the news meaningful'. Their linguistic and visual style, their presentation and format, their address to audiences and topics, their rhetorics and appearance offer us the vital clues to their collective identities.

Such matters of style and appearance are not simply referable to

7 Gregory Stone, 'Appearance and the Self', in *Human Behaviour and Social Processes*, ed. Rose, Routledge & Kegan Paul, 1962.

the production and presentational choices of the editorial team and
its managers. Though speaking to readers from a position outside
their 'world', and about topics on which it is well informed and they
are relatively ignorant, the newspaper is, nevertheless, the product
of a *social transaction* between producers and readers. Successful communication in this field depends to some degree on a process of
mutual confirmation between those who produce and those who
consume. At the same time, the producers hold a powerful position
vis-à-vis their audiences, and they must play the primary role in
shaping expectations and tastes. The notion that the *Mirror* or the
Express simply reflect the society as it is, and 'give the people what
they want', begs the crucial question of how 'the people', who do not
have the means of communication at their command, know 'what
they want' until a model has been offered to them. The point has
been forcefully made with respect to the growth of the modern
popular press by Raymond Williams:

> ... the way of seeing this history that I now want to suggest is
> first, the emergence of an independent popular press, directly
> related to radical politics, in the first decades of the nineteenth
> century; second, the direct attack on this, and its attempted
> suppression, in the period up to the 1830s ... ; and third (and
> most important as a way of understanding our own situation)
> the indirect attack, by absorption but also by new kinds of
> commercial promotion, which aimed not at suppressing the
> independent popular press but at *replacing* it, in fact by the
> simulacrum of popular journalism that we still have in such
> vast quantities today.[8]

Newspapers' styles, identities, are chosen and maintained with
continual reference to some notion of who their readers are, what they
will understand, what their social position is, what is their state of
knowledge, and so on. Newspapers must continually situate themselves within the assumed knowledge and interests of their readership, consciously or unconsciously adopt modes and strategies of
address: they must 'take the attitude of their significant others',
their 'imaginary interlocutors', in order to communicate effectively
in any particular case about any particular person or event. Language, style and format are therefore the products of a process of
reciprocal symbolic interaction between the newspaper and its
audiences; and matters of presentation are not only expressive
indicators of the newspaper's collective identity, but forms of address

8 Raymond Williams, op. cit. The argument was also developed in
Raymond Williams, *The Long Revolution*, Chatto & Windus, 1961.

to an audience, requiring reciprocal confirmation, and continually underwritten by a structure of informed but informal assumptions.

Such modes and assumptions will not necessarily be consciously recognized by every journalist on the paper, just as a man will not necessarily recognize his own psychological structure; that is why we cannot, as historians in particular tend to suggest, simply go and ask the editors the questions we are applying to the papers.

One of the central ways in which a newspaper presents itself, is in terms of its 'tone'. Tone (the term is derived on the analogy of speech[9]) is a rich and complex mode of linguistic registration. It indicates to the reader an evaluative 'set', or stance, towards a certain topic (or range of topics) taken by 'the speaker'; and it invites the reader to assume a similar stance. Tone is another way in which the underlying assumptions behind an explicit rhetorical style can be traced out and shown to be at work.

We may now return to the point made at the opening of this section: the separation between two kinds of research into newspapers—that which focuses on the social processes by which newspapers are produced, and that which focuses on newspapers as symbolic artefacts. Our point is that these are *not* two opposing types of research, but essentially complementary. The producer-reader interchange is registered in and mediated through the symbolic structure of the newspaper itself. Without this symbolic mediation, no transaction between editors and readers would be possible. Therefore, the study of the symbolic construct in itself cannot be a subsidiary part of any inquiry, but stands at the very heart of the relationship. Our working hypothesis was that every significant stylistic, visual, linguistic, presentational, rhetorical feature was a sort of silent witness, a 'meaningful disguised communication',[10] embodying and expressing that relationship: a 'message' (or metalanguage) about how the 'messages' (items) should be understood. Similarly, every shift in tone and rhetoric, every change in the balance of content, every move in the implied

9 On the use of 'tone' in cultural research, see Richard Hoggart, appendix to paper delivered to Conference on the Role of Theory in Humanistic Studies, sponsored by *Daedalus*, the Journal of the American Academy of Arts and Sciences and the Ford Foundation, at the Villa Serbelloni, Bellagio, Como, Italy, September 3–7, 1969.

10 *cf.* C. Rycroft: 'It can be argued that much of Freud's work was really semantic and that he made a revolutionary discovery in semantics, viz., that neurotic symptoms are meaningful disguised communications, but that, owing to his scientific training and allegiance, he formulated his findings in the conceptual framework of the physical sciences.' *Psychoanalysis Observed*, Pelican, 1968.

'logic' in the newspaper signified something more than a mere stylistic shift. At these points, we suggest, we encounter the core meaning-structures of the paper, the value-sets which give the paper a consistent identity over time: we are watching the relationship between paper and readers, defined in one historical situation, being reshaped and redefined under the pressure of new events, new social forces. It is only when we penetrate to the deep structures of the newspaper that we really understand *how* a paper stands in relation to the society which it 'mirrors' day by day, in the kaleidoscope of items which go to make up that construction of reality we call the news.

We argue that such a structure does emerge from our study of the *Mirror* and *Express*. Increasingly, the central point of the study became the effort to trace this structure out precisely, to account for its historical genesis, to watch its evolution, and disintegration over time. We should say structures rather than structure: for we found nothing so solid or uniform as a single, over-arching structure in either newspaper, nor any moment in which every item in a single day's newspaper seemed to be coherently orchestrated by a single set of meanings. Every newspaper is a coalition of interests, a negotiated compromise between variety and coherence: so we are speaking of overlapping structures of meaning, rather than *a* single structure; and of degrees of convergence and structuring rather than of absolute unity. Despite these reservations, we think we located a pattern of recurring meanings and assumptions in different parts of the world of each paper; these patterns seemed both distinctive in their own right, and different from one another.

2

EXPRESS, 1945

A T any time, Winston Churchill was beyond reproach in Lord
Beaverbrook's papers. Arthur Christiansen, who edited the
Daily Express from 1933 to 1957, wrote in his memoirs, on the
subject of Churchill:

> It was axiomatic that if you wished to remain a Beaverbrook
> editor you did not permit any word of criticism to creep into
> the leading articles. The historical researcher will find much
> criticism of Churchill's colleagues in his war-time and peace-
> time administrations, but none of Churchill.[1]

It is not surprising, then, that the figure of Churchill bestrode the
Express's columns during the 1945 General Election campaign,
when he was regarded by the Conservative Party as their chief
electoral asset, and Beaverbrook, a close political associate of
Churchill, was strenuously advocating the Tory cause at public
meetings. Analysis of the *Express* from June 16 to July 5 (polling
day) shows that of the total space given to the election 20 per cent
concerned Churchill's campaign tours, which did not begin until
June 23. Furthermore, that 20 per cent represents only the space
given to the circumstances of his tours: reports of what he said, and
of his other activities during the period (he made no campaign
appearances, only broadcasts, before June 23), are classified below
by subject-matter.

Matching the hero figure of Churchill was a villain figure.
Harold Laski, the chairman of the Labour Party's National Executive
Committee, was painted by the *Express* as the enemy of the 'universal
desire for privacy and freedom of choice' that even so committed a
Socialist as Aneurin Bevan sensed in the postwar mood.[2] Laski, with
22 per cent of the relevant space, alone exceeded Churchill's coverage in the paper.

Of other subjects, government direction of labour (also relating to
'freedom of choice') occupied 12 per cent of the space, foreign
foreign policy, nationalization and housing occupied 9 per cent
each, and less than 2 per cent each was given to such issues as social

1 Arthur Christiansen, *Headlines All My Life*, Heinemann, 1961.
2 Michael Foot, *Aneurin Bevan*, MacGibbon & Kee, 1962.

security, health, education, food and clothing supply, trade, and commerce.

With that analysis by subjects might be compared the results of a British Institute of Public Opinion poll[3] which asked, 'What questions do you think will be the most discussed in the General Election?' The main answers were Housing 41 per cent, Full Employment 15 per cent, Social security 7 per cent, Nationalization 6 per cent, International security 5 per cent.

The election occupied in all 31 per cent of the *Express* during the seventeen issues in question. When comparing that figure with other elections the newsprint shortage in 1945 must be borne in mind. All papers were allowed a small increase of newsprint for the election period, which could be used either to swell the paper occasionally or to print more copies. The *Express* increased from four pages only once, going to eight pages to print the full election results on July 27. (The gap of three weeks between polling and results was caused by the gathering of service votes from abroad.) Its circulation during the campaign rose to 3,300,006 copies a day in the month of June, the highest sale ever recorded for a daily newspaper at that time.

Of that total space given to the election, 56 per cent reported or discussed Conservative views and public appearances, 26 per cent those of Labour, and the remainder concerned the smaller parties and the election process; 11 per cent of it was visual matter, photographs and cartoons. Of Laski's 22 per cent, text accounted for 21 per cent and visual matter for only 1 per cent (of which a single cartoon on June 18 accounted for just half). Churchill's 20 per cent, in contrast, breaks down as $13\frac{1}{2}$ per cent text and $6\frac{1}{2}$ per cent visuals. During the period there was no photograph at all of a Labour politician except Laski; the only visual representation of Attlee, Bevin and Morrison was in the June 18 cartoon of Laski, plus a minute column-breaker of Laski trapping Attlee in a net. As well as the generous photographic coverage of his tours, Churchill appeared in three cartoons before the tours. There was one photograph and one cartoon of Beaverbrook, and five Conservative candidates—all ex-RAF pilots—appeared in photographs: one of them was Max Aitken, Beaverbrook's son. With only four pages a day the paper could not afford to give much space to photographs, but considering that photographs and cartoons of Churchill during his tours altogether totalled 241 column inches, one might think that the leader of the Labour Party was not handsomely treated.

3 See McCallum and Readman, *The British General Election of 1945*, Oxford, 1947.

The 12 per cent figure for employment reflected Beaverbrook's animosity toward Bevin's Control of Engagements Order, which was intended to direct scarce post-war labour where the national economy most needed it. Beaverbrook's part in the election campaign was generously reported in his paper, including attacks on him. A front-page panel on June 22 read:

> To make space for Mr Churchill's broadcast speech, all reports of attacks on Lord Beaverbrook last night have been held over.

Christiansen tells us: 'As for Lord Beaverbrook, he had the time of his life. Throughout the campaign he was in high good humour.'

These figures alone make it clear that the *Express* was heavily committed to the Conservative Party, though it digressed quite often from the official party line, as when Beaverbrook advocated a policy of high wages, or hinted at 2s. 6d. off the Income Tax. The thoroughness of the commitment, and the energy with which it was expressed, can be seen in Christiansen's feelings when the result (the Conservatives were beaten by 295 seats) was known:

> From his penthouse Lord Beaverbrook telephoned me for the latest news. As I told him, I broke down. I was suffering from acute shock. I had believed that the *Daily Express* campaign would swing the election for the Conservatives. I had thought that my Press propaganda machine was invincible. I had been proved wrong and hurt where it hurt most—in my professional pride. . . . Politics had never moved me deeply prior to the 1945 election, and I vowed thereafter that they would not do so again.

Lord Beaverbrook's consultations with Churchill about the *Express*'s election policy have been documented by Kenneth Young.[4] Christiansen was happy to describe himself, apropos Beaverbrook, as 'his creation . . . under his spell'.

The *Express* thus occupied a peculiar position in this campaign; anti-Tory papers constantly pictured Churchill, Beaverbrook and Brendan Bracken as cronies, and so created the impression that the *Express* was to some extent the reproduced voice of Churchill himself. And since Churchill, Beaverbrook and the Tory Party all promoted Churchill as the unanswerable reason for voting Tory, the Tory case must have seemed to many to be rooted in the *Express*. That Christiansen felt this to be so can be deduced from the quotation above.

4 Kenneth Young, *Churchill and Beaverbrook*, Eyre & Spottiswoode, 1966.

That the Tory Party to some extent felt it is evidenced again by Christiansen:

> As we left Lord Beaverbrook's apartment together at 2.30 a.m., Brendan put his arm around my shoulder and said, 'Chris, the Conservative Party will never forget what you have done for us.'

Churchill too, according to Lord Moran,[5] blamed his defeat on Beaverbrook, and so affirmed the *Express*'s central part in the election.

Although the total Conservative vote, 9,960,809, was a figure oddly similar to the *Express*'s 9,900,000 readership at that time (if we take three as the readership-per-copy then), not even the paper's editor could believe that all the Tory voters were *Express*-readers. But it would be misleading to conclude, with Christiansen, that the paper's campaign was simply a failure. The mass media are seldom able to alter voting intentions; their most successful role is that of reinforcing trends or raising issues. Whether the *Express* could have raised more telling issues is hypothetical; but a critical analysis of the issues that it did raise, particularly of the themes embodied in the stories of Laski and of Churchill's tour (both of which were drummed up much louder by the *Express* than by any other paper), will give us harder ground for speculation.

*　　　*　　　*

The party leaders in the Coalition Cabinet disagreed about the timing of a dissolution and General Election. Most of the press thought the election unwelcome. There were two notable enthusiasts for it, however: the Labour Party conference, which met at Blackpool on May 20 and urged its leaders on, and the *Daily Express*, which greeted the announcement of the election with: 'July 5 a glorious date', and continued in euphoric voice. On June 7, for example, William Barkley, the Parliamentary reporter, called:

> Hit the cymbal, bang the drum! Walk up, walk up, to the greatest sales circus of all time, the biggest most important General Election in the history of mankind, or the British nation.

The paper strove to make the campaign into, precisely, something as entertaining as a circus; finding, apparently, no disparity between a circus and the 'most important General Election in the history of

5 Lord Moran, *Churchill: The Struggle for Survival 1940/65*, Constable, 1966.

mankind'. Why should it? Christiansen tells us often of his conviction that news must be *made* 'interesting', to overcome the 'dreari-
ness' of life in Derby and Rhyl.

The country, only a few weeks after defeating Germany and still
at war with Japan, did not share Beaverbrook's high spirits; but
whereas the *Mirror*, for one, interpreted this quietness as a tired but
determined mood, and addressed its readers soberly, the *Express*
diagnosed it as a repressed vitality, waiting only for the lifting of
controls to express itself. Christiansen sought to open up this vein,
to 'combat the public mood. Cheer them up when they are depressed
. . . Make it exciting even when it's dull.' This approach inevitably
merged into Beaverbrook's policies: for high wages, against controls and bureaucracy. The *Express* was an entertainment that
embodied the promise, if the electors took its advice, of more
entertainment to come in the form of released enterprise and
vitality. It presented itself as the model of society under Tory rule.
In this it ran counter to official Conservative policy which, like
Labour's, held out no promise of instant rejuvenation of the country.

Churchill's first election broadcast, on June 4, was the crucial
episode in the early part of the campaign, and the *Express*'s enthusiasm now found an issue instead of just a mood. The essence of his
argument was bannered next day on the front page: *Gestapo in
Britain if Socialists win*, and expanded in the leader:

> Voters of Britain! Will you go down to history as the men and
> women who smashed the inhuman tyranny in Europe but
> were too tired or too bewildered or too dazzled by your own
> glory to save yourselves from tyranny at home?
>
> After ripping the Gestapo out of the still beating heart of
> Germany, will you stand for a Gestapo under another name at
> home? . . .
>
> Were you shocked to learn from Mr. Churchill that State
> Control leads to Fascism?
>
> Think hard about it, and see how true it is.

The broadcast, containing references to Englishmen in their
'cottage homes' and phrases like 'in thrift and toil accumulated',
was expressed in the prose-style which Churchill had deployed for
his famous war-time addresses and which he sustained throughout
the election. A. H. Booth,[6] among others, tells us that Churchill's
solemnity became a joke among the forces who, attached to David
rather than Goliath, to the 'little man' of British sentiment, found
Attlee's waspish stings much more to their taste. More resented than

6 A. H. Booth, *British Hustings 1924–1950*, Muller, 1956.

the style of the broadcast, however, was Churchill's swift exploitation for party-politics of the prestige he had gained in the war. One
might guess that the serving forces were made to reflect that it was
they who had fought the war. As for the 'Gestapo' threat itself,
taken seriously it would have bewildered people who had seen the
Labour Party's leader, Attlee, and several of his lieutenants working
closely with Churchill in the war-time Coalition Cabinet. How
could Churchill have tolerated such sinister figures as colleagues?
The *Express* realized the bewilderment of the question and, with
Churchill, found a way of answering it.

How far this speech, which has been called 'silly' by some historians and which 'opened the gutters' according to Michael Foot, was
the responsibility of Beaverbrook has been argued ever since. The
following night Attlee, in his first broadcast, said 'The voice we
heard last night was that of Mr. Churchill, but the mind was that of
Lord Beaverbrook.' Kingsley Martin[7] said that Beaverbrook persuaded Churchill to it, A. J. P. Taylor says he 'egged him on', but
Tom Driberg,[8] R. A. Butler[9] and Kenneth Young maintain that the
idea was Churchill's own. It is worth noting how similar Churchill's
methods could be to Beaverbrook's. An apt illustration is the way in
which Churchill directed *The British Gazette*, the Government's
daily paper during the 1926 General Strike:

> Churchill directed all operations with enthusiasm and urgency
> . . . He loved running a newspaper; it was, as he himself said
> with relish, 'the combination of a first-class battleship and a
> first-class general election.' The *British Gazette* made no pre-
> tence to impartiality . . . It was, in short, an inflammatory,
> one-sided, highly provocative propaganda broadsheet, 'a
> first-class indiscretion, clothed in the tawdry garb of third-rate
> journalism,' as Lloyd George described it . . . The avowed aim
> of the *British Gazette* was to keep the temperature up, indeed,
> to force it up, when almost everyone else was trying to keep it
> down . . . The *British Gazette* contributed in no small way to
> the degeneration in the atmosphere of the strike.[10]

Churchill once said, 'I like things to happen, and if they don't
happen I like to make them happen'.[11]

7 Kingsley Martin, *Father Figures*, Hutchinson, 1966.
8 Tom Driberg, *Beaverbrook*, Weidenfeld & Nicolson, 1956.
9 *The Listener*, July 28, 1966. In a letter to *The Observer* on October 9,
1966 John North suggested that Churchill was influenced by August von
Hayek's *The Road to Serfdom*.
10 Robert Rhodes James in *The Observer*, September 4, 1966.
11 Quoted by Robert Rhodes James, loc. cit.

Attlee's broadcast on June 5 crystallized the disapproval of Churchill's. The *Express*, which had already spoken of the 'dismal, doctrinaire bletherings of the Socialists', headlined its front page report *The National Socialists* and in its leader drove home the point, the same as the previous day's:

> After last night's broadcast who would raise his hand and call Mr. Attlee fuehrer?
> Not a soul. Not a single, solitary soul.
> And who would suspect the innocent and mild exponent of the Socialist creed of totalitarian ambitions? Not a soul.
> Does this prove that Mr. Churchill was talking through his hat on Monday night? Not a bit of it!
> Mr. Attlee is the decoy-duck of Socialism.
> It has been the steadfast aim of Socialism to conceal from the people the means it intends to employ to achieve its ends.
> It uses fancy words like 'central planning', fancy phrases like 'the will of the people', to conceal the methods by which it intends to work.
> And they all boil down to the simple device of telling the ordinary citizen what he must do, and seeing that he does it, with no argument.
> Slavery? The Socialists will be the first to repudiate the word. They will give lip-service to freedom to the end and beyond it.
> Do not be deceived. There is no freedom under Socialism, except such 'freedom' as is tolerated by the State, for its own purposes. It can be taken away by a stroke of the pen.
> Cripps has outlined his party's technique for by-passing Parliament and the courts of law. Attlee has publicly approved the method. And it is exactly the method used by Hitler to turn the Reichstag into a mockery in 1933 . . .

Apart from the renewed attempt to associate Socialism with the most hated element of a detested enemy, and the tone of keen-eyed scepticism ever watchful on behalf of the ordinary, unadvised citizen, the most interesting point in this leader is the description of Attlee as 'the decoy-duck of Socialism'. This is the first answer to anyone who asked how Churchill could have worked for five years with crypto-Gestapo colleagues: Attlee is only the front-man. It is not until June 16 that the *Express* tracks down the head of the sinister organization he conceals and serves.

Whether it originated in his mind or not, there is no doubt that Beaverbrook's paper took up the 'Gestapo' allegation and fomented

it with zest. Meanwhile, its other leading issue was developing, as in
the leader of June 11:

> The main issues are clearly set forth upon which the electors
> have to make their decision.
>
> On the one hand is an invitation to join in the great effort of
> reconstruction. And an effort to give the natural genius of the
> British for personal enterprise and initiative full play.
>
> And on the other hand is a desire to extend bureaucratic
> ownership and perpetuate direction of labour, along with all
> manner of hampering and vexatious restrictions on the people's
> ancient liberties.
>
> Vast reforms in the social system are contained in the
> Churchill programme. Their virtues cannot be gainsaid by the
> Socialists, so they say that he is not a likely man to put them
> through . . .
>
> There is the smear which the Socialists are trying to put on
> Churchill's name. And what impudent nonsense it is!
>
> They know full well that in the history of social legislation in
> Britain in the last forty years there is only one name to be put
> alongside that of David Lloyd George—and that is Winston
> Churchill. The people of this country have received countless
> blessings from the reforming zeal of Mr. Churchill . . .

The leader goes on to attribute many reforms to Mr Churchill's
zeal.

That piece is virtually the whole Tory case as the *Express* was to
develop it: the contrast of 'natural genius', 'personal initiative' and
'ancient liberties' with 'bureaucratic ownership', 'direction of
labour' and 'hampering restrictions'; the ready and unexamined
concession of 'vast reforms' in the Tory programme; the representation of the Labour Party as reacting, never acting, in open argument
('*so* they say . . .'); and above all the total reliance upon Churchill's
reputation. The broad strategy was to exalt the premier as the very
embodiment of the traditional values in defence of which the war
was assumed to have been fought, and as the only conceivable
choice to lead the country through the post-war reconstruction; and
to represent the Labour Party as being in breach of the country's
traditional values, especially personal freedom. In an early campaign
speech Beaverbrook had not hesitated to make his line plain: 'It is
no use supposing the electorate, after ten years of political truce, is
informed on public issues . . . We have to show them that our
Prime Minister, Mr. Churchill, must lead us through the days that
lie before us.'

Attlee had pressed for a dissolution because of 'acute party differences' about reconstruction policies. The most familiar Conservative election poster bore a picture of Churchill and the slogan: 'Help him finish the job.' The job included the war with Japan, post-war foreign policy (in which Churchill was much more interested, says Michael Foot, than in home affairs), and economic reconstruction— as a continuing part of the accomplished job of beating Germany. The emphasis in Labour's propaganda was rather on getting on with the next job, the fresh one of reconstruction. These were obvious emphases to make when the electorate was being asked to choose between the present leader and a new one, but historians generally agree that 'getting on with the next job' was closer to the electors' mood. They were predominantly concerned with social security; the labour controls of war time, conscription, the worker–employer boards that Bevin had created, wage agreements, industrial welfare provisions, evacuation, rationing, school meals, welfare orange juice (the health of children actually improved during the war)[12]—by these things the public had been accustomed for six years to the feeling of collective security and, if not equality, at least the absence of conspicuous inequality.

There is a strong presumption, borne out by the election result as much as by anything else, that the electorate credited the social security measures of the war-time Cabinet to its Labour members; and an even stronger one that the Conservative Party was still associated with the economic hardships of the inter-war years. 'Political trends were boxed off by the war, not deflected', wrote Anthony Eden.[13] Labour, who had held office (but not power) for only two brief periods between the wars, had in 1940, with the Liberals, overthrown the discredited Chamberlain government and joined Churchill in a coalition where they experienced, and were seen to experience, true power. They had, for the first time, 'ceased to look like a faction'[14] and become a credible national party. The Tories in the war-time government, on the other hand, are thought[15] to have damaged themselves in their inept handling of the Beveridge Report on social welfare. The Report, explicitly based on the war's social levelling, spoke of 'A revolutionary moment ... Freedom from want must be won ... needs a sense of national unity overriding the interests of any class or section.' These sentiments were

12 These facts were pointed out by L. C. B. Seaman, *Post-Victorian Britain 1902–1951*, Methuen, 1966.

13 Earl of Avon, *The Reckoning*, Cassell, 1965.

14 Anthony Howard in *The Age of Austerity*, ed. Sissons and French, Hodder & Stoughton, 1963.

15 By L. C. B. Seaman, op. cit., for example.

close to the hearts of people both at home and fighting abroad, as the *Mirror* realized. Churchill called it 'dangerous optimism'. Morrison and other Labour M Ps were wary of the promises but voted against the Government. Copies of a summary of the Report, specially prepared by the Army Bureau of Current Affairs, were withdrawn by the War Office after many servicemen had read them. The Forces demanded that copies be reissued, and they were. Eden, who at first thought that most servicemen had no politics, was warned by Trygve Lie, among others, that the army and young people at home were 'very Left', and after the election he saw that 'the young were protesting at a return to old forms and faces'.

*   *   *

The Laski affair began on June 16 and remained in every issue of the paper until after the election on July 5, providing nearly a quarter of the election coverage in the world's largest-selling daily paper at that time. In five of these seventeen issues it led the front page, and in three more was the most prominent subsidiary story; it failed to make only five of the front pages. It was the subject of seven leading articles, and either wholly or in part the subject of seven other leader-page features and one cartoon. In all, in a paper reduced by newsprint scarcity to only four pages, it provoked forty-eight separate stories. All those figures represent direct references to Laski by name: a great deal more matter derived from the implications that the *Express* decided the affair had.

In all this coverage there were two issues, two news-stories: the influence that the Labour Party's National Executive Committee would have over an elected Labour Government; and a statement attributed to Laski that the party would if necessary use violence and revolution to achieve its ends. The first story arose out of a letter from Churchill to Attlee, and led the paper on June 16; the second, June 20's lead, arose from a speech made four days previously by Laski. The double issue led the paper on June 21, the occasion being a speech by Lord Beaverbrook which amplified the *Express*'s deductions about Laski; and again, for the third day running, on June 22, this time deriving from a broadcast in which Churchill made similar points to Beaverbrook's. The fifth time Laski led the front page was July 3, following another letter from Churchill to Attlee.

Three of the five lead stories, therefore, were not news but reports of politicians regurgitating news that had already been printed. All the other forty-three articles were concerned with political speeches or letters that referred to the affair without adding news to it, or were leading articles or journalists' background-filling.

If those figures alone do not make the case that the Laski affair was inflated, we have Christiansen's own word for it. Writing about the story as it developed after June 20 (the 'Socialism even if it means violence' issue), he makes the paper's treatment of it quite plain:

> I confess that at the *Express* office we were carried away by the excitement of the story. I thought we had an election weapon as good as the Zinovieff letter . . . It is a fault of newspapermen that they can be carried away by their own efforts and believe they are having the same effect on the readers as on themselves.
>
> Even the Socialists on the staff—and there were plenty—carried out their briefs with professional gusto. It was all-in wrestling, hand-to-hand fighting, commando stuff, and we were, we thought, very good at it.

The lead headlines on June 16 were:

> Socialists split: Attlee repudiates Laski order
> Strong line against party bosses
> Behind-scenes rule

Order, bosses, rule—antonyms of freedom—were to recur again and again in the paper's handling of the affair, always with the behind-scenes implication; rule by unknown bosses. The story begins:

> Mr. Clement R. Attlee, Parliamentary Leader of the Socialist Party, last night repudiated a statement by Mr. Harold J. Laski, the Socialist Party's chairman. He is taking a strong line in a political storm of the first magnitude.

'Repudiates' and 'storm' indicate a divided party; and one grievously divided ('the first magnitude'). The ostensible purpose of the story, over the next weeks, was to stress this division, but underneath a deeper key was being struck, the question of freedom *v.* control. Attlee himself, the 'decoy-duck of Socialism', is presented as a victim of control by the 'party bosses', those shadowy, unelected, 'behind-scenes' figures, in comparison with the untrammelled leadership of Churchill. The paragraph seeks solemnity with 'strong line', 'first magnitude', and the punctilious use of the middle initials in the men's names. (The initials, not the paper's normal style, at the same time distance the men by an air of quaintness.)

Given this dramatic setting, we are now told the facts. Churchill has invited Attlee, his potential successor, to attend the Potsdam Conference with him; Laski has asserted that a Labour Government could not undertake to be bound by agreements entered into by Churchill, despite Attlee's presence. Attlee has assured Churchill that 'There was never any suggestion that I should go as a mere observer', in reply to Churchill's expression of concern at a departure from their war-time agreement of foreign policy. On this basis the *Express* erected 132 column inches of copy on June 16. The reasons why, its potential as an 'election weapon', soon emerge.

The story continues by telling us that Attlee is taking 'a serious view' of the matter, and that the question of how much policy-making power Labour's National Executive Committee has over the Parliamentary party is one that 'has caused crises in the party in the past'. The reporter, Guy Eden, heats up the controversial effect of his story by introducing contentious views in the third-person-neutral:

> It is felt that the electors have a right to know whether in returning Socialist MPs to Parliament to form the possible basis of a Socialist Government, they are sending representatives of the people who will act in accordance with the needs and interests of the nation, or servants of the party machine who will obey nobody but the party bosses.

That paragraph is the true reason for the *Express*'s excitement at the affair: it is not, of course, news but a signal to the reader to tell him how to feel about what news the story does contain. The air of responsibility—'right to know', 'representatives of the people', 'interests of the nation'—both dissociates the paper from the squalid events it is witnessing—'party machine', 'party bosses'—and invites the reader to feel that his attachment to Parliamentary dignity and ancient freedoms will be outraged by a Socialist Government. Throughout these seventeen issues there will not be a word of rational argument about the policies of either main party; nor any examination of the country's economic condition, either at government level or at the personal level (which the *Mirror* was concentrating on day after day), except for an occasional factory worker found to complain about direction of labour; nor, in the case of the present story, any evidence whether the constitutional structure of the Labour Party was more (or less) open to factional pressure than the Tories'. The entire political message of the paper was conveyed by striking emotional attitudes which sought to manipulate the reader's emotions into the same attitude: commando stuff with the emotions.

Once the story has found its way to this tone of emotional appeal to democracy, antonyms of freedom proliferate. A 'statement' develops into a 'demand' and on to 'dictation from the party bosses.' The pseudo-dignified tone reappears:

It was taken for granted that ... Mr. Attlee was acting as responsible leader of the Socialists ... should not be a mere dummy figure.

Churchill/Attlee relations are characterized in words connoting breadth and magnanimity:

> The whole object of Mr. Churchill's invitation. ... Mr. Churchill fully intended ... Mr. Attlee all along fully agreed
> ...

We come back to 'impose conditions', hints of 'a great disservice to world peace', and 'interference with the elected representatives of the people by Socialist bodies having no responsibility to the electors.' Juxtapositions of that sort (people/bodies) are the most characteristic figure of all in this prose. Further intimations of a tightly-knit politically-motivated group seeking to usurp the traditional cradle of democracy are 'party caucus', 'providential for the nation' (that Mr. Laski showed his hand when he did), and 'make the Government of Britain answerable to it'. The story ends on that favourite tense of political correspondents, the future predictive: Socialist leaders 'plan to make a public statement defining Mr. Attlee's position and openly repudiating Mr. Laski, their chairman ... Every effort will be made to convince voters ... But Government supporters will press the matter ... Mr. Attlee and other Socialist leaders will be asked ...' Readers informed what will happen tomorrow are not likely to be taken in by it when it comes. The future is defused. It is castrated too, in the sense that when politicians can be thus predicted, not only in action but also in reaction, they are in effect puppets directed by the dramatizing hand of the journalist.

Throughout the story runs, behind the surface events, a myth which the choice of vocabulary creates and sustains now and up to July 5. The myth is enhanced by four other stories on the front page, and by the leader inside.

1. 'Alone I did it—Laski. "Now satisfied."' The smugness of the headline is a perfect clay-pigeon for the dignified worry of the main story, yet the story itself almost annuls Guy Eden's. Laski is quoted as saying that he is no longer concerned about Attlee's status at Potsdam, which had not been made clear to him previously. Both Churchill and Laski are quoted to the effect that Labour and Tory foreign policies are alike only in 'some of the main aspects', which effectively conceded the only real principle at stake, whether Attlee is free, and known to be free by Churchill, to alter course.

The story ends with the gratuitous paragraph: 'He has never been an MP'—the theme of an unelected man seeking power in a democracy. The point of the story is to suggest that Laski, though tripped up this time and putting a good face on it, is not likely to remain in the wings, with the rest of the party bosses, if Labour is returned.

2. The letters that passed between Churchill and Attlee are printed without comment, though the headlines are careful to pick a contentious word from Churchill's letter: 'Come—but not as a mute observer'.

3. 'Laski on the throne.' A brilliant example of *Express* ambiguity: the first meaning, before the story is read, must be that Laski is abrogating supreme power to himself. The text turns out to be a quotation of some of Laski's pre-war observations on monarchy in a Socialist democracy. At a time when loyalty to the King was running high, simply to raise the issue is tendentious, even though nothing in the quotation raises stronger feelings than 'a monarchy and a Socialist democracy are not, in the long run, easily compatible'. A photo illustrates this piece—placed between headline and copy with the effect of heightening the ambiguity mentioned above; the portrait chosen is one in which Laski peers through his glasses, shadow emphasizing the tired lines on his face and making his mouth obscure. He is evidently not one to hit the cymbal or bang the drum.

4. 'Whole country is shocked—this is a warning.' A party-political speech by Brendan Bracken is quoted at unusual length, more than a column.

5. The attitude of the leading article is at one with the front page stories; the issue is presented as a package by the whole paper. The sideheads alone (there are no headlines) in the leader tell us its direction: 'Laski—edict/Caucus rule/Attlee goes too/Decide nothing/ The prisoner/One more proof/The junta.'

The text starts by seeking credentials:

> Mr. Harold Laski is chairman of the Socialist Party. When he says that the Socialists will not be bound by any decisions taken at the forthcoming conference between Mr. Churchill, Marshal Stalin and Mr. Truman he speaks with the voice of authority.

Partly by the use of his Christian name, Laski is distanced, made to seem slightly upstart in comparison with the trustworthy figures at the conference. The leader continues:

Last night Mr. Laski tried to cover up. He declares that publication of the letters that passed between Mr. Churchill and Mr. Attlee clarifies the position. But it does nothing of the kind.

Mr. Laski knows the rules and regulations of the Socialist Party. He was entirely within his rights in making Thursday night's statement.

Those credentials satisfy the *Express*. It does not offer its readers any gloss on the party's constitution, save the implicit judgement in 'rules and regulations'. As for Laski, we now know that he is given to evasiveness when the going gets hot, but that the *Express* at least is not going to lose his trail ('. . . tried to . . .'). Now the *Express* establishes its own loyalties:

> Mr. Laski's words administer a shock to the whole traditional method of conducting British affairs.
>
> They are, of course, familiar in the narrow conduct of Socialist Party politics.

The *Express* is on the side of all the resounding overtones in 'traditional' and 'British', leaving no alternative to Laski and his like but to be seen in breach of those values; as the sneer in the second paragraph crudely makes clear. The word 'Socialist' has now been girded with associations that have nothing at all to do with policies and everything to do with personal behaviour. The invitation is, and will be, to judge the men, not the issues. Throughout this election the *Express* invariably referred to the Labour Party as the Socialist Party: the three or four exceptions were always in quoting from someone outside the *Express*. The reason was stated in the paper: that the party presumed too much in adopting the name of all working men. One might think, too, that the theoretical feel of the world 'Socialist' suited the party as the *Express* determined its readers should see it.

To continue:

> But they become a most grave departure in the wider sphere of British foreign policy, showing plainly that the rule of the secret party caucus completely nullifies the position of a British representative if he is merely the leader of the Socialist Party which hopes to govern this country.

The paper is now set portentously in the saddle of British democratic tradition, inviting us to look severely askance at such Socialist 'hopes'. The word 'secret' echoes 'behind-scenes' on the front page but has not yet been orchestrated into the leading position that the *Express* will find for it. Now the tone alters to sweet reasonableness:

> The facts are quite simple. Mr. Churchill proposed to take with him to the conference the leader of the party which makes the principal claim to be the alternative Government.
> The Prime Minister's motives were perfectly clear. At the time of the meeting the result of the General Election will be in doubt in the sense that the votes will not then have been counted.
> So Mr. Attlee was asked to go along with Mr. Churchill.

We remember the front page phrases like fully intended . . . fully agreed'; and we note that the Labour Party is making a 'claim' but that its hopes will be dashed when the chips are down and the votes counted; a different use of the future predictive, this, discouraging anyone who may be considering a pro-Labour vote by suggesting that it is scarcely worth his trip to the polling-station, and heartening the faithful. The tone switches again, melodramatically:

> But watch your step, Mr. Leader Attlee! At once the fulmination goes out from Laski, the party chairman: 'You will be there as observer only!'

This remarkable paragraph, written in a hoarse whisper between clenched teeth, seems to be addressed to a quite different audience from the one expected in the earlier dignified sneers. The case is being presented in the tone of Bulldog Drummond. Laski, bereft of all titles of address, can now be chairman only of something like a Hong Kong drug ring. (And indeed it was only three days later that the far-East joke—we were still at bitter war with Japan—was made manifest in the large feature headline: 'Goody, goody! But Mr. Attlee will have to ask Mr. Laskee!')

The next paragraph returns to something nearer a level keel, though neither Attlee or Laski has yet regained a 'Mr.':

> Obviously, says Laski, Attlee should know what is going on. But he warns that no decision arrived at in this three-Power meeting can commit the Socialist Party.

It may seem reasonable that a newly elected government might want to retain at least the option of departing from the recently defeated Government's policies. Not so to the *Express*, capriciously restoring its courtesies:

> Mr. Attlee, who is merely the leader of Mr. Laski's party, cannot have power to accept agreements on topics which have

never been debated by the party executive or by the parliamentary party.

This is profoundly shocking doctrine.

The sententious tone of the opening paragraphs is returning:

> In this country we have always worked on the principle that you pick a man, you trust him, you support him against all critics, and if a time comes when he is clearly wrong you replace him.

Two interesting doctrinal points are made here. One is that the notion of a democratic Opposition seems to be ruled out; the other is that charismatic expediency is precisely the principle which the *Express* is using in support of Churchill, as we shall see later.

> But the Socialist doctrine, according to Laski, is that you appoint a man to be your leader, and then send him abroad in chains.
>
> Your leader is your prisoner. You say to him: 'Take no decisions. Never make up your mind. Your mind is not your own. Come back and report, and then we will see whether we think you are right or not.'

A decoy-duck is flapping around the column once more. Attlee is 'merely the leader of Mr. Laski's party'. By now the *Express* feels that it has erected a sufficiently stable slipway to launch its chief message:

> It becomes clearer every day that it is madness to think that anyone can represent this country today other than Mr. Winston Churchill.

This is again a slightly different tone from any that we have heard before. It is the simple outspoken man; and accordingly the version of Churchill's name suggest a simple humility. It is quite a different usage from the 'Mr. Harold Laski' that started the column: there, when a more patrician dignity was being assumed, the Christian name distanced him from 'Mr. Churchill, Marshal Stalin and Mr. Truman.'

The simple tone, slightly warmed up, lasts for another paragraph:

> This Laski-ism is only one more proof that at this dividing of the ways Mr. Churchill should be returned to power.

And it grows hotter still, melting into threat:

> If the Socialist Party were to win this election the Laski law would see to it that there could be no three-Power meetings

*B

such as occurred so effectively during the war without the constant fear that their decisions would be overthrown at a later meeting of the Socialist junta in London.

'Junta' reminds the attentive reader of their 'Gestapo' stories a few days previously. Now, for the last time, the tone veers once more, into rhetorical questioning:

> And what is this Socialist junta? It is difficult to assess its importance and membership.
> But at the Blackpool conference three weeks ago a big movement developed among the delegates to re-open discussions for the inclusion of the Communists inside the Socialist Party. This demand was beaten by only 1,314,000 votes to 1,219,000.
> So what would be the Socialist foreign policy? The nation is entitled to know.

'Communists' is clearly being used in menace, although Marshal Stalin, already exalted as a principal in the three-Power conferences earnestly desired, was a well-known member of the Communist Party.

To say no more of the quality of political address, what is really interesting is the wobbling of tone. It is as though the *Express* was not sure that anyone was really listening, like a comedian with a thin house who knows that his material is not very good. What confidence there is in the writing is the confidence of a bully, someone who discounts the humanity of those he deals with. A good deal of that may be attributable to a hangover from the rhetoric that was more appropriate, or at least acceptable, in war time. Then the common enemy was universally identified and hated. Now he has to be created.

That, with the addition of a brief report of a speech in which Hore-Belisha described Attlee as Laski's 'office boy', was the *Express*'s coverage of the Laski affair on the first day of it. Most of the guidelines were laid down, but the emphases altered as the days went past. Themes that implicitly buttressed the message of Laski—stories that distinguished between the two parties by relying heavily on words like 'order', 'control', 'compulsory', 'regulations', and those that associated the Labour Party with the 'Gestapo'—were running throughout the period.

Guy Eden's headlines on Monday June 18 were:

> Laski widens the split
> But Attlee says nothing at all

The story accepts without question the fact of a 'split' in the party, and concentrates on dramatic 'evidence' of the dismay it is causing, 'despite efforts behind the scenes to close it up'. It is a classic instance of scaremongering; without substantiating its own facts, it seeks to put the onus of disproof on those it represents as disarrayed. Its purpose is to arouse suspicion: not of the 'split', but of the absence of any attempt by Labour to come clean about it, or to deny it. 'Mr. Attlee himself was careful to make no public mention of it . . . gave the puzzled electors no explanation.' 'Professor Laski, technically subordinate to Mr. Attlee . . . still in defiant mood . . . offered no apology.' After quotations from a Laski speech, in which he redefined his objection to the doctrine of 'continuity of policy', the 'reporter' comments: 'All of which flouted Mr. Attlee's solemn undertaking to Mr. Churchill.' (Attlee had in fact spoken only of 'great public advantage' in maintaining a common front on foreign policy, which falls short of a 'solemn undertaking'.) 'Back in London', we learn, 'Socialist leaders, alarmed by reports pouring in of the stir caused in the constituencies, debated how to get round the trouble.'

> A formal statement may be made by one of the highest bodies in the party—perhaps the National Executive itself, of which Laski is the chairman—turning him down and stating that Attlee is right.
>
> Socialist apologists have found during the week-end that voters all over the country have refused to accept the plea that the incident 'is only another Tory stunt'.
>
> They also found demands for two assurances:
> 1. That a Socialist Government would act according to the wishes of Parliament and not those of a party caucus or other body in no way responsible to the electors;
> 2. That there will be no violent changes of foreign policy under a Socialist Government.
>
> Guidance on how to answer these questions is being sent to Socialist speakers this week from party headquarters.

Like Churchill, when things don't happen the *Express* likes to make them happen.

A cartoon on page 2 represents a diminutive Attlee perched on Laski's knee, crying 'But I'm no dummy'. Bevin and Morrison smirk ambiguously in the wings of the stage. Although it may superficially seem to support Attlee, it allows him none of the dignity of an aspirant Prime Minister. The 'split' is once more taken for granted. Attlee henceforth makes no appearance in the *Express* except in connection with Laski. Of Labour leaders, only Bevin is granted

much non-Laski coverage (the actual result of the election appeared
under the main headline: 'Bevin for Potsdam'). His Control of
Engagements Order obviously recommended itself to the paper as a
target; but also on record is Christiansen's belief that he and Bevin
liked each other, and possibly Bevin had a more acceptably 'push-
and-go' character in Beaverbrook's eyes than the other Labour
leaders. (Bevin had certainly pushed Beaverbrook to go out of the
war-time Cabinet.)

On the same page the leader betrays the wobbling images of its
audience, and the search for emotional response, that the previous
day's did. It is addressed to the Forces:

> Soldier abroad, mind where you cast your vote. What are you
> looking for—a change?
> You're dead right. You're entitled to a change.

That change, we find, is from being ordered around.

> It is only fools who resent discipline in the Army. But who
> welcomes it in private life? Who wants to give orders and take
> orders in civilian clothes?
> Look at your candidates with that in mind.
> Like as not there will be among them a Socialist who hopes
> that you are so used to discipline by now that you won't
> resent a good dose of it in civilian life.
> Don't expect him to say so in his election address. He will
> talk about 'planning' and 'centralised control'.
> But . . .

And so on. The extraordinary profession-of-arms romanticism of
'Soldier abroad . . .' recurs, sorting oddly with the last, and direct,
threat: that Socialistic 'cat-and-mouse control' can send some
demobbed men back into uniform. It will be 'a world full of sergeant-
majors', 'led by Plain-Clothes-Field-Marshal Ernie Bevin'. The
Conservatives, on the other hand, 'want you not only to feel free
but to be free as soon as possible'. That freedom is at once identified
as 'giving full rein to the skill and ingenuity and enterprise of
Britain's industries'. The words 'free' or 'freedom' occur four times
in the three paragraphs devoted to the Conservatives, and three
times in an inch in the adjacent column. Socialists—or rather that
distanced 'a Socialist'—have been characterized in terms of order,
deviousness, 'anxious to cover up a mess', 'furious when they were
rightly told . . .', malicious and secretive as cats.

It is interesting that a paper that consistently seeks emotional
responses should brand its opponents as emotional in order to

discredit them. The kind of political judgement offered, and invited, is entirely a question of creating subconscious images, by seeking, as advertisements do, to manipulate subconscious fears and desires.

On the 19th the *Express* picks up a phrase from Harold Macmillan, 'Gauleiter Laski', to head its front-page story; the subsidiary heading is 'Attlee pressed to reply'. The story is not much advanced: 'speakers up and down the country' and 'many leading Socialists' are agitated, Socialists have been 'given the tip' not to say anything until their leaders have told them what to say—a sly, underhand directive, that tip; Bevin is quoted criticizing Laski, in a quite different context and nine months previously; and decoy-duck Attlee 'lies low and says nothing', clearly having something shameful to hide. William Barkley, in the 'Mr. Laskee' headline already quoted, exploits the threat of an unEnglish name; and also defines for *Express* readers the fallacy of nationalization: it suits those who want 'a quiet life', 'the Tired Tims who fear the competitive life of nature'. Conservatism, we deduce, looks to Darwin as its philosopher.

On the 20th 'Laski unleashes another General Election broadside: Socialism—"Even if it means violence".' This is a new emphasis. It is based upon words alleged to have been used by Laski during a meeting in Newark. In the libel action[16] that Laski subsequently brought, the jury found for the defence after many conflicting testimonies of what had actually been asked, heckled and answered in the Market Square hurly-burly.

The content of the story is what the headline leads us to expect. It starts 'Professor Harold Laski . . .', describes the report as 'sensational', and expands into three articles on the feature page. A leader, firstly, argues that, whereas 'Conservative policy is laid down in the House of Commons and debated there', the Socialists' is decided by a 'completely obscure . . . secret caucus', which has no responsibility to the electors, and which has 'snubbed . . . a political leader who until recently enjoyed great eminence as Deputy Prime Minister.' Attlee's powerlessness is not a new line; secrecy and violence are. A second feature, 'Sayings of the professor—"Revolutions are not made in rose-water"' (a misquotation, incidentally), strings together some of Laski's more radical observations of the previous dozen years. The 'professor' emphasis, already made twice, is the main theme of the leading feature: 'This Man Laski. He is the power behind the Party—and why', wherein Trevor Evans, beneath another sinisterly lighted portrait of the Professor, describes the man who, luckily for *Express*-readers, had once been a neighbour of Evans.

16 See *The Laski Libel Action*, Daily Express, 1947.

A professor then, and perhaps even in our own technocratic age, had, among its folklore connotations, absent-mindedness and potential madness. The 'mad professor', usually foreign, often German, was familiar enough in popular fiction. A professor who speaks of violent revolution may well have bubbling test tubes to support his case. But he is also academic, intellectual, somewhat ridiculous, not downright like you and me and Trevor Evans.

The burden of Evans's piece is Laski's allegedly self-confessed and self-deplored 'mental aloofness' from the working-class roots of his party, which has affected 'his judgment of the moods of other people, particularly those for whom he has worked so assiduously in the last twenty years on the preparation of beliefs and principles they *ought* to hold'. (*Express* italics.) He is 'complex . . . intellectual . . . his sole weapon is intellect . . . sardonic . . . good company when you are mentally alert . . . a terrific worker . . . tiny crabbed script . . . books everywhere . . . he reads at the rate of 260 pages an hour . . . works far ahead'. This emphasis of the remote and ineffectual don having been made, the portrait is actually much less rebarbative than the presentation, and the news-stories and leaders, have suggested. It may be that Evans, one of the Socialists on the *Express* of whom Christiansen spoke, was not carrying out his brief with the 'professional gusto' that he might.

Beaverbrook leads next day's paper with 'Shall the Laski "25" rule Great Britain?' The strapline, referring to Labour's National Executive, is frankly insulting:

> Who are they?—Binks, Burke, Clay, Dobbs, Earnshaw, Heady, Knight, Moody, Openshaw . . . and so on

It is not only that men you have never heard of cannot be trusted, but that they must moreover be ridiculous ('and so on') because they have never been heard of. The very ordinariness of their names is exploited: in alphabetical order, they sound like soldiers on parade being 'called off', and are thus privates, not officers. And these men presume to rule a country with the resounding name of Great Britain under another who, as the photograph of Laski (hand resting on hip) clearly shows, is a manifest crackpot. How readily we prefer the familiar figure of Beaverbrook, pictured in staunch forthrightness next to him.

Beaverbrook's speech attracted 'an immense gathering'. A 'great batch' of critics 'quailed under Lord Beaverbrook's eye.' 'It was a warm and heartening occasion.' The word 'freedom' occurs three times in the first two paragraphs of the reported speech; the word 'secret' also occurs three times in three paragraphs after the name of

Laski has been mentioned. 'Caucus', 'dictatorship', etc., are also much in evidence. 'This audience of people from hard-boiled Streatham heard with enthusiasm Lord Beaverbrook's powerful call.' At the end 'it was on its feet in an instant, clapping and cheering'. The Lord was mobbed by autograph-hunters.

It is Beaverbrook Day generally. There is a report of an Attlee speech that attacked him, and the main feature is on the Beaverbrook plan for high wages. The latter begins:

> Lord Beaverbrook's election speeches are having their usual effect. They are enraging his enemies, delighting most of his friends (and alarming others) and winning reluctant approval from some of his political opponents.
>
> Beaverbrook has many of the attributes of Lloyd George . . .

In the next-door leader Socialists are again 'furious', and Morrison is 'white and incensed': the cause is opposition to their desire to 'clap on controls . . . even stricter than those which were found necessary to beat Germany'. We are threatened with 'social revolution, even if it means the wholesale slaughter of the ancient rights and liberties of the people'. The *Express*'s basic polarity has now matured into its characteristic expression: a party given to violence and controls, ruled by an obscure, unelected caucus, emotional (because guilty) when opposed or found out, *versus* an entertaining, enthusiastically welcomed party devoted to ancient rights and liberties, led by an ineffable statesman.

That statesman himself leads the June 22 paper: 'Obscure Laski caucus will give orders'. 'Churchill explains how the Socialists would run Britain. Do this, do that; go here, go there—or you will be punished.' Even the *Express* has started to run out of new phrases of threat; but it adroitly colours its headlines by running them round two sides of pictures of a very alien-seeming and intimidating military courtroom. Close inspection reveals that the pictures are wired from Moscow, and nothing to do with Churchill's remarks.

On the same page:

> Socialist candidates complain—
> Laski's policy means defeat
> 'Tell us what to say'

It is another thrombosis for the 'inner-circle of leaders' of the Party, who want

> to find some way of 'disowning' the professor's views . . . the professor's friends are making it clear that he will not 'go

quietly' . . . Any plan to hold a secret meeting of the National Executive has also had to be abandoned.

The ironic quotation-marks proliferate:

> Candidates and speakers all over the country have been told to keep quiet and evade questions on this Laski affair, which is described as an 'indiscretion' . . . Yesterday a hunt for a 'formula' was going on for a form of words designed to reassure worried Socialist voters without at the same time provoking Professor Laski into any 'indiscretion' in self defence.

Possibly—no attribution tells us—we should think that the quoted words are actually quotations.

Socialist candidates, finding that 'questioners refuse to be fobbed off' and worried that the whole thing is becoming 'hopeless', have made 'urgent appeals . . . to party headquarters for more positive guidance'. Guy Eden understands that two courses of action are meditated:

> The first is to include reassuring words in the party's election manifesto this week-end.
> The second is to put words into the mouth of the party's final election speaker on the radio in the hope that it will then be too late for the professor to do much harm.

An inside page carries the full text of Churchill's broadcast, as always, a coverage extended to Anthony Eden's one broadcast but never remotely approached by Labour broadcasters. Trevor Evans, again with more sympathy, describes the composition of the National Executive: such an article seems to counteract the *Express* policy of representing the Socialist leaders as clandestine. Perhaps journalistic inquisitiveness overcame election policy on this occasion. There is, true, the telling sentence, 'No one, except party officials, has ever seen the executive at work'.

Now, from June 23, Churchill's tour takes over the front-page leads, and there are only some small Laski items to note before the final exposé. The 'obscure caucus or junta who are not answerable to the electors', the 'totalitarian despotisms . . . conspiracy . . . tyrannical power', are contrasted with the 'swift authoritative mind' of 'Our Churchill'. In the same leader, which denies that 'Laski-ism is obscuring the issues of this election', there is a curious example of the self-fulfilling prophecy; we are warned not to trust those who 'may look soft and easy going, with the right hand outspread in persuasion and the other resting on the hip . . .'. Where have we seen such a precisely-described posture?—on the front page two days ago. The paper is drawing on its own mythology. The leader questions 'Socialist experimentation', and concludes with the words 'the mess that we have been thrown into by German National Socialism'.

The main headline on July 2, is 'Socialists decide they have lost'. 'Opposition experts' have 'combed' Churchill's speech but their 'recommended' answers are unenthusiastically received by speakers who find that 'abuse of Mr. Churchill is received with open resentment, even in places which are usually regarded as Socialist strongholds.' The leader disparagingly analyses all those strategem (they have sought to 'laugh the whole thing off', then to 'talk it away', and finally to 'yawn it off'), and concludes that Laski's 'cool, calculating brain' is leading the Party into Communist domination.

The affair finally bursts back into 60 point headlines on July 3, two days before polling.

Premier rebukes Attlee, says nation must know the truth
Churchill forces Laski show-down
Attlee gets letter—then disowns the Professor
Grave issues at stake

The story, its first paragraph in six lines of four-column bold caps and the body all in double column, the most forceful presentation of the whole campaign, starts:

Mr. Attlee has thrown Professor Laski overboard. His hand was forced last night by a new note from Mr. Churchill which stated bluntly that grave constitutional issues were raised by Laski's orders to Attlee ... The Professor is now repudiated completely—after 18 days.

The blunt and irresistibly righteous leader has exposed what plainly ('show-down') must be furtive and shameful. The cause-and-effect of '—then disowns ...' reminds us of the use of 'so' in other stories: Attlee is liable to be 'forced' into courses of action he was unwilling to adopt. 'Rebukes' expresses the master-and-pupil relationship. The 'grave issues' remind us of what this election is all about; they also lend their gravity to this story. We are promised 'the truth', which someone must have been trying to cover from us till now, for his own secretive reasons.

Although we are relieved that Attlee has been forced into a rightminded course of action, what are we to make of a party leader who throws overboard one of his colleagues? He is clearly unstable emotionally, something Churchill has known all along:

'The discussion of grave constitutional issues,' he is quoted as saying, 'cannot be prevented by anger or strong language'.

> This emphatic statement brought Mr. Attlee into the open at 9.30 last night.

The usual image of emphatic/into the open is given a circumstantial authority by the naming of the exact hour. Politicians, we are told, were 'astonished' at the strong tone of Mr. Attlee's reiteration of the party's constitution, which was available for a small sum from Transport House. The party's 'internal disruption' must soon come to a climax, despite 'strong efforts' to gag Laski (a typical Socialist evasion). The trouble is that it is now too late for the Socialists to present their foreign policy, such as it is, to the electorate. (The following day the *Express* thought it necessary to print an 'Easy-to-read summary of the Prime Minister's policy for Home Affairs'. It begins: 'What is the constructive Home Policy of the Conservative Party? At the request of many readers . . .'—an extraordinary request on the day before an election during which, the *Express* was later to claim, it had 'striven by argument' to present the issues.)

Yet another letter from Churchill to Attlee keeps the story going as second lead on July 4 ('I think that you underestimate the intelligence of the public' Attlee said in his reply). The leader speaks of Churchill's 'deadly criticism' of the 'angry, frightened' Socialists, to whom unspecified policies of violence are accredited. Laski breathes his last in a mere quip from a Churchill speech on polling day, and a headline, 'Split, split, split.'

It seems fair, before reflecting on some of the wider implications of the Laski affair, to allow Christiansen to define his attitude to news-reporting:

> Always, always, the news should be presented fairly in our columns. We will, of course, give prominence to those who support Empire policies and that sort of thing, but we will not be unfair to those who oppose us. So far as the news columns of the paper are concerned, we seek only one thing—absolute objectivity. And I call upon the staff to help me in this task.

No historian believes that the Laski affair, which the *Express* started (as far as the press was concerned) and billed biggest, had any influence upon the election result. It seems to have been regarded with scepticism or puzzled indifference. McCallum and Readman say that it failed because the public had been warned by the Labour Party to expect stunts:

This part of the Labour Party's campaign is perhaps the most brilliant piece of prophylactic political medicine ever achieved in electoral history. When the 'Laski Affair' appeared the Labour Party was ready for it.

One might feel, however, that more credit should be given to the untutored intelligence of the public. The affair, and Laski's own disingenuity in it, is said to have 'irritated' Attlee. Christiansen of course defended it, in phrases that make his cynical exploitation of it quite clear:

> By the time Harmless Harold had been through the wringer, my poor paper had been accused of conducting the dirtiest election campaign of all time . . . But everything we printed was based on the news.

He could hardly make a lesser claim; a coal merchant might deliver a sack of nylon stockings and defend himself by claiming that they are based on coal.

*   *   *

Churchill was the instigator of new chapters in the *Express*'s Laski story. There seems to have been no speculation upon how great a part he played in deciding to keep the story going: certainly his harping on it was convenient to Beaverbrook. The reason may have been the same for both men, want of a real issue. Churchill was out of his element in this election, so soon after his unchallenged and celebrated war-leadership. He later wrote, 'The incongruity of party excitement and chatter with the sombre background which filled my mind was in itself an affront to reality and proportion.'[17] He was 'bored' by home affairs, according to Michael Foot, and ignorant of the realities of Labour thought and policies. He was clearly content to go along with Beaverbrook's and the Tory Party's policy of no policy but Churchill's leadership. He was the leader you know, Laski was invented as the leader you don't know. The *Express* placed great value upon that which was known, as can be seen in its handling of Churchill himself.

The *Express* more than once thought it necessary to warn its readers against a dangerous rumour, 'that it will be possible to have at the same time both Churchill as Prime Minister and also a Socialist majority after the election'. No: 'It is one thing or the other. It is either Churchill or the Socialist Party'. The emphasis is square. Conservative policies or, of course, Socialist leadership are

17 Winston S. Churchill, *Triumph and Tragedy*, Cassell, 1954.

subordinate; you must choose either this man or that body of theory; this national hero or that gang of gauleiters; this embodiment of the national pride and memory, or that 'fantastic leap in the dark' to land in a mesh of rigid controls. Deep in that dark, unknown, un-elected, is a coldly remote caucus whom 'no one has ever seen at work'; 'Our Churchill', in contrast, stands upright over us in the clear light of day.

The appeal to loyalty was of course meant to feed off the dedication to a cause that had been won only a few weeks before. The Socialists were not offering an alternative policy but a hostile one, hostile to the man who had commanded the nation's loyalty for five years. How could a decent-minded nation be so capricious as to consider re-nouncing its loyalty now? And beneath the appeal to loyalty runs another, even closer to the British heart, the appeal to gratitude: didn't everyone feel an inalienable gratitude to the man whose voice had heartened them in the darkest days of 1940? Lest we forgot, there were, before Churchill's tour started on June 23, stories to remind us: '"Thank Churchill"—Eisenhower to US' was June 19's main lead.

The picture of themselves that the *Express* gave back to its readers here was that they were loyal to the point of unrestrained sentiment; grateful to an extent that pre-empted reasoned argument for political choice. They detested disloyalty—party splits—of the kind that riddled the Socialists. They were people who never changed their mind once it was made up. And they were people who needed a national figurehead to symbolize the victory they were celebrating: a leader. A capacity for reverence is the most strongly held assump-tion in the tone of the *Express*'s presentation of Churchill, 'The greatest man now living'. It is something quite different from Christiansen's assurance that no word of criticism should creep in. It is the treatment of Churchill as partaking of the divine. How else can we read a passage such as the start of the July 3 leader?

> *They laughed at him.* They shouted and jeered and called him a warmonger.
> But he was right.
> What bitterness arises in the souls of the Socialist politicians at the thought of their past mistakes!
> They howled him down. They thought that Hitler himself could be brought into a brotherhood of love—that the tiger could be trained to pull a governess cart . . .
> *Then they turned to him.* Then, when they knew that their homes and their children were threatened . . .

Then for a time they fawned on him . . .
And now—now that it is safe—they have turned on him . . .
Angry and jealous at the warm-hearted reception he gets
from the people, they liken the cheers of the multitude to the
swooning of bobby-socks girls at the sight of Frank Sinatra.
Yes, they even said that.

[*Express* italics]

This man of sorrows is described in the rhythms, the syntax and even,
allowing for the usual veering of address, the vocabulary of Isaiah
Chapter 53. Similar examples are easily found; the leader of June 22
('Obscure Laski Caucus' day) starts:

Faith of a man
Who shall govern the people wisely in the early years that
follow the slaughter of war?
Who shall guide the people in the tasks of the Peace Con-
ference?
Who shall be trusted with the immense tasks at home and
abroad?
'I sincerely believe', says Churchill, 'that I can help you.'
This man, who dedicated himself . . .
[See Isaiah Chapter 6.]

Five days later a short leader on Churchill ends, 'Truly this Churchill
of ours is a man worth following.'

It requires no very long leap in the dark to attribute the Old
Testament tone to Beaverbrook's Presbyterian upbringing. It invites
us to defer to Churchill with a scripturally unquestioning reverence.
By the same token it also seeks to make a humble congregation of us,
a multitude that defers to the interpreting ministers. The biblical
usage has another intention, that of associating its subject with the
deepest traditions of British life by summoning up the sort of
language that might evoke great national occasions, pageantry, and
also the notion, still widely held then, of Britain as a Sunday-pious
country.

In this context, it is not surprising to find that Churchill's electoral
tour, as reported in the *Express*, took on the lineaments of a messianic
progress. The multitude flocked to hear him preach.

The first report, on June 23, was headlined:

VE Day all over again for Mr. Churchill
Thousands cheer speech in street

The strapline was: 'Premier loses cigar as surging crowd try to carry
him from car.' There is a 7 in. × 5 in. column picture of Churchill,

a lion statue and a vast throng, headed: 'The lion speaks beside the lion'. We read that Churchill 'had the greatest electoral reception of his life' at Uxbridge, that 'he was almost torn out of his car by cheering supporters . . . they struggled to grasp his hand . . . Mr. Churchill had to cling to the seat of the car', and much else in the same vein, 'enthusiastic', 'triumphant'. His tour during the coming week, variously described as a 'friendly pilgrimage' and a 'wayside crusade', is detailed in a separate itinerary.

The report from Birmingham on June 26 opens: 'Never has there been a tour like this . . . It has not been an election tour at all. It has been a victory tour, a roaring helter-skelter triumph for the man who won the war . . . Those people who could not hear him speak were content to see the man, to cheer him and to thank him for his great leadership.' The next day 'The North gives him his greatest day', said the headline, only to be upstaged immediately by Scotland, 'outdoing even the acclaim of England.' But London rallied at the end with 'a tumultuous reception surpassing even those accorded him in Edinburgh and Glasgow'. Headlines, photographs and copy continue to hammer the point of multitude: unlike the secret caucus of the Socialists, never seen at work, this Churchill of ours must have been seen by nearly every man, woman and child in the country. The progress is punctuated by many informal moments: the farm-girl whose cows got mixed up with the procession, the boy who snatched a ride on the back of Churchill's car, the woman with a bunch of flowers and 'tears of happiness welling in her eyes', the 'grey old farm horse . . . bearing on its back a white-bearded old gentleman aged about 80 . . . carrying in his hand a Union Jack which he waved vigorously at the Prime Minister.'

A sentimental journey calls for sentimental copy. From Edinburgh on June 29, for instance, there came the headlines:

Clydeside and Edinburgh speak for Scotland
Churchill back today after final triumph
'Carry On' Call
The scene that will live in his memory

After the last headline is an arrow cut into the big picture of Churchill, taken, as often, from his back so that the 'Silent Multitude', as the caption calls it, faces the reader. 'Every eye in this vast multitude is fixed on Winston Churchill as, in the final speech of his tour of triumph, he addresses the throng in Princess-street Gardens, Edinburgh.'

We read that Churchill is returning to London 'tired but in-spirited', with 'the slogan cry: "Carry on, Winston", ringing in his ears'. He has been moved to tears by 'a day in which Scotland rose in all its pride to greet the Premier . . . the crowds have been quite out of control in their frantic effort to show Mr. Churchill that he is a greater fighter and a man after the Scots people's own heart'. Edinburgh, fittingly, was 'a little more solemn and calm' than Glasgow, but still their cheers 'echoed . . . round the rock on which beautiful Edinburgh Castle stands'.

The tour's climax merited four front-page pictures headed: 'This was London Pride'. We are told of the 'tumultuous welcoming' of 'The Churchill tornado'.

> Old women came out and sat in their little front gardens on wicker chairs; Chelsea pensioners stood awkwardly to attention; street hawkers left their barrows to their fate—but the crowd wanted Churchill and not the cherries. And some— daring much in this great crowd—booed. Mr. Churchill had a word for them, a softer word . . .

The sentimentality is conservative, seeking, in its plurals, to evoke a fixed order of society where people know their place and the behaviour expected of them. To stereotype people like that is to diminish them to Happy Families.

All hecklers at Churchill's meetings are shown to be at best eccentrics, more likely motivated by malice and jealousy; they are invariably laughed out of court by the common-sense majority, or shamed into silence ('Churchill . . . thus swept away the Socialist contention . . .'). The picture on polling day includes Churchill, two policemen, A Union Jack, a rosette, a carnation, ancient buildings, a pressing throng, and the inset headline, 'Hand of friendship'. The main heads are:

'We are winning'
Churchill: I feel it in my bones you will send me back with a great majority
Blitz people give greatest ovation

And, above, 'Roar of London's cheers gives nation lead for today'. Churchill is reported as describing Socialist policies as 'a vile form of Communism'. Adjacent headlines tell us 'Socialist chance is remote'; 'Premier says—Morrison did a cowardly thing'; and 'The man from Burma', another story of a serviceman testifying for Churchill. Familiar keys are being struck: multitude, confidence, indignation, and the classifying 'Blitz people'. Only inside the paper, in William Barkley's article on page 2, is an uncertain note heard: '. . . surely he will not be rejected on any cry that this is fuehrer-worship'. The unspecified reference is to an accusation by Arthur Greenwood, which reversed Churchill's 'Gestapo' smear on him.

Whereas the paper had printed the full texts of Churchill's broadcasts, it seldom gave great space to what Churchill actually had to say on his tour. He was cast in a part of modest pride. As late as July 3 we read:

> It was here I heard him indulge himself for the first time since his tour began in a personal note.

We are invited to marvel at the self-restraint. Churchill (unlike Laski) is a man like us, subject to physical tiredness (understandable after all he has been through), to mild indulgence and to deep but controlled emotions; and he is among us, seen, known and trusted. But he is somehow more a man than any one of us is: touched with greatness, endowed with solemn dignity, more wise, farsighted and confident than any ordinary mortal can aspire to be. It is not necessary to report every wisdom: the mere fact of his presence, and the effect on those he passes among, is sufficient. When we see how the multitude behaves, we cannot assume but that someone mighty, truly a man to follow, is there. To this man, to be measured only in traditional rhythms and cadences, we flock to warm ourselves at the ancient ways and manners he embodies: 'Trust the time-tried qualities of initiative and enterprise which have made us great. Trust the well-tried leader Churchill . . .' The hero has proved himself in the ritual test of battle; now we reverence his prowess in time of peace.

Anthony Eden thought later, 'We fought the campaign badly. It was foolish to try to win on Winston's personality alone instead of a programme. The modern electorate is too intelligent for that, and they don't like being talked down to'. Churchill himself seems to have sensed early in the campaign that victory was far from assured: he told Eden that he foresaw a period in opposition. (Eden thought it 'a tease'.) And a bold headline in the June 18 *Express*, '48 in 100 say "Give us Churchill"', might have provoked the thought, *only* 48? By the climax of the campaign, however, Churchill, in common with most people and most newspapers, expected that he would win. Eden tells us that the result came as 'a devastating, and especially a personal, defeat' for Churchill, who was 'wretched'.

* * *

The material within this period that did not form part of either the Churchill or the Laski stories was aligned to the same polarities, and sounded a very similar register of tone.

Every opportunity was taken to drive home the leader column's theme of Socialist orders, controls, punishments. A Tory speech reported on June 16 mentions 'repression . . . Socialist repression . . . action by Order . . . take away the citizens' right of challenge . . . dictatorship . . . dictatorship.' The story next to it reports Bevin defending 'regulation . . . restriction . . . restrictions . . . regulations'. The main speaker reported on the page, Beaverbrook, speaks of 'compulsory directions . . . controls . . . direction . . . There must be control where there is shortage of supply. But the real job of government must be to make up the shortage of supply . . . controls . . . the Socialist Party like regulations. They want control. They believe in direction . . .' On the front page is the headline: 'Bevin Order keeps men from jobs'. Elsewhere we read of a 'pre-war air of rebellion against autocratic and bureaucratic control' at the Milk Marketing Board.

Grotesque ineptitudes on the part of Labour candidates were common currency. A notable one was a story that gleefully described. how posters bearing Morrison's smudged face were scattered in a parcels jam at Euston. On the front page that was dominated by 'Scotland rose in all its pride to greet the Premier' Labour politicians were having a less dignified time: all the headlines they rated were 'Alexander loses his ninepence' and '20 wait in vain for Morrison'. Labour speakers were in fact also drawing large crowds, though no *Express* reader was told about them. There was a photograph, in an issue outside this sample, of Bevin addressing a handful of children; Bevin later commented that he had sent his audience under the trees to get out of the rain, but the camera-angle did not include trees or audience. A brilliant small example of the sub-editor's power of keying a story can be observed in one that opened:

> Mr. Ernest Bevin, at a Socialist rally on Brentford Football
> Club ground last night, expounded *his* plan for housing.

The jaded italics could imply that this is just one plan among a pack of others, or that it is an eccentric plan; either way, it certainly does not prepare us to take the rest of the report seriously. A similar example is in the headline immediately beneath: 'My plan for the Bank of England By Herbert Morrison'. Morrison's views are at once insulated: the tone of the headline reminds us of a schoolboy's essay, little Herbert piping up about an august institution.

Beaverbrook, figuring largely in his own newspaper's campaign, is presented as fluctuating between dynamic, aggressive energy and impish wit. Headlines often show him in combat: 'Speak, Sir Walter. Beaverbrook attacks Labour direction'; 'Aren't you

ashamed, Mr. Cadbury? Lord Beaverbrook on nationalization'. He
has a way with audiences: 'The meeting hushed as Lord Beaverbrook
tackled this issue . . .'; 'Paddington's noisiest meeting . . . gradually
dominated by Lord Beaverbrook'; 'Thunderous applause greeted
this powerful passage . . .' Beaverbrook always has the quick and
last word to make hecklers 'quail' amid loud laughter, or to reduce
them, by a dazzling display of facts, to 'an air of gloom'. The content
of his speech invariably deals with the right policies for 'getting
Britain moving again', and fast. Like his paper, he believed that the
country was straining at the leash, and the only problem was how
best to slip the collar off: the dog would know where to go. He
sets out lists of necessary freedoms (his assertion of the need to
be free from the 'tyranny of labour direction' generally elicits the
reporter's note, 'loud applause'). 'Speed the demob', his headlines
cry. 'Silence the voices of free men? Never.' Attacks on him, it has
been said, were generally reported with relish in the *Express*. One
attack, by Attlee on Beaverbrook's 'insatiable lust for power',
was not reported; instead, the following exchange was described
next day:

> When asked a question about Daily Express politics Lord
> Beaverbrook replied: 'I have no time to give to the Daily
> Express. The Daily Express was built up by me from a strug-
> gling little undertaking. I worked pretty hard on it and there
> it is to give you pleasure or to annoy and anger you, just as you
> like. (Loud laughter.)
> 'But I cannot answer questions about the internal economy
> or political attitude of that newspaper because I am never
> there and I do not know it. I am elsewhere.'

  William Barkley was Beaverbrook's personal reporter. He also
wrote an occasional election column. The most remarkable one was
saved for election day. Headed 'THE GLORY of the BRITISH
WAY of LIFE . . .', the first paragraphs deserve quoting in full:

> Last night I invaded with consent a Londoner's castle to
> telephone to the Daily Express. The Londoner welcomed me.
>   He put his sitting-room with telephone at my disposal. When
> I had finished he brought me food, prepared by his wife, and
> drink. It was in a district of London badly bombed by the foul
> Germans.
>   Presently I said to him: 'How did you get on in the blitz?'
> He and the dear woman exchanged glances, and he said to me:
> 'My wife was killed in that heap of rubble across the road,

and the elder of my two boys—you see their photographs on the mantelpiece—was badly injured.

'This dear lady,' said he, smiling and bowing across the table to the woman of the modest house, 'takes my wife's place. She is my second wife.'

I said: 'I wish I had not mentioned it.'

They said, in duet: 'Please do not feel embarrassed.'

This passage, written by the paper's chief political columnist on election morning itself, vividly illustrates what assumptions the *Express* was making about its readers, in Derby and Rhyl.

The article continues with talk of 'this old country', 'the Socialists have been screaming and squealing', 'Great is the British Constitution, the wonder of the world, the marvel of the ages . . as near as may be in this finite world it is eternal', the 'working man', 'this old House of Commons', 'Let us hold to the old and tried ways', and 'the bomb-blitzed homes of Britain'.

Manipulation of the war sentiment was naked on election day. The leader, in unusually large type, starts 'Rejoice and be glad. For this is the day of the people', reminds us that 'men have died to secure this right of the people' (to vote), and continues:

We, the people, make our crosses with a sense of deep responsibility. We remember how near in 1940 we were to slavery and degradation.

We remember the beat of the Luftwaffe's engines in the sky. We know that once only a handful of young RAF pilots stood between us and destruction, death, utter defeat.

The *Express*, claims the leader, has 'presented . . . vast issues . . . without fear or favour'; now, reminding us of our 'liberties' and 'sovereign independence of Parliament', it attacks the Socialists, 'destructive of liberty', and equates Churchill with 'free enterprise and equal opportunity'. We are exhorted to vote for 'the Churchill candidates'. On the back page Lord Woolton's 'solemn eve-of-poll declaration' is reported under the headline: 'If you now change the government—Despair (in America); rejoicing (in Japan).' The same paper contains pictures of Churchill headed, without fear or favour: 'Don't let him down'.

*   *   *

The mood of the electorate in 1945, according to Michael Foot, was one in which the nation reflected 'on its whole history since 1918'; the war had awakened 'a more radical impulse than anything Britain had known for centuries.' Other historians agree: the election result, says L. C. B. Seaman, was the 'most decisive verdict in favour of radical change the British electorate had ever delivered'. Bevan, for one, had foreseen a 'stupendous revolution' in the electors' minds. A. J. P. Taylor, an historian of whom Beaverbrook approved (and vice-versa), goes so far as to say, 'In the Second World War the British people came of age.'[18]

The *Express* knew, or admitted, none of this. It is not simply that the paper backed the losers (and, as we have seen, expected to win), but that its entire address to its readers was dislocated from what proved to be the dominant feeling in the country. The evidence is that it was not calculation (a deliberate decision not to acknowledge the feeling for radical change) but ignorance that so divorced it: the same ignorance as Churchill's, a remoteness from real social life severer than any professor's. And that ignorance of fact, of what really concerned people, was compounded with a deep under-estimation of their intelligence. The people were in a questioning mood: the *Express* gave them personalities, not arguments. The people were, as Bevan put it, 'suspicious of being had': the *Express* gave them Laski, a stunt explicitly acknowledged as such by Christiansen. The people were profoundly glad the war was over, and what patriotic pride they felt centred on their own sufferings (more than it had done in 1918): the *Express* gave them a continued diet of war-time rhetoric and vituperation, and proposed Churchill as the messianic sufferer. The people associated the Conservative Party with the economic hardship of the 1930s, and felt the war to be an end and a catalyst, enabling the radical changes that were already discussed in the 1930s to be more expediently effected: the *Express* exulted in the chance of returning to some ancient, misty sceptr'd isle. The people were ready for further hardship in order to achieve a real change from the old order—'when the British know they are in for a hard time, they elect Labour', says Colin MacInnes:[19] the *Express*'s circus-entertainment style predicted instant beer and immediate skittles.

A paper for which the word 'freedom' was the soberest of all its expressed values constantly trespassed on its readers' freedom to know, to judge and to act. Instead of the 'free use of ideas', in Matthew Arnold's phrase, it took a politician's decision that the readers' votes were all that mattered, not their understanding. It did not suppose its readers competent to judge the issue but supplied their opinions for them.

18 A. J. P. Taylor, *English History 1914–1945*, Oxford, 1965.
19 *New Society*, September 8, 1966.

To do so, it assumed that people in Derby and Rhyl were bored by politics until made otherwise. The relief of boredom was to be effected not through the intellect but through the emotions, by 'commando stuff', in Christiansen's phrase. The election was presented as a conflict of heroes and villains, motivated by feelings, not reason: and readers were invited to engage themselves in the same way. 'The Tory', said Bevan, 'never addresses himself to the merits of political issues, but rather to the subjective attitudes of the electorate.' Instead of attacking the Labour Party's programme, the *Express* attacked clusters of feelings about the abstract notion of Socialism, feelings that it supplied with fictive licence. As Hitler had recently been a potent symbol, so Laski was first found, then 'revealed', as the head of a caucus, and used as a symbol: that he was used to symbolize something very like what Hitler had symbolized was a shameful development of the method. Churchill was used in a similarly totemic manner: instead of supporting the Conservative programme, the *Express* invited its readers to immerse their democratic freedom in Churchill's charisma. Adopting the priestly function of witness on behalf of Churchill, the paper assumed that its readers would deferentially accept being talked down to from the pulpit, midway between heaven and earth. It was in this vertical sense that the paper saw itself as a medium of news, news that was presented, to borrow a phrase from Graham Martin,[20] with 'the implication that without their colourful intervention there is no meaningful relationship between the events which they dramatize and the readers for whom the show goes on'.

All the evidence suggests that Labour would have won heavily whatever any newspaper said. That Beaverbrook's papers never had an ounce of real influence, distinct from Beaverbrook's personal involvement within the government, is a very old joke. The bitterest joke of all, in 1945, was played on Beaverbrook, when later in the year a meeting of Tory candidates turned on him for having, they said, betrayed the Conservative cause at the election by employing left-wing editors.

20 Essay on The Press in *Discrimination and Popular Culture*, ed. Thompson, Pelican, 1964.

3

MIRROR, 1937–1945

THE *Mirror* plainly advised its readers to vote Labour in 1945, though never in quite as many words. Labour's unexpected and huge victory led some, at the time and since, to credit the *Mirror* with a large responsibility for the result. One cannot know what truth there is in that. Experimental evidence about attitude-formation suggests that the paper is not likely to have changed many voters' minds, but it may have played an important part in getting the already decided Labour vote out to the polls, and particularly in mobilizing the Forces vote, which historians have guessed to be around 90 per cent for Labour. The paper's great popularity among servicemen is not in doubt,[1] and it helps to account for estimates of up to 11,000,000 readers in 1945, although the printed copies averaged 2,400,000 daily. If the *Mirror* did significantly influence the pattern of voting it must have done so by crystallizing a new mood that was already strong and widespread among the electorate.

In documents discussed later in the chapter there is firm evidence that a new mood of radical populism had seized many in 1945. A reading of the *Mirror* in the election period, and at intervals during 1937–45, suggests that the paper did develop a congruence with that mood. It may thus have served to crystallize the voting intentions of many of its readers: not only those who would have accepted the *Mirror* as their spokesman even if it had not changed (just as many *Express* readers presumably felt that their paper continued to speak

1 In *Newspaper Reading in the Third Year of the War*, Allen & Unwin, 1942, P. Kimble found that 30·3 per cent of servicemen and 32·4 per cent of servicewomen read the *Mirror* in late 1941; the corresponding figures for the *Express* were 26·5 per cent and 13·6 per cent. No other paper approached the popularity of those two among servicemen, of whom nearly half read them in 'institutions'—canteens, etc.

Kimble's figures for civilian readership are also pertinent. Among factory workers the *Express* reached 22·6 per cent of men (*Mirror* 24·9 per cent) and 10·1 per cent of women (*Mirror* 24·5 per cent), but among men doing other work (presumably of higher status on average) the *Express* with 26·9 per cent easily beat the *Mirror*'s 19·8 per cent. Among women non-factory workers, also, the *Express* narrowed the gap: 17·2 per cent against the *Mirror*'s 21·0 per cent. Thus there is evidence that the *Express*'s war-time appeal was typically to a higher social class than the *Mirror*'s. Among all women readers the *Mirror* had 23·5 per cent against the *Express*'s 13·8 per cent, which seems to validate the *Mirror*'s special direct address to women, discussed later in the chapter.

for them) but, crucial to the question of influence, existing readers
who responded politically for the first time, and perhaps new readers
too, attracted by finding their mood articulated. The *Mirror*, then,
may not only have confirmed but also helped to spread the new
mood, during the later war years.

The evidence of the *Mirror*'s congruence with the populist mood
will rest mainly on the paper's relationship with its readers. First, an
astonishing proportion of the paper in 1945 was given to readers'
letters, and stories derived from readers' own experiences. Sixty-five
per cent of the election coverage on July 4 was contributed by
readers, and from June 13 to July 5 readers contributed on average
nearly thirty per cent of the paper's electoral material. For the
possibility that the reader feedback was substantially invented by
the paper's staff, that they wrote most of the letters, there is little
evidence, and sheer mass and variety against it. The second striking
element in the relationship was the directness of the paper's address
to its readers, felt as much in its sympathy with distressed readers as
in its brusque admonitions to others who had only to get on with
their jobs like everyone else in a difficult time. The latent but powerful function of the direct mode of address was that it had about it the
feeling of democracy, of people talking straight to each other in
'real' language about their lives and hopes, and by the same token
an anti-authoritarian feeling: we, the people, can get things moving,
and done—anyone who directs us can do so only with our consent.
The directness was embodied in the *Mirror*'s main campaign slogan
in 1945, 'Vote for Him' (characteristically started by a reader's letter,
though the authenticity in that particular case is dubious)—an
appeal to wives whose husbands in the Forces had not registered as
Service or proxy voters, asking them to cast their votes as they
believed their husbands would have done. Two assumptions under-
lay the appeal, that women needed chivvying into voting at all, and
that the Forces were predominantly for Labour.

Around those central elements, the rest of the *Mirror* formed a
convincing totality, in the coherence of its parts, the matching of
tone to content, and the confident ability to assimilate and make
sense of new facts. There is also evidence from opinion polls that the
election issues most often treated by the *Mirror* closely conformed to
those thought most important by a majority of voters. The same was
not true of the Express.[2]

2 A comparison between topics covered by the *Express* and those rated
most pressing in public opinion polls has been made at the start of the
chapter on the *Express* in 1945. A direct statistical comparison between the
Mirror's and the *Express*'s coverage would require a percentage content

It is not plausible that the *Mirror* could have conjured up so convincing an appearance of confident exchange between itself and its readers expressly to fight an election. The question is one that Hugh Cudlipp has also asked: 'The intriguing point is not that the newspaper was accurate but why it was accurate'. An answer is that, in its election manners, the *Mirror* was cashing credit that had been banked over a period. To prove the hypothesis, a longer back-perspective than 1945 is required. The year 1937 was chosen as the start of the sample, because by then the new regime of Guy Bartholomew, Hugh Cudlipp, Basil Nicholson, Cecil King and Cassandra had begun to alter the paper from the quite different character it had during the first thirty years of its life. The sample comprised the papers of May and June every year. For reasons explained later, a sample was also made of a Forces newspaper, *Good Morning*, which was associated with the *Mirror*.

The main sample concentrated on material principally addressed to the Forces, and that directed at women, the two paper-reader relationships that were dramatized in the 'Vote for Him' campaign in 1945, and that most clearly embodied the mode of direct address. As a control sample of the rest of the paper, attention was also paid to Cassandra, and readers' letters. The development of each kind of material will be examined in turn, at periods from 1937 to 1945. Having seen what credit was banked, in the second part of the chapter it will be possible to consider the 1945 election material as the encashment.

*   *   *

1 Into Battle

In 1938 the *Mirror* demanded a National Government, National Service, a joint command with France, urgent re-armament, and 'the best brains in the country to direct us'. In the following year, impatient with the 'old men' and 'Munich Muddlers' of Chamberlain's government, it called for Churchill to form a new one. Ten days after war was declared, the paper said: 'In 1939 we cannot endure fools in high places as we did after 1914. The self-revealed blunderers must go. We endured muddlers too long in the last bitter

---

analysis of the *Mirror*; but its *forms* of content, including a very high contribution from readers, make content-classification so complicated as not to be worth the labour. Evidence of which election issues were most prominently treated by the *Mirror*—housing, above all—can, however, be found in the analysis of the 1945 *Mirror*'s principal themes later in the chapter.

struggle.' The Ministry of War was described as 'The Museum Ministry'.

When Churchill became Prime Minister in 1940, the *Mirror* assured him: 'You need not worry about the men and women of Britain, Mr. Churchill. The common people of this land have the courage . . . above all give them LEADERSHIP.'

It will already be apparent that for the *Mirror* there were two wars to be fought: the military war against Hitler, to 'rid the world of tyranny', and the war to win that war, against 'fools in high places' at home. From this second war was later to emerge a third, the war to win the peace, the decisive battle of which was the 1945 election. By attending to the way in which the paper fought the first two wars, one can see how its credit then banked was cashed in the third war. The processes were not, of course, clearly separate in time.

Also apparent in the brief examples above is one characteristic address of the *Mirror* to its war-time readers. By a kind of ventriloquism, it is not speaking *to* its readers but assuming what it took to be their voice, and letting its readers overhear it addressing those in power. It was not always thus: the *Mirror* was later able to address its readers plainly.

No one has doubted that the *Mirror's* readers, on the whole, accepted the paper's ventriloquistic voice as their own. It was, said Aneurin Bevan,[3] 'in a special sense the paper of the Armed Forces'. The war-time *Mirror* was the first daily paper to be read by 'other ranks' in the Forces and at home, according to A. J. P. Taylor.[4] Maurice Edelman[5] explains that Guy Bartholomew, the *Mirror's* editorial director from 1934 to 1951,

> was pre-occupied with the links between the home front and the Forces. Bart had appointed Greig to write a regular column dealing with soldiers' grievances. The idea had immediately caught on. Thousands of letters flooded into the office, not only with servicemen's grumbles but their wives' as well. There were down to earth complaints about delays . . . red tape . . . unfairness and a hundred other things.

Hugh Cudlipp mentions that the paper deliberately kept itself informed about its Forces readers by asking those staff who were in

3 Quoted in Cudlipp, *Publish and Be Damned*, Dakers, 1953. All quotations from Cudlipp in this chapter are taken from the same book.

4 A. J. P. Taylor, *English History 1914-1945*, Oxford, 1965.

5 Maurice Edelman, *The Mirror, A Political History*, Hamish Hamilton, 1966.

uniform to feed back the atmosphere 'in their articles and letters'.
Cudlipp also illuminates the historical development of the paper's
ventriloquism:

> the battle conducted in pre-war years against the smothering
> of legitimate grievances by military red tape explains much of
> the paper's war-time and post-war acceptability to the Forces
> ... the Mirror needed no second thoughts in determining the
> path it should pursue in the Hitler War. Here above all was the
> newspaper of the masses, the bible of the Services rank and file,
> the factory worker and the housewife. No daily journal was in
> a better position to register the people's pulse beat, reflect
> their aspirations and misgivings, and make articulate their
> relation or censure on the progress of the war. All the clues were
> in the Mirror's postbag from its readers.

Cudlipp quotes Roy Lewis to the effect that the Mirror described the
war in terms of 'the man at the receiving end ... the Mirror settled
down to fight his fight and air his grouse ... as everyone now knows,
the Mirror was in fact an integral part of Service morale ... it was
in touch with Service feeling as no other paper. It was the paper ...
of fighting men innocent of ideologies.' 'It regarded itself,' says
Cudlipp, 'as a paper with a mission and it was accepted as such': a
vital part of that mission, he says, was to provide matter for the
serious debate that took place in Nissen huts and air-raid shelters,
at home and abroad.

At this point the question is the Mirror's relationship with the
Forces, but the references to 'the factory worker and the housewife'
will be important later in the chapter.

The theme of the 'war to win the war' was most explicitly drawn
out by Tom Wintringham in a series of articles beginning in 1940.
Wintringham was a well-known and controversial representative
of the Popular Front when he began writing for the Mirror. He had
been active in the politics of the 1930s, had fought in Spain, and had
set up a centre for the training of an efficient Home Guard, the need
for which he often argued in his weekly column. Later in the war he
was to stand as a Common Wealth Party candidate.

Wintringham's articles spoke to the Government for the soldiers,
complaining of shortages and inefficiency, ending on the note of
'And let's get it done quickly'. He reaches the centre of his argument
in an article on June 5, 1941, where he is proposing that the men
saved from Crete should be brought home to teach the British forces
how to fight warfare from the air. He then looks at the conventional
opposition to such an idea and spells out his answer to it.

Responsible soldiers may object: 'We fought in several wars, in 1914–1918 on the North West frontier. Our experience of war is much greater than that of these boys.' Yes; there are soldiers with as many years fighting to their credit as these boys have weeks. But you learn more about modern war from one day under the dive-bombers than anyone would learn in the whole four years of the last war.

Therefore the leaders of these men from Crete, when they are brought here, should not be made to listen to any authority on tactics who belongs to the past. They should be given a free hand to train anew first a number of divisions, then the whole army and the Home Guard. We need a clean sweep, away from the old days of war. We need a war to win the war.

Call that 15,000 home to start this offensive. And tell them to get on with it at a blitzkrieg pace.

Setting the past against the present, the article questions the value, in this completely new situation, of that last defence of the old against the new, 'experience'. It is not simply that the older, 'responsible soldiers' are a little out of date; they are unable to comprehend the realities of modern warfare because it is different in quality from what they have known. They have not had the modern experience, and therefore have missed the modern meaning.

Thus a radical break with the past is necessary, 'a clean sweep'. Within the larger conflict against Nazi Germany there is a struggle to be won at home, a struggle to change a traditional thinking which is merely irrelevant now. This change will not be easy—Wintringham talks of 'a war to win the war', 'this offensive', 'a blitzkrieg pace'—but on its success the outcome of the larger war depends.

Not only is the structure of the argument significant; its tone has a relentless authority behind it, an assurance that the writer is empowered to speak for one group to another. The beginning catches a note of fairness:

Responsible soldiers may object . . . Yes, there are . . .

The writer sees the point and admits its superficial authenticity. But then he confidently hammers home his points, and moves to the imperative mood.

If you are to launch an 'offensive' to win the war, it must be launched against certain ideas and certain individuals who hold to them. It is here that an Us/Them consciousness, with deep roots in working-class mistrust of shadowy authority, enters, in battle-dress. The *Mirror* is for *us*, the ordinary soldier trying to win a war, against *them,* politicians, industrial magnates, civil servants, top brass, whose inefficiency makes them 'the tools, unwitting perhaps, of Britain's enemies'. This Us/Them consciousness is latent in all the common-sense advice given to soldiers, but seldom explicit.

Wintringham's central theme, the need for a radical break with the past and the struggle at home against those in the War Office, and elsewhere, who were making such a break necessary, recurred in his column throughout the period. He invited soldiers to write and tell him what they thought of the conduct of the war, and summarized their answers under the headline 'Give us the right fight'.

> Blanco and brass, polishing things that shine already, or ought not to shine for action, are the main grouses.

On July 17 he spells out the message:

> And how to get such a modern Air Force? Obviously the first thing to do is to get rid of the men at the top, who understand so little of the changes in warfare that they have prevented our having modern dive-bombers.

The authoritative tone of June 5 is also characteristic.

> News from Egypt is so scanty that we cannot tell if the fighting near Sollum is the beginning of a drive or not. Since Italian troops played the main part in it it is probably not.

This is the tone of the military expert, the man who can tell us, later, 'Crete is NOT a rehearsal for the invasion of Britain', and lecture the military or the Government:

> That, in outline, is the story of Greece. It is not a good story. It is a story of men wrongly placed, made to fight in an obsolete way. That their courage and endurance redeemed the story must not blind us to the need for modern tactics and strategy.

That Wintringham should consult, or appear to consult, the soldiers themselves, and speak for them directly to the Government, gives the column an authority different in kind from that of the military expert. It can speak from one group to another, the stance which the *Mirror* was to adopt at the 1945 election. Wintringham had both kinds of authority, and in his *Mirror* columns one could feed the other.

Wintringham spoke for the *Mirror*, not merely in it. Elsewhere in its pages, the *Mirror* can be heard speaking in a similar way:

> Shall we never get rid of these boobies who cannot understand that *Anything* may happen to those who will not be

prepared in time for the new form of war, which is war in the air? They utterly lack imagination, foresight, speed in preparation. They are the victims of the slap-dash touch. And they exasperate this nation by their everlasting rot about valour and one Briton being the equal of a dozen Germans. (Leader column, June 4.)

Zec's cartoon showed a huge alarm clock (Our War Effort) with the caption 'Still Going Slow'. Three days later, Live-Letters, answering a reader's criticism that the *Mirror* is over-critical of the Government, expressed approval of 'any sacrifice that will rid us of slothful politicians, of old-fashioned soldiers and of parasitic communities, both rich and poor, who are indifferent to our cause'. Cassandra on the same day wrote:

> To those who are worried, critical or alarmed about the events in Crete, I offer as balm the soothing ointment of General Sir Charles Bonham-Carter: 'Criticisms, however, would be more helpful if a greater understanding were shown of the present difficulties of supply and administration due to long postponement in beginning our preparations for war . . .' Isn't that the same answer that can be so glibly proffered if we lose the war? When all is at stake, is it enough to say we weren't ready? Or that we were too late? Or that Hitler had the start on us? As a prelude or a postscript to past and possible future disasters, I find the General's inane remarks peculiarly disturbing.

His attack on Them, who are losing the war, continued the next day:

> Lord Teviot, in a remarkable exposition of complacency, even goes so far as to advise us to say, 'Well done! Well tried! Carry on. If there is anything more any of us can do to help just tell us about it.' . . . nobody can say that an encounter in which we were forced to leave about 15,000 troops on the island and lost four cruisers, and six destroyers, is a sufficient cause to shout 'Well done!'
>
> And if you still think so, ask the relatives of the men who have not returned . . .
>
> As a parting shot, Lord Wolmer thoughtfully reminds us that 'we have still many months of deficient equipment before us and that victory cannot be attained until that has been made good.' I doubt if there is a single elector in the country who is unaware of this crushingly obvious fact. The revealing thing about these peers, with their compulsory ear plugs for all, is

that they cannot conceive a government virile enough to welcome criticism and benefit by it.

What do they want—an Anglicised Reichstag egged on by
organised cheer leaders?

On June 12 the leader column refers back explicitly to the 'War
to Win the War' column (by 'Our Military Correspondent, Tom
Wintringham') and summarizes the argument: 'in these critical
times dead wood isn't even of use for the coffins of those martyred
through muddle.'

To gauge the *Mirror*'s distinctiveness among other newspapers of
the period, the leaders of *The Times*, *Daily Express* and *Daily Herald*
at the time of the Crete evacuation may be compared with
the *Mirror*'s, on June 10, which tried to separate what was fair
and unfair criticism of the Government's conduct of the war. It
opened:

> Another small piece of good news!—the parliamentary debate
> on the evacuation of Crete and the situation in the Mediter-
> ranean will *not* be secret. We are to be allowed to know where
> we stand, or whence we have retreated—and perhaps why!

The tone is that of superior surprise: at last the Government is
beginning to move in the right direction ('our' direction). There is,
therefore, another *small* piece of good news to report. Only small,
but in these hard times that merits an exclamation mark. 'Not'
is in heavy type in '*not* be secret', since the Government has
now reversed a previous decision to fall in line with what 'we'
have already argued. We are to be 'allowed to know'—at last
we, the people, are being conceded some democratic rights; the
sarcasm rings bitterly on in 'where we stand, or whence we have
retreated'.

A later paragraph articulates the ironic tone into a parody of
upper-class speech, to criticize 'ministers or generals who just can't
believe that a nasty move will be made, as really it wouldn't be the
right move on gentlemanly lines.'

The Times, in its first leader on June 9, saw the problem more
philosophically:

> A certain lack of foresight, failure to see things whole, seems to
> have dogged our war effort from the first. Men change, and,
> though the changes have often been for the better, the failure is
> not remedied. May it not be that it is the system that is chiefly
> at fault? Too much weight seems still to be put on the shoulders
> of the Prime Minister, strong and unbowed as they are.

The language is constantly qualified, and the criticism is levelled not at personalities but at 'the system'. The Prime Minister is carefully protected in his dignity ('strong and unbowed') from any slight sting that might be implied.

On June 10 in its Opinion column the *Express* was also finding fault with the system, and appealing to MPs to get at the facts during their recess:

> The Daily Express hopes that MPs have been finding out about things in their constituencies, that they haven't just been playing golf, or lolling about.
>
> We hope that they have been working as hard as they demand the industrial masses should work, that they have discovered the where's and why's of the war factory bottlenecks.
>
> It is because they are short of this and that piece of equipment that our generals are often made to look inferior. And it is because Goering has screwed so much out of the German Home Front that the German High Command looks so brilliant.

The *Express* is concerned to mobilize all the resources of the nation, but it is not the generals who are at fault. Rather, it is the 'war factory bottlenecks', an impersonal object of criticism again. The people directed by the Government are no less impersonal, 'industrial masses'. On June 4 the *Express* outlined what it saw as necessary in the present difficult situation: 'At this time, of all times, the crowning needs of the people are faith and understanding'. On June 6 it argued that 'the mood of the nation is to say to its rulers: "take us and get something done with us. You can still have greater power with us and America than Hitler can squeeze from all his conquests"'. A popular demand for leadership is echoed here as much as in the *Mirror*, but the relationship between leaders ('rulers') and led is notably more deferential—we, the people, are to initiate change by provoking the government, but we are to provoke them to 'take us and get something done with us'. This 'get something done with us' is quite different from the *Mirror*'s mood of 'let's get something done'. It suggests that the role of the people is essentially passive, to be led, to take orders. We are to offer ourselves for their use. The *Mirror*'s stress is the reverse: people demand a government they can use. On June 9, the Opinion column summed up the hour as being one of 'endeavour and of sacrifice. We will win this war quickly only if our leaders and our people together answer every demand made upon their energies.' The syntax of the last sentence is fascinating. To whom does the initial 'we' refer, when the sentence refers both to 'our leaders' and 'our' people, ending with 'their' energies? Who is speaking here?

On June 10 the *Daily Herald*'s long editorial is highly critical of the way the war is being conducted at all levels:

> And, most regrettably, ostrichism has its representatives among the organisers of war industry, its vital efforts are to that degree enfeebled; even among the military minds to whom we should be able to look for the grimmest and most penetrating assessment of our task.

The editorial sharply attacked the 'national complacency' which would allow the war to be lost.

> It is *not* easy to offer the hard talk of realism to people who believe that soothing syrup is the only food fit for human consumption.
> And a great many of our people are still like that.

And again:

> . . . there is a large and influential section of the public which insists in regarding the war as a walk-over for Britain—somewhat prolonged, perhaps, but a walk-over all the same.

The *Herald*'s criticisms are similar to those of the *Mirror*, attacking the military leaders for trying to paste over the problem. What is missing from the *Herald*'s editorial is the aggressive Us/Them tone of the *Mirror*. The *Herald*'s remarks are addressed to 'those who are in a position to comment and to criticize'; they are made in a tone of democratic debate—'most regrettably . . . to that degree . . . a great many of our people . . . somewhat prolonged, perhaps'—to which such highly-placed people are thought to be accustomed. The *Herald* seeks to persuade, the *Mirror* threatens. Implicit in the *Herald*'s tone is an acceptance that other points of view are in debate; its own argument is made firmly, is more sharply critical than *The Times*'s, less readily passive than the *Express*'s, but it remains a *contribution*, on behalf of the national interest. The *Mirror*'s ventriloquized sarcasm sounds as though it issues from the object itself of the debate, the people; pressing behind its tone is the populist feeling that if, in the last resort, the debate is ineffectual, then the debaters will be by-passed by the *Mirror*'s readers. It is against the *Herald*'s residual tolerance that the *Mirror*'s aggressive tone is most sharply distinguished.

The two most popular papers are also the two most in contrast.

In between are *The Times* and the *Herald*, both moderately critical, one blaming 'the system' from a traditional fourth-estate posture of armchair statesmanship, the other more squarely aimed against persons, or a type of person, but both mediating between government and people. The *Mirror* situates itself solidly among the people, a tribune[6] loyal to its readers and owing no obligation of respectfulness to the government it criticizes. The *Express* seems to speak from a position above debate or society: its first-person plurals are normally used only by the sovereign. It is speaking out of its idea of the nation—grand, imperial, but addressed to suburban readers, who passively wait, wanting to be led by 'rulers', because they wisely understand (the *Express* assumes) that to be the principle of greatness in a country.

* * *

During the war Tom Wintringham, Bill Greig, Garry Allighan and Ann Towers were all writing for the Forces, Allighan's column being the most regular during 1942–1945. Its tone is like that of an elder brother, firm, well-informed, but basically 'on your side'. It is a friendly, relaxed tone:

> Don't worry chum. No declaration of banns is necessary for a Register Office wedding.

but scrupulously fair. Allighan has no time for slackers, for those who don't realize that 'we're all in this together'. Thus a soldier aged 41, who enlisted for four years in 1938, writes asking whether he can get his discharge now that his period of enlistment is completed, and receives the reply:

> Not on your life. You're in—for the duration.

There is a level voice behind the banter. But whilst Allighan keeps firmly to the army rules, within the limits of law and order, the tone of his answers often moves against the authority which he is explicitly buttressing, so that he is also able to be on the side of the soldier, to apply the service regulation and still be 'one of the boys'. Answering a soldier's inquiry as to why he has not been promoted, Allighan picks up the fact that the soldier lost a good conduct badge in 1940:

> That's the solution to your problem. You've got to regain the time you lost for being a bad lad.

6 The characterizations of Armchair Statesman and People's Tribune are borrowed from Graham Martin's essay 'Public Voices' in *Your Sunday Paper*, ed. Hoggart, London University Press, 1967.

Allighan here does not question the regulation, made by Them, but the use of 'being a bad lad' is a signal transmitted and received within 'our' group, a group which knows about the abstract rules but makes allowances for people. Sometimes this sympathy is sharply linked to the critical vocabulary of the 'war to win the war'. Asked why service letters have to be written in formal circumlocutions, Allighan replies:

> Because—it is in the rules. It's an official 'must'. To cut the flowery language and get on with the war would upset the rule book.

Allighan's column gives the impression of being itself very efficient. Information is succinct:

> Demobbing will be on a planned basis so as not to throw too many men on the labour market at once.
> Bevin means to 'feed' men back into industry so as to avoid mass unemployment. Nothing has yet been decided about gratuities.

There is an official impersonality about this tone which contrasts sharply with the humanity of 'bad lad'. Nevertheless, this efficiency is deployed on behalf of those in need:

> The Ministry of Pensions, when I reported the facts, agreed to put Tilbury on full pension, are providing surgical boots, and promised that he will be looked after.

The sentence moves with a neat efficiency: Allighan is tidily prepared to fight the powers-that-be when injustice appears to be being done. 'Blighty', RASC, writes to ask Allighan: 'Can an OC stop a man having his wife with him in a town which is *not* a restricted area?' Allighan replies:

> He certainly can't. If he attempts to, send me full particulars, and it will soon be altered.

Allighan's self-confidence in his column's ability to 'get things done' is communicated very clearly here. But it is not just a matter of 'getting things done'. It is a matter of getting things done for Us, the men in the ranks, often over against Them, the officers and the service bureaucracy. Allighan is a figure who can talk Their language, play the game according to Their rules, but, basically, he's still one of Us. His tone, which shared its brisk efficiency with the women's pages, is as representative of the *Mirror* as Wintringham's. Allighan is another link in the binding of the *Mirror* with Us.

The concepts and imagery of 'The War To Win The War' are extended into the third theme, 'The War To Win The Peace'. By 1944 the *Mirror* clearly sees the defeat of Hitler as only the first step in a two-stage process. This is brought out by the editorial of June 14, 1944, 'Votes For Heroes'. The first paragraph praises the heroism of the British soldier, 'the individual Tommy'. The editorial continues:

> These gallant men are fighting and they know what they are fighting for. Their first task is to rid the world of tyranny. Their second, no less important, is to create a 'new world' in which men may live in peace and fairly shared prosperity. But how is this to be done? Do the soldiers realise that just as they fight now for military victory, they will have subsequently to fight for political victory?
>
> Their weapons will not be guns and grenades but votes— a prosaic word among so much glory, but one of profound significance . . .
>
> Votes are weapons fit for heroes. Our soldiers should make sure they have got them.

The editorial moves from the level of general assertion to that of more detailed advice, but it speaks on behalf of the soldiers—'these gallant men'—in a tone curiously civic by comparison with its address directly to soldiers or women. 'No less important' has a pedagogic air, which increases with the question marks. The questions are not direct—'Do you soldiers realize . . . Your weapons will not be . . .'—but 'Do the soldiers realize . . . Their weapons will not be . .', as though the *Mirror* wishes to allow the soldiers to overhear a more general, public conversation. The unwillingness to address the soldiers directly, in sharp distinction to the public-forum role the *Mirror* had developed elsewhere, may have been calculated to bring pressure on the soldiers through their families at home.

The war imagery of the editorial is significant, centred on the phrase 'political victory', another extension of the theme of the war to defeat Hitler. Unlike the 'War To Win The War', however, it is not a preliminary battle necessary for the successful execution of the Hitler war but rather its logical sequel. Just as the soldiers have fought Hitler to defend one kind of freedom, so at home they will have to fight to win another kind of freedom, the freedom to

> create 'a new world' in which many may live in peace and enjoy a fairly shared prosperity.

In the same paper on the same day Garry Allighan was also writing his weekly Forces column, and the war imagery and sense of wider struggle is also caught in that. He writes:

> Beware, lest, when the next election comes—which will be your opportunity to compel the politicians to give you 'the better Britain' they now talk about—you have not left yourself voteless, and therefore powerless.

The word that leaps from the page here is 'compel'. It suggests the unwillingness of the politicians to do what the soldiers want unless the soldiers make sure the politicians are left with no alternative. There is a suspicion of the whole political process, which underlies the implicit contrast between 'give you' and 'talk about'. The passage stresses the importance of the soldier taking part in the democratic procedure—it equates 'voteless' with 'powerless'— and, most important of all, it asserts that real power lies with the electors, not the elected, with the people, not the politicians. The *Express* saw the voting procedure as the privilege of concelebrating the triumph of the hero; in comparison the *Mirror*'s political imagery is radical. We, the *Mirror*'s readers, are the masters now.

*   *   *

Information about its Forces readers reached the *Mirror* through letters from them and from its correspondents in uniform: among the latter were Hugh Cudlipp and Cassandra, both of whom worked on Forces newspapers. Another important channel was *Good Morning*, a daily paper for the submarine branch of the Royal Navy. It was published between 1943 and 1945, the issues being undated but numbered for distribution on board during the course of the voyage. As the papers were all printed some time ahead of the voyages they were unable to carry news but were filled instead with educational articles, quizzes, 'things to think about', pin-ups and cartoons, including the celebrated Jane. *Good Morning* was published by the *Mirror*, with the enthusiastic agreement of the Admiralty. It was run by Bartholomew—with such success, says Cudlipp, that Bartholomew could have been rewarded by almost any honour he chose. The *Mirror* did not advertise its control of *Good Morning*, but the regular appearance of Jane, among other things, must have suggested the paper's parentage to its readers. It seems likely that the *Mirror* picked up new readers through *Good Morning*. It can be seen as an instrument for learning, even practising, modes of address that would feed back into the *Mirror*.

The sailor readers were repeatedly invited to send the paper their views, and requests. A paragraph in issue No. 675 gives one some idea of the kind of relationship that *Good Morning* was building up with its readers:

> Of course, I know you will appreciate that it is more than one man's job, now, to cope with all your letters—the answers alone, apart from requests for gramophone needles, baby shoes, and gold braid, etc., for which we have to comb London, take quite a while.

It was a relationship of trust, very similar to that being built up by Garry Allighan in the Forces column in the *Mirror* itself.

Perhaps to make up for its inability to publish replies to readers, *Good Morning* began a series of interviews with the relatives of men who were serving in the submarine branch. Readers were invited to:

> Make this your own newspaper by sending us the address of your wife, your mother, your girl friend, so that we may photograph them, and publish their pictures and greetings in these papers.

At first these interviews were published irregularly, but by issue 55 they had become a daily front page feature. Each bore a photograph of the family and then an interview, which carried snippets of information about home life and greetings to the sailor whose name was headlined at the top of the article. The language of the interviews has a peculiar authenticity about it; the language moves into a private, working class, colloquial idiom, very different from the public populism of the *Mirror*'s leaders.

Here is one fairly typical interview from the middle of the run examined, interview 671, quoted in full.

> Your father is hoping to beat you in a game of darts at the King's Head next time you come home on leave to 9 Salisbury House, St. Mary's Park, Islington N.1., Stoker Bill Armstrong.
>
> He's been getting in some practice lately and seems quite confident of wiping out the defeats you inflicted on him last time you went there together.
>
> Both your mother and father are keeping well, Bill, and so for that matter are the rest of the family. Doris is working hard at her dressmaking and Rita is busy learning machining. Nellie and Edie are keeping the railway going, and Esther is still on government work, we are told.
>
> Ethel, too, has a full-time job on her hands, for young Carol is just getting to the stage where she makes her presence known.

As for the other members of the family, Bill, there is young
Beryl who is still at school and John, who has just about seen
enough of Italy after three years with the army in that area.

Joyce is waiting to welcome you home and so are your
nephews, Bernie and Brian, who were very anxious to stay
away from school so that they could send their own messages
to you. Needless to say, school won.

Billy Fowler is keeping fitter now, and he, too, is hoping it
won't be long before you are able to visit the Odeon and see
some more thrillers.

Until then, Bill, all the family are thinking of you and all
send their love, but with it comes a request. Please write a
little more often, Bill.

The first impression is a special quality of 'flatness', the flatness of the
everyday. The repetition of the name Bill, the names Edie, Rita,
Carol and so on, all are exposed in a moment of intimacy to the
public world. A number of expressions belong very clearly to a
spoken, informal language, and one of them in particular, 'Nellie
and Edie are keeping the railway going', embodies a homely, wry
humour which is rooted deep in working-class experience. It is a
phrase used by people who realize that they are seen by 'the bosses'
as very small cogs in the industrial machine, and to that extent the
phrase is defensively ironic. At the same time there stands behind it
some muted consciousness that, quite literally, it is such people who
are 'keeping the railway going'.

These phrases, though, pick up only one tone within the article.
There is another more formal tone:

> We are told
> makes her presence known
> who were very anxious to stay
> Needless to say

Such phrases belong to a more literary, middle class idiom, of a
kind that does, however, occur awkwardly in letters to and from
'respectable' working-class people. The use of a phrase like 'we are
told', which occurs in the same sentence as 'Nellie and Edie are
keeping the railway going', indicates an important tonal divergence.
Contrasting with the earlier phrase it immediately distances the
experience described so that, with some sense of shock, we remember
that we are reading the report of the visit in a semi-public printed
medium. The position of the reporter seems to have shifted from
inside the family experience he is describing to a position outside,

from which he comments, asserting his identity and establishing his credentials.

The use of working-class idioms, a use which we have not seen made in the same way by any other *Mirror* writing, may be an example of the *Mirror* staff skilfully employing a style which it feels to be suitable to this particular audience of this semi-public medium. It may be that the *Mirror* writers caught in the course of the interviews, unconsciously or semi-consciously, the colloquial idioms of those people with whom they were speaking; or that they had heard the idioms in letters from readers; or that they summoned them up from their own background, as Cudlipp says they could. Whichever explanation is correct, ears sensitive enough to catch this kind of speech would surely hear also these people's ideas and sense their attitudes, ideas and attitudes which could be played back to the *Mirror* for use in the shaping of its election campaign in 1945. If one looks for evidence of the *Mirror* having a special relationship to the Forces, of the *Mirror* having learned how to speak to people in the Forces and to their relatives at home, the language of Garry Allighan's column and of the *Good Morning* interviews provides some of it.

A characteristic of the *Good Morning* interviews is an effort to evoke a generalized response, available to a wide range of readers, by focusing on particulars:

> There's another addition to your home, Ordinary Seaman Alan Cliffe, of 4 Hollyhey-drive, Wythenshaw, Manchester, in the form of 'Sacha', a brown, sleek-haired pup. He is full of life and gradually making friends with 'Simon' and 'Peter'.
>
> Everybody was in the best of spirits when 'Good Morning' called, and this is what they all had to say to you:—
>
> Your mother is now back to her old self once more and waiting for the time when you will be strolling along the Parkway with her. The Parkway is looking really grand, these days, Alan, and, in fact, your road looked a picture of green with the sun shining brilliantly when we called the other day.
>
> Dad—as busy as ever at the Post Office—is tickled to death about the expressions in your letters. Keep them up; the family loves them . . .

The dogs, the Parkway, the mother's recuperation, and the father's amusement at his son's letters, these details, while particular to Alan Cliffe's own home environment, are likely to have sounded undertones of immediacy in many of *Good Morning*'s readers. Not everyone lives near Alan Cliffe's Parkway, but a great many of us could readily substitute another name for it, especially if we had been in a submarine for weeks. Such selection reinforces the similar use of a generalized working-class tone. The whole endeavour seems to be to write a letter to everyone at once.

Working-class idioms appear and disappear in the *Good Morning* interviews with no discernible pattern. Sometimes the reporter's 'letter' is condescending to its subjects. Quite the opposite attitude is at work in this example:

> I got off the train at Liphook, Hampshire, and walked slightly uphill through the station yard. I was the only moving thing in sight—the sun was warm and the two porters sitting with brown cigarettes in their mouths, were relaxed and didn't move a muscle—it must have been siesta hour . . .
>
> The road was a long, winding lane—when I had walked a mile I went into the butchery—the straw-hatted shopkeeper told me that 'Farthings' was five hundred yards further on, on the other side of the road.
>
> The gate was open and I was met by a brother and sister— the girl was three and a half, but her brother hadn't yet celebrated his second birthday.
>
> They were happy kiddies in their place in the sun— they had toys and books and a nanny, who humoured them when they fell off or got scratched by Sherry, the cat. Richard wore a Panama but Cecily had a mass of golden curls that protected her head from the sun . . .
>
> When I went into the gate the kiddies ran into the house for their mother. Mrs. Wingfield thought I was a Hoover salesman, but she was kind. I told her the Editor had recently had a letter from her husband, Lt.-Cdr. M. J. R. Wingfield, D.S.O., D.S.C., and that he would like to photograph the kiddies and publish the family picture in the paper.
>
> 'Certainly', Mrs. Wingfield said, and she produced a tin of toffees and some kiddies' books to put the children in the mood for photoplay . . .
>
> Everything is ship shape at your home, Sir—the lawn needs your attention and the borders are just a trifle ragged, but the family is happy and well. The garage, of course, needs a little tidying—Cecily's tricycle and Richard's toys are draped round the walls, and the pram just inside the door is hard against your bicycle, which, by the way, has two soft tyres.
>
> But apart from that, and your absence, everything at 'Farthings' is as it was—and everyone is happy as ever at the Hampshire retreat.

That one is quoted almost entire since it points up so sharply the tone of other *Good Morning* interviews. Of course it is not meant to be typical. It is distanced in many ways: in the heading the interviewer is named as Ron Richards, one of the prominent members of the *Good Morning* staff, whereas the other interviewers remain anonymous—it is a sort of courtesy to the Wingfield family to select a man specially for them. It is also distanced by the long walk necessary to reach the house from the station; by the presentation of credentials from the Editor; and by the absence of references to friendships outside the family which serve to place the other interviews socially. Yet it is placed in the interview series and maintains the normal format.

After the first two slow, descriptive paragraphs, the tone moves interestingly in 'but her brother hadn't yet celebrated his second birthday'. A long-winded way of saying 'he wasn't yet two', it would be more at home in an official announcement.

The fourth paragraph is amazing. Is it possible that this writing is being held straight? Could a *Mirror* writer say 'their place in the sun', or 'a nanny, who humoured them when they fell off' without being aware of the *Mirror* tradition which was to make 'hours in the sunshine at home and abroad' the salt stoked into a sensitive wound? (See later, page 97). Could the interviewer describe the Panama hat and golden curls, with Sherry in the background, without calling to mind the *Good Morning* photographs where a child clutches its mother's skirt on the gravel path in front of a red brick council house?

'Mrs. Wingfield thought I was a Hoover salesman, but she was kind.' Kind. But. Why, one wonders, are the other families who anxiously peer into the camera, posed before oval photographs of their parents over a wooden clock, not usually described as kind? The other *Good Morning* families are seldom heard to say 'Certainly'. Nor, for that matter, are their borders often 'just a trifle ragged' in their Lancashire 'retreats'. This world of discourse is far removed from that of 'Nellie and Edie are helping to keep the railway going'. It is not simply that the Wingfields' social milieu is in a different class, and so different particular details are chosen to evoke the generalized picture, but that, unless the interview is thought to be ironic, the interviewer adopts a quite different attitude towards his material on behalf of his assumed audience. Wingfield is addressed as 'Sir', and credited with all his decorations; the homely news about the garden has about it an air of nervous banter, a wariness of going beyond the bounds of respectfulness. By no means all this deference could be attributed to the respect towards their officers enjoined upon men in submarines, or the respect owed to a man with the D.S.O. and D.S.C. There remains a surplus of instinctive forelock-touching not found anywhere in the war-time *Mirror*.

The possibility remains that the tone of the interview is ironic, and viciously so, the writer speaking to a known, sceptical audience over the heads of the people interviewed. But more probably the paper wanted to include an officer's family in the series, for demo-cratic diversity, but felt it had to suppress any note of class hostility because it was read by men of all ranks living close confined together in submarines.

* * *

Within the limits mentioned, the *Mirror*'s own Forces column always took the soldier's side against the 'old men' in authority who were allegedly hampering the war effort. The criticism of authority ranged from naming the units in which blanco and 'bull' were more rigorous to such outspokenness as 'the accepted tip for Army leadership would, in plain truth, be this: All who aspire to mislead others in war should be brass-buttoned bone-heads, socially prejudiced, arrogant and fussy.' Hugh Cudlipp calls the column a 'safety valve', but there was a time early in the war when it was accused of being something much graver. In 1941 Winston Churchill pointedly told Cecil King how a Fifth Column would work: 'a perfervid zeal for intensification of the war effort would be used as a cloak behind which to insult and discredit one Minister after another. Every grievance would be exploited to the full, especially those grievances which lead to class dissension . . . The Army system and discipline would be attacked.' The Government continued to be disturbed by the *Mirror*'s criticism of the direction of the war, and after private recriminations it culminated in a debate in the House of Commons. The Government's case was led by Herbert Morrison, then Home Secretary, and Aneurin Bevan was the *Mirror*'s principal defender. He asked the House why men in the Army weren't treated as adults, and argued that the *Mirror*'s criticism of the Army would have effect only if it was confirmed by the soldiers' own experience. Comment in other national newspapers generally supported the *Mirror* against the Government. It is worth noting that several MPs, including Chur-chill, made enquiries at that time into who *owned* the *Mirror*.

* * *

The *Mirror* had been born in 1903 as a paper for gentlewomen, written by gentlewomen. Although that proved a false start, women predominated in the paper's readership for many years. The 1938

PEP Press Report stated: 'The *Daily Mirror* in 1935 was a paper with a definitely upper and middle class appeal, though again, nearly half its sales were in the fourth income group, and only thirty per cent of its readers were men.' In the years 1935–39, during Bartholomew's revolution, that confusing mixture of 'upper and middle class appeal' aimed at a lower income group, especially women, produced an odd bran-tub of items. It was a fat tabloid, often 32 pages, bent on amusing and provoking its readers, but it seems to have had no clear impression of who those readers were, of how they located themselves socially or politically.

Cudlipp reveals that the paper had at least one kind of audience in its sights: '. . . a section of citizens much neglected by newspapers of the time. Girls—working girls; hundreds of thousands of them, toiling over typewriters and ledgers and reading in many cases nothing more enlightening than *Peg's Paper*.' The working girls were accordingly fed with dream interpretations, tennis tips, 'Lover's Log' by Clarissa Lynn, 'the famous numerologist', gossip about 'Paris, the fairy book city of gaiety and romance', 'The Secret Diary of a Doctor', serials, features about film idols; but also advice, about dealing with problem parents, bosses, boy friends, cooking, complexions and fashions.

Several women columnists addressed themselves to women's interests, and a few men implicitly aimed at the same audience. Some of the women were well known writers. Emily Post, for instance, gave advice on etiquette: 'Emily Post tells you . . . How to light a cigarette . . . How to Answer a Wedding Invitation . . . How to talk to a Golfer . . . How to Greet People'; 'Lord Baldwin's son insults Emily Post!' Elinor Glyn wrote on such matters as The Meaning Of The Marriage Service ('If he is utterly despicable you *cannot* honour him.') Dorothy Dix, 'the woman who knows everything about love', wrote a homely agony column: 'If you want your husband to chum with you, you have to be interested in the things that interest him.' Others were *Mirror* specialist writers. Eileen Ascroft's Sanctuary column, subtitled 'A message of peace and comfort', and later her 'League of Loneliness', a weekly letter, asking 'Are you the sort of woman who makes for herself a private hell?'— such features, and many others like them, supplied what Cecil King has described as 'buckets of sentiment'; 'Eileen Ascroft sat on the grass by a baby's side. And in that baby's eyes she saw all the mystery of Love fulfilled.'

Prominent among the men who wrote for *Mirror* women was Godfrey Winn: 'I have to be honest with you always, for otherwise this page can have no reality for any of us.' It was called his

Personality Page, and certainly Winn's own personality bulked large. 'Dashing up the Kingston by-pass on my way to keep a date for lunch at the Ivy', and on the same day 'having to dash to Grosvenor House for a dip in the pool, where I find Osbert Sitwell', and later having to 'Dash back to town again to have a cocktail with Noel Coward in his studio', Winn was always well connected, and he sought to connect his readers too:

> It was Wordsworth who said . . . Such a moment of revelation came to me on Friday evening as we drove over to Eton to see the fireworks. The light was fading rapidly along the banks of Runnymede.
> In the car the wireless was turned on, and under the wand of Toscanini the Adagio of the Eroica took on a new significance.
> Perhaps you were listening in, too, that night, and the same burst of immortal exultation filled your hearts.
> I only wish you could have been with me.

There was another regular column in the paper, Cassandra's, in which Wordsworth, Eton, and the Adagio of the Eroica could have appeared only in a very different social light. Winn exulted: 'how damn lucky we are to be members of a democracy like our own . . . where the poorest subject has equal political and legal rights with the richest men and women in the land, where so far the stench of corruption does not permeate the atmosphere of high places.' Cassandra was later, after Winn left the *Mirror* in 1938, to make hay of 'my favourite tennis player, Mr. Winn' precisely for his generous sympathy for those in 'high places'.

Two other colunists should be mentioned briefly. There was the author of *Ivor Lambe's Tales*, a gossip column inhabiting almost exclusively the drawing-rooms and coming-out parties of the fashionable. 'Miss Symons-Jeune will be among the loveliest brides this season.' And there was Dr. Ivor Beaumont who, dealing with infected gums and impetigo, could start a column with:

> This isn't a pleasant article. Don't read it at all if you can't face facts.
> What's a kiss?
> A bit of heaven snatched from a sordid world under an understanding moon, a gay bit of fun, meaning nothing and earning, perhaps, a laughing cuff on the ear.
> Yes, it's all that, BUT—
> It's rather horrid sometimes being a doctor . . .

Women were constantly regarded only in their traditional roles of wife, mother or sweetheart; their interests were private, domestic ones. As late as June 1939 the women's page chirped:

> Readers eager for the latest news from the Polish corridor or the Suez canal had better turn to other pages. I have to deal with a sterner, starker social problem. STOCKINGS.

The women's pages often stressed value for money, estimating that many readers didn't have much to spend, and continually helped them with economical ways of keeping up with fashion, in a no-nonsense, girl-to-girl tone: 'One snappy suit . . . hot from Paris. Make it from an old frock—like this. Unpick the waist. Cut the top up the middle . . .' and so on, ending with 'It's effective. We know—we've done it ourselves'.

Almost every feature page of the time exhorted its readers to write in with their views, or ask for help, or for various offers. 'We are calling this page YOU', women were told. And as war approached, housewives were advised to stock up their cupboards and plant vegetables. It was these two functions, participation and advice, that were, in the long run, to prove most enduring and influential in all the *Mirror*'s address to women.

The pre-war address varied widely. It was not a simple question of modifying the tone according to the subject: fashion advice or high society gossip was sometimes delivered with gushy delight and at other times with the brisk, downright edge of Cassandra. The paper's readers, that is to say, were offered no consistent attitudes: fashion, or 'society', or politics could be matters of common sense, or of frivolous indulgence. It is hard to imagine any one sort of woman who could feel every day that the paper was talking to her, for her. But the *Mirror* was learning, perhaps by its mistakes: and the communal stresses of wartime were to produce a far more homogeneous view in the paper.

From the confused molecules of the pre-war period, two elements survived and became dominant in the *Mirror*'s wartime address to women readers: its encouragement to them to participate in the paper, even if only by writing for a free offer of powder, and its direct, brisk advisory function. What had before the war been principally devices, among several others, to boost circulation turned into an instrument for sensing social change, articulating it and seeking to direct it. The seeds of 1945's *Mirror* were in these two pre-war *tones*. It is hardly too much to say that the later content was a consequence of the tones: it was by learning how to talk to its readers that the paper learned what to talk to them about.

The *Mirror* in war time developed a point of view about what sort
of people its women readers were, and what sort of social attitudes
should be enjoined upon them. It is characteristic that it seems to
have pieced together this point of view by listening to its readers and
deducing its own opinions from what it heard, rather than, as in the
Express's case, basing its views aprioristically upon those held by
authority, in the paper's offices or the government's.

In the first month of the war, a *Mirror* leader advised those who
were being evacuated, or whose children were: 'Do all you can to
help those who are trying to help you. Keep steady and cheerful.
Be kind to one another.' The simple second-person address, the
friendly homilectic authority: even in the atmosphere of September
1939, it was surely an extraordinary role for a mass newspaper to
adopt so confidently, especially a paper with a highly frivolous
flavour only a few days previously. If the *Mirror*'s readers accepted
the paper's role, then clearly such a newspaper might exert an
intimate influence over them when the time came to persuade them
into a positive course of action, such as voting.

The *Mirror*'s war-time pages for women were virtually one long
advice column, characterised by the use of direct address, which
tended to the imperative mood, and the constant encouragement to
readers to participate, feel part of it. The effect was of a two-way
dialogue, though not quite as between equals. Although the paper
felt able to admit, on occasion, that it didn't know the answer to
this or that problem, it remained in the stance of, roughly, a welfare
worker, with that kind of acceptable authoritativeness, seldom exerted to the full. In the dark uncertainties of the early war the paper
continually encouraged, chivvied, organised and consoled its women
readers, ran campaigns to educate them in such economies as
not throwing away useful rubbish, or not listening to rumours.
There were schemes for renovating clothes and sharing them, anti-
Haw-Haw labels for radio sets, a 'family spy system' ('the idea is
that one member of your family shall be appointed as official
spotter of wasters'), Victory Circles for 'women who want to do
something of real help'. Constantly, too, the *Mirror* tried to cheer
up its readers, not by concealing the darkness of the war situation
but by appealing to the spirit of patriotism, communal self-help
and common sense.

Once the war was on, many of the pre-war mixture of tones to
women, the frivolous, arch or feminist ones, disappeared at once.
Apart from the participatory and imperative styles, the only other
pre-war tone that survived for any time was sentimentality.

And if there is a quiet tear, late at night when no one sees, that tear is a safety valve which makes for renewed courage on the morrow.

But the strain is there all the same and tense nerves may sometimes be better for a mild sedative.

You don't need drugs for the duration, British mothers and wives—but some of you, just now, when you feel you've got to clench your fists or bite your lower lip, would be helped a lot if your doctor gave you a mild bromide for a few days.

That appeared on June 3, 1940, the week of Dunkirk, and it may be that the sentimentality, which did not pervade most of the war-time *Mirror*, was acceptable to many women then. Here is an example of another sort of sentimentality, from the same week:

CALLING EDITH

As a train load of soldiers home from Belgium passed through a station near London yesterday, a soldier threw a post card message to his wife from a window—as did also hundreds of others. But this particular soldier forgot to put the address on the card. The finder brought the card to the Daily Mirror and here's Norman's welcome message to you, Edith, wherever you are.

With the confidence with which a lost child might be taken to the police station, the anonymous card was taken to a newspaper that could be trusted to bother with a relatively trivial matter, though one that was immensely important to Edith. As in the *Good Morning* interviews, or in the BBC's *Forces' Favourites* programme, the assumption was that the public enjoyed overhearing a little personal exchange, and could identify themselves with it. The paper's role in this case was that of a lay fairy godmother. Wishes could come true in the *Mirror*.

But with equal aplomb orders could be given. On June 6, 1940 the paper said:

We've told you dozens of times that it's your duty not to let your appearance go ragged on you just because there's a war on ... never let it be said that just because she has a job of work to do, the Englishwoman is content to look a mess.

This nagging tone persisted throughout the war, and became an electoral weapon in 1945: 'I told you last week that nobody could threaten you about how you should vote. Now here's a woman who writes to me ...' Other examples between 1940–45 could be multiplied indefinitely:

> Never spin a handkerchief out too long!
>
> It's not beyond your power to wash a [mascara] brush each time after use.
>
> Plan your meals now for the week. And see they are properly balanced by following Josephine Terry.
>
> A war is won by preparing for the worst, even if you hope it won't happen ... REGISTER YOUR CHILD FOR EVACUATION NOW.
>
> Have YOU—as a war time working mother—yet found out whether ... It is not a bit of good waiting until the last day of term, and then grumbling at the local authority ... if there are enough mothers like you—then something will be done.
>
> Look at the clock now—time to go. Quick—fold the paper—grab your hat. Up and away—you're on the job. Feeling Mondayish? Not you—no time. This is war—this is speed.

The author of many of these injunctions was Janet Grey. Here is a longer example of her style, which is tougher in manner than anything the *Mirror* ever directed at its Forces readers, who presumably were thought to be chivvied enough already. It was headed 'You Women are Lazy Minded!' and appeared on May 7, 1941. It harangued women for not having written to their MPs about the Personal Injuries Bill, and continued:

> You knew that the Personal Injuries Scheme was going to be debated. And if you didn't, you ought to have done—it's been mentioned in the papers often enough ...
>
> It's no good your thinking that what goes on in Parliament is nothing to do with you. You may feel that you have got your hands full with your home and babies or your job.
>
> But don't you see that without being 'in the know' about every plan that has anything to do with women, you're not being fair to your children or yourself?
>
> And how many women aren't in the know is proved daily by the letters that come in here, asking questions about small and big things that have been settled and made public long ago.
>
> Don't think we mind answering your letters. We want to help you, but the point is, you shouldn't have to ask us questions like:
>
> When does cheese rationing start? How do I get free milk for

my children? I have to register on Saturday, do I have to go into munitions?

If you had read your paper with intelligent interest, you would have read and remembered all these things . . . Look—you're right bang in the centre of this war. You're in the front line as far as raids go, and if you're not being mobilized for industry or one of the forces, you've got the big responsibility of your home and family.

For heaven's sake, then, shake off your feeling that the world is bounded by your front gate, or a visit to the pictures with the boy friend next Saturday, and realise that you've got to be ready to take a part in the running of things.

The *Mirror* was in a large degree fighting the Government's home battles for it, by pushing its readers into the necessary frame of mind for carrying on the war; the paper's personalized admonitions were more acceptable, and possibly more trustworthy, than any official directive. The corollary was that the *Mirror*, as we have seen, was all the more ready to turn and kick Ministers if it thought that the Government itself was not pulling as hard as it could on the same rope.

While mobilizing and hectoring its women readers, the *Mirror* did not lose its habit of regarding them as wives, mothers and sweethearts, nor shrink from advising them in the etiquette of war-time behaviour. Janet Grey ran a 'campaign against starchiness':

Supposing you are walking down the street and a lorry load of soldiers goes by. They wave at you, laugh, and yell out 'Hello beautiful!' What do you do? You do not turn a haughty head and show them a pair of indignantly raised shoulders.

You laugh and wave back . . . as gaily as you know how.

She explained why:

You and I know that we are the fighters on the Home Front . . . Upon the background of solidarity and cheerfulness that we can provide, depends the morale of the men who go out there.

Female emancipation was to be tempered:

Let it be a quiet strength. Something restful and noble. Never should the strong side of a woman's nature become too obvious. Men do not want to be commanded by women: they want to be admired and adored.

Granted that the grave circumstances of the early war were bound to press the *Mirror* away from its pre-war leisurely, sometimes flippant style, and that, on a practical level, the newsprint shortage, which cut the paper to eight pages, deterred prolixity, yet it should be clear that the *Mirror* did exercise choice in its mode of address. There were other options than the one it chose, the imperative mode; other possible approaches to women's feelings than the *Mirror*'s emphasis on solidarity. It could have spoken to them as it did only on the assumption that two other channels of advice to women were for the time being muddied: their husbands, who were likely to be stationed away from home, and official government advice, which, the *Mirror* may have supposed, could not speak to women with its own direct, daily effectiveness.

Cecil King,[7] many years later, thought:

> It now seems inevitable that the *Mirror*, ruthlessly outspoken, strongly emotional, powerfully projective, brief and simple to read, should have had enormous appeal in war time. It identified itself with the serving man and woman, with the workers and their children. In the restless atmosphere of the barracks and the war time factory canteen, it was the easiest paper to read and understand and the most entertaining too.

Perhaps: but it was not inevitable that the *Mirror* should have chosen those roles. It is true that war restrictions and shortages called for a multitude of improvizations, wresting women from their mothers' way of doing things: but the progression from being told, before the war, how to make Popeye soup and not to mix old vermilion lipstick with fuchsia rouge, to being exhorted to act politically, in 1945, for the sake of home and family, that was not inevitable. Under the bombs, a family and a nation drew closer together; Megs Thompson wrote in the *Mirror* on June 7, 1941:

> This time at least, I said, we are all in it together, not just the young men. And we can share the grimness and the lighter side, talk things over, help one another along. And maybe, now that for the first time in history EVERYONE is being made to realise what war means, we shall at least make the tremendous effort needed to prevent it again.

That 'we are all in it together' was the *Mirror*'s war-time starting point in addressing women; by the end of the war the 'tremendous effort needed' was in the forefront.

The *Mirror*'s transition from enjoining solidary self-help upon

7 Granada Northern Lectures, October 1966.

women to mobilizing them politically, in preparation for the General Election, was explicit:

> What you say and think—added to what other women all over the country are saying and thinking—makes 'public opinion'. And public opinion counts.

> After this war there is going to be a General Election . . .

That appeared on June 19, 1944. A week before, the paper had sounded the same tocsin in more elementary tones:

> And I don't mean the X that we used to put on a picture postcard to show which was our room in the hotel on the sea front.
> THIS X is the one that goes on the ballot paper against the name of the man or woman you want to vote for, because you think he or she is the candidate who expresses *your* views . . .
> At the next Election, every man and woman over twenty-one will be able to write that X. And anyone who doesn't will be betraying the principles for which our men are fighting today.
> Why? Because if you are too lazy to use your vote you give a chance to others, not so lazy, but perhaps more unscrupulous, to get into power to run *your* life.

Women are clearly expected to require as much chivvying into voting as they had been given in the campaign against waste or rumour, and the same imperative mood serves. Just as common sense reasons had been bluntly advanced for those early war exhortations, so were they now. Women were appealed to as responsible members of a democratic community, and sometimes as sectionally interested members: women, said the paper in 1943, 'are through with accepting now. There are some things they want run their way.' They were also to influence their husbands:

> Your man, serving in the Forces, *must* vote at the next General Election. By fighting for his country he has won the right to have a say in its peace time running . . . It's more likely that your man will bother if *you* ask him to. Write NOW and get him to get hold of the form . . .

—an abbreviated version of the *Mirror*'s translation of the war to win the war into the war to win the peace.

June 1944, the month of D-Day, was also the month in which the *Mirror* began an onslaught on its women readers with the intention of making them politically conscious, at least sufficiently so to vote. Apathy was assumed:

We can start working out just why this war happened, and what we are going to do about stopping other wars.

We can think about the future . . .

And to be a thinking woman doesn't mean that you have to be highbrow, to have won all the prizes at school . . .

It just means that you are sensible enough to feel responsible for things that affect you and your family.

Cicely Fraser hectored her readers every Monday. 'Now's your chance—grab it!' she wrote. 'A chance to realize how much power you hold in those two hands of yours—and to learn how to use it.' She discussed women MPs ('No, they aren't so very different from you') without mentioning their party affiliations but dwelling on personal details, such as how many children they had, or what previous jobs they had held. She concluded:

And maybe that's the one thing where they ARE different from most other women.

They were interested in politics. They believed that women had a job to do in helping to run the country. They didn't sit back and leave it all to the men.

Whereas:

Lots of you are interested all right, but when it comes to doing things it's different.

You feel, perhaps, that you don't count, that you're alone in your new interests.

That isn't so. If you start talking with your friends about serious matters instead of just trivial day-to-day events, the odds are you'll find they are interested too . . .

On your judgement depends the whole future of your children and this country.

Your children, this country: mothers were voters. The *Mirror* had no qualms in conducting their adult education:

We've received letters asking us if we can 'explain politics' to some of you who have never had the time for them.

When I tell you about Parliament, that is what I'm trying to do. Because it's no use talking about the theories of the various parties unless you can understand just how they put them into practice.

And the place where this happens is Parliament. But if you feel there are things I haven't told you, I'll answer any letters you care to write me about them.

And, predictably, women were encouraged to participate in the *Mirror*'s enthusiasm. On June 26 a questionnaire was printed, asking questions which, if answered by enough women, would not only give the readers the sense of sharing in the paper's drive but would also— perhaps the chief motive—tell the *Mirror* a lot about their political and social preoccupations. 'You women are important' said the *Mirror*; 'what you think and what you want done should be known . . . today we give you the chance of "putting it across" by answering these questions.' The *Mirror* was not only talking briskly, it was listening very hard too.

What it heard was, we might guess, encouraging for the Labour Party; certainly the *Mirror* felt no more need in 1945 than it had earlier to direct its women readers explicitly into party preferences. It was enough to activate them, as it had been doing, in various causes, throughout the war. For the rest the *Mirror* could rely on the promise of a new deal to be attained by the solidarity it had so sedulously cultivated. Women 'in it together' could be trusted not to be dazzled by the slogan of free enterprise, nor to vote in simple gratitude for the war time leader. The *Mirror* had, to a considerable extent, pre-empted that role, by translating government into its own voice.

*　　*　　*

For thirty years, until his death in 1967, Cassandra (William Connor) was the *Mirror*'s, and possibly the country's, best known columnist. Having joined the Forces in 1942, he did not contribute to the paper during the latter half of the period under consideration, but his columns from 1937–42 should be mentioned here. In the late '30s his virulent tone stood out from the generality of the *Mirror*, but it was the paper, not Cassandra, that changed in the early war years, with the effect that Cassandra became a central tone in the *Mirror*. What he specialized in—short-tempered debunking of autocracy, bureaucracy, injustices and mealy-mouths—became a natural stock-in-trade of the *Mirror*'s war-to-win-the-war campaign. On Hugh Cudlipp's evidence, Cassandra was always permitted to digress from the paper's line if he felt strongly inclined to do so: but there can be no question that he was entirely representative of the paper in the early '40s, and always remained close to the paper's editorial directors.

Cassandra's characteristic tone was heavy irony, easily moving into articulate sarcasm. He would sometimes include in his armoury words such as 'pharisaical' which, though not in an every-day vocabulary, were presumably allowable as rhetorical licence, in the tradition of the gifted, articulate populist, such as you might meet on a soap box or at a miners' gala. Cassandra assumed an audience of decent, extravert, unillusioned, unafraid, patriotic, democratically-minded people, quickly sensitive to injustice, stupidity and pomposity. Here is an example from June 1, 1938:

> William Sidney Challis, age 33, embezzled three half-crowns from his employers.
> Now it seems that on an occasion before William had pinched another small sum—which was foolish of him.
> He was on a salary of thirty bob a week and he was engaged in collecting hire purchase rents.
> The justices in their wisdom and mercy said:
> 'That it was a very serious case and defendant would have to be sent to prison for three months with hard labour.'
> Challis's mother pleaded desperately for him and said she would pay any fine.
> Before they threw him in gaol she was allowed to kiss him goodbye.
> It makes me sick!
> The sanctity of property in this country!
> You can rot your guts out in some landlord's slum and all the rigorous mechanism of the law will see that you pay your rent for that privilege.
> And if you try to sneak seven and six and get caught—then God help you!
> When I think of the vast frauds put over on this country by crooks in the City of London who go unscathed, and when I hear of poor devils like Challis who get three months hard for grabbing a handful of small change it makes me proud to be an Englishman.
> Does it hell!

The virulence could as readily be turned to overtly political ends:

> I wonder what the civilians in Spain who are being blasted to bits by aerial bombing would think if they read these words spoken by Mr. Neville Chamberlain:
> 'His Majesty's Government have on more than one occasion expressed to both sides in Spain their profound concern at the intensification of aerial bombardment resulting in serious loss of life among the civil population, and have drawn attention to the universally accepted principle that aerial bombardment of military objectives is alone admissible.'

A fat lot of good that'll do!

And what's the good of drawing attention to 'the universally accepted principle of bombing military objectives alone' when it's brutally plain that nobody intends to take the slightest notice of such a ruling?

The dead in Shanghai and Barcelona testify to that.

If we aren't going to do anything about this unspeakable slaughter, then for heaven's sake let's admit that these women and children are going to be left to die in the welter of their own blood.

The charge of vile hypocrisy against us will then not fit quite so neatly.

The next example is from 1939. At a time when the *Mirror*'s politics were not much concerned with parties but concentrated on strong government action to prepare for war, Cassandra shared the *Mirror*'s general approval of Churchill's sombre appreciation of the international situation, but he also remained partisan:

One of the big trade union bosses is reported to have been entertained to dinner the other night by a wealthy group of city bankers.

Just as he was about to embark on the sumptuous meal, he turned amiably round and remarked to his host:

'When we get into power, we'll smash all you fellows!'

I like that.

Such refreshing candour, crude to the point of brutality, is a pleasant change from the mealy-mouthed hypocrisy that is the basis of most conversation in the upper crust.

The only trouble is, of course, that the valiant stalwarts of Labour are dangerously susceptible to the blandishments of High Society.

The spectacle of Ramsay MacDonald and his boiled-shirted satellites obsequiously revolving in the glittering Londonderry orbit is not one that is easily forgotten by those who value their self respect.

At the time of Dunkirk, Cassandra waxed against 'the political botchers who, guided only by supreme ignorance and stubborn selfishness, did nothing during the first eight months of the war.' A year later, when Hitler was 'rocking us with desperate, skilfully-timed blows', he complained:

We are *still* not fully geared to fight. Our effort lacks punch. Hundreds of thousands of men are not full out . . . The careless apathy of many of our people is not the only thing we have to dispel. There is plenty of evidence that some of the Service Chiefs are still thinking along the lines of strategies that they were taught about a dozen years ago at Sandhurst, Cranwell, or Dartmouth. Even politically many of our old Chamberlain chums are still lumbering up the scenery to our grave disadvantage.

It would, he said, be 'political infamy if we allow the guilty ones to escape into the House of Lords'.

This was not simple populism, however. Not only Churchill, the war leader, won Cassandra's approval; so also did Lord Gort, Commander-in-Chief of the British Expeditionary Force, who had stayed with his men in Flanders on a dangerous beach until the last possible moment. Cassandra was exactly in tune with the rest of the paper. He flayed those who, he alleged, were not doing all they could for the war effort: from 'stupendous bureaucratic asses' in charge of factories, to aliens and conscientious objectors. He was particularly vitriolic about a male ballet dancer who was discharged as an objector; his attitude to the fine arts seems to have been philistine at all periods.

In the war years, Cassandra was not just thumping large, obvious, inflammatory tubs. As well as his popular pungency, there was a willingness to stand out for what, in the context of the *Mirror*, might be thought quirky points of view, without apparently doing so just to establish himself as a character. In 1941, of all years, Cassandra, having attacked hotels for profiteering, parenthetically observed that dressing for dinner was 'laudable enough in its way as a habit'. In the same summer he noted, with what could have been supreme insensitivity (or bitterest irony), that in the bombing of London there was some benefit, the free demolition of 'wretched slums and hideous commercial buildings', and he advocated a very modern style of rebuilding. In the previous year he had directed his admiration to an improbable quarter; the context was an attack on the aircraft supply system, 'this rich and powerful cabal':

> It is being dismantled by a tough, stocky little egotist who for fifteen years has been chasing moonbeams, arguing ridiculously about ten ton railway trucks, shouting about isolation, bickering noisily with farmers, surrounding himself with yes men, infuriating his enemies, coining money and generally carrying on like an infuriated blue-bottle in a deserted cathedral. His name is Beaverbrook.

This ten-stone parcel of angry brilliance has been unleashed on the industry that has the fate of Britain in its hands. I am told by people who are in the business and who are in a position to know that the new Ministry is making a shambles of all the cowardly bureaucracy that has been strangling the finest air force in the world.

Cassandra did not hesitate to tackle the professional undertones of his praise: if Beaverbrook could bring it off, 'it will be a triumph that will do something to atone for the balderdash we write. The silly tricks we get up to, and all the footling mechanism we've devised to sell more bits of paper than the other fellow.'

An opportunity for trying to place Cassandra in the context of the *Mirror* is supplied by an incident later in the war, in 1944, when Captain Henry Longhurst made an attack in the Commons on Cassandra, alleging that he was using his position on a Forces newspaper to spread subversion among the men. The *Mirror*, challenged in what it held to be its sacred trust to speak for the ordinary man, made its position very explicit:

Captain Longhurst has recently written a book, 'IT WAS GOOD WHILE IT LASTED'—a book of pleasant memories, a record of life in soft places; hours in the sunshine at home and abroad.

Cassandra did not lead that kind of life. He was of the people.

And the people from whom he sprang, for whom he wrote, were not those who had found it good while it lasted.

Captain Longhurst wrote for the well-clad well-fed golfers of the more expensive golf clubs; Cassandra for the scorned, the rejected, the men hemmed in with spears, and that is his crime.

That is the full measure of Connor's subversion.

So the ranks divide.

Indeed they do. But seldom so sharply as here.

It is interesting to observe how the rhetoric of this defence is constructed. It is the phrase 'in soft places' which pivots the first sentence. The title of the book and the description, 'a book of pleasant memories', are held neutral, non-committal, just as 'hours in the sunshine at home and abroad' could have been held neutral if it were not for the drop to 'soft places'. As the argument gathers strength from the next paragraph's comparison of this way of life against Cassandra's way of life, the reader becomes aware that only some people, more precisely only a certain kind of person, could afford to spend hours in the sunshine *abroad*.

The language now becomes terse, the syntax precise, the tone authoritative. 'Cassandra did not lead that kind of life. He was of the people.' Behind this use of 'people' presses a weight of democratic definition. It is also a slightly abstract use of the concept of 'people'; as again in the next sentence: 'the people from whom he sprang', that use of 'sprang' draws its strength from classical and abstract usage, rather than from the language of vigorous, everyday speech.

The following paragraph is remarkable. 'The more expensive golf clubs' suggests finely the social stratification which is exploited in the rest of the paragraph. For it is not 'for the poor, the unhappy, the men who were unlucky' that Cassandra wrote, but for 'the scorned, the rejected, the men hemmed in with spears'. In other words, for those at the receiving end of social activity which had resulted in their demoralized situation. And when one poses the questions: scorned by whom? rejected by whom? hemmed in by whose spears? the rhetoric refers one back to 'the well-clad well-fed golfers of the more expensive golf clubs'. The irony of 'Connor's subversion' is hardly necessary. Having so carefully constructed the basis of its argument the editorial now moves easily in the next paragraph to identify Captain Longhurst, MP, with his colleagues 'on the Right' and to suggest that 'for the safety, security and happiness of this country they should stick to the links'.

The *Mirror*'s confidence in speaking for the victims of social injustice; its assumed stance of addressing the Government for the 'people'; the underlying Us/Them consciousness; the feeling that the people who wrote for the *Mirror* were sending 'a letter home to the family'; the stylistic roots in biblical imagery and classical political thought; the relish of the phrase or sentence which is almost a detachable slogan; and the *Mirror*'s self-assured irony—all are focused most strongly here, where the *Mirror* is attacked at its most sensitive point of self-identification.

From that, and from what Cudlipp and others have said, it is plain that the *Mirror* looked on Cassandra as especially embodying much of its character; that the paper found in him a forthright, decent, sceptical patriotism which it was glad to acknowledge as its own, and implicitly to offer as a standard of discourse among democratic men.

*   *   *

The 1937 *Mirror* was packed with human interest stories. In issue after issue there was no home political news at all in the seven news pages that the paper customarily carried, and often only the briefest mention of foreign affairs, such as Hitler's rallies. A feature called 'The one minute world news tour' consisted entirely of trivial, amusing snippets. The leader column felt only slightly more obliged to refer to political developments, in Spain, Germany and elsewhere and did so with sketchy superficiality, tending simply to shake its head over such matters and propose disarmament. Trade problems at home received no deeper analysis than the comment: 'This is the riddle of the hour'. The paper's interest was outstandingly rooted in human behaviour, sensational or trivial; nothing suggested that it was aware of any social concern in its readers that might seek political action.

The correspondence columns were equally apolitical. Cudlipp says that the paper was 'setting out to prove that the experiences of ordinary men and women could make exciting reading . . . here at last was a national newspaper dealing sensibly, sympathetically and understandingly with their own problems and which published their own views.' Readers were accordingly assumed to be bursting with a long-suppressed desire to make themselves heard; columnists daily repeated their address for correspondents, and would often comment on the size and variety of their regular postbag. 'Don't bottle it up', the *Mirror* encouraged its readers, and Cudlipp estimates that they received a thousand letters a day 'blowing off steam'. Very little steam seems to have been generated by politics, although a remarkable number of the letters made themselves heard in the paper. On June 1, 1937, thirty-seven letters were printed, quoted in excerpt, or confidentially answered. Most were grouped into five separate features; others were referred to by columnists Cassandra and Bernard Buckham, the radio reviewer. Topics in the letters included; nine on 'the man or woman they DIDN'T marry' (a series); nine heartache letters to Dorothy Dix; and one or two on subjects such as the price of a pot of tea, the use of beer to forecast the weather, the law on suicide, nursemaids, etc. Only one letter could be considered as remotely political; it was about personal relationships between English and German people, and wondered if bees might be trained to heil.

The *Mirror* had yet to find an editorial stance amid all this steam. In 1937 it was still content to invite and print as much correspondence as it could. Its only printed reply to any letter on June 1, 1937 was a sentence of legal advice. By June 1938 it had invented for its main correspondence feature, Live-letters, the Old Codgers, whose replies below every letter revealed them as a repository of general knowledge, broad humour and, on occasion, sharp rebuke. It was a persona that was to spread throughout the war-time *Mirror*. To a

boy at Marlborough College who complained about the conditions
at his school, the Old Codgers answered:

> You're getting big ideas, sonny—would a sunk marble bath
> with solid silver taps please you?
> We know there's a lot of bunk talked about Spartan condi-
> tions being good for youth, but a lad who gets such a flying
> start in the world, as being a Marlborough boy, shouldn't start
> whining about the size of his bath.
> Among the things that YOUR parents are paying a con-
> siderable sum for, is that their offspring may learn a little
> common sense.
> It seems, in this respect, that they are not getting very good
> value for money.

The sarcastic appeal to the class prejudices of *Mirror* readers is a
confident one. But the Old Codgers' impatience with 'whining', or
with any other sort of pretension or ignorance, was as readily,
indeed eagerly, turned upon those who might be supposed natural
Mirror readers. 'Listen, you . . .' was a characteristic opening to a
reply; it might end 'Now hop it and don't be so confident about your
phoney facts in future.' Here is an example from 1939. 'Regular of
Catterick' wrote:

> I see that we regulars have got to go into tents so as to make
> room for the Militiamen.
> Why don't they bring nurses with them? We who are serving
> should be thought a lot of, we are the mainstay of the army.
> Why should we be driven from our barracks into tents to
> make way for a lot of featherbed soldiers?

Regular's sarcasm was turned on him:

> And you, you blanket-hugging, mattress-pounding sluggard,
> have the hide to call Militiamen 'featherbed' soldiers? 'Fraid of
> the draught, dearie?
> May you have to kip on an old coalsack filled with brass
> nails.

Behind these answers, and hundreds more, was the clear assumption
that *Mirror* readers liked a barney, and enjoyed the spectacle of
pretension vigorously dethroned. The Old Codgers had much in
common with working-class back-chat. They never proceeded from
simple spite, always located themselves squarely as men of sound
common sense, ready to entertain a good argument, but having no
truck with stuff and nonsense. The flavour, in fact, is a slightly more

knockabout version of Cassandra's, and sometimes indistinguish-
able: 'thus one-maid Suburbia lies smouldering behind its impenetrable wall of snobbery, untroubled by any subversive thoughts
of true democracy or even common courtesy'; or, 'when you're older
you'll find out that the West End of London is largely owned by a
few rich men, who don't really worry whether boys can find a little
open space to play cricket'.

The Old Codgers had several other tones of voice, all of them as
informal as that one: 'By the way, we don't think much of the boss's
son or your girl—you're well rid of her'; 'sorry to pull you up, lads,
but you're barking up the wrong tree'. Readers quickly learned to
join in the game: 'The bloke who sits in the corner of our local said
that . . .' Both correspondents and the Old Codgers were fond of
mock aggressiveness: 'So you won't talk . . . blowed if I don't feel
like paying you a violent visit' wrote a reader, and was answered:
'You'd never come out alive'. When readers were encouraged to
write, it was with the warning: 'But mind the rotten tomatoes!'

The Old Codgers liked to picture themselves as overworked:
'We've got such a heck of a lot to do and such a short time'. They
enjoyed jokes about their age, too: 'If those bleary old eyes of ours
don't deceive us . . .'; and about their 'cussedness'. Altogether, the
Live-letter Box as ardently inculcated the family feeling as any
holiday camp. According to Cudlipp, letters were the most popular
of all the paper's contents.

As well as in the Live-letter Box, and in columnists' references to
their postbags, letters were introduced in other sections of the paper.
One leader began: 'Several readers have asked us whether it is not
true that Russia is becoming a little too difficult . . .' The *Mirror*
also found a way of incorporating letters into the news pages: readers
who had a funny or significant story to tell were invited to send it
in: 'News to you—news to us. Most information is of national
interest. Don't keep it to yourself.' Such contributions (exclusively
human-interest) were paid for, and signed with the contributor's
name, although they were obviously rewritten in the *Mirror* style.
In this instance the paper found not only another channel for
reader participation but also a cheap source of news. A similar
effect was achieved by its solicited letters on set themes, sometimes of
a confessional nature ('the frankest page you have ever read!'; or,
seeking specimens of good angry letters to other people, the paper
asked 'ever written a snorter?') and sometimes in the form of
'reader's Parliament', wherein issues of general interest were in turn
debated. 'It was the unorthodox approach to serious social issues
that stimulated the talk and the criticism', wrote Cudlipp; and the

circulation, he implied. Yet another way of involving readers in the paper was to go out and find them: 'Cyril James may be breaking into your office tomorrow. He's going to reconstruct in the Sunday stillness the story of that office. It may be yours. So be careful what you leave behind today.'

In response to the international situation during 1938–9 the *Mirror* began to give more space to politics, but tentatively. If British sailors in Spanish waters were killed by Franco's bombs, then naturally it was news to the *Mirror*: more than news, in fact, for the unnamed reporter was allowed to express his opinion that Franco 'must be told firmly once and for all . . .' But when it came to debating the Spanish war in a leader, the paper did little more than express dismay.

The *Mirror*'s gauge of its readers' political concern can be assessed in a series of brief little articles at this time in which Philip Buckman explained a political 'ism'. For example, 'this is YOU—if you're a Tory', was the headline to a chatty, unpolemical glance at elementary Conservatism. An occasional sharpness against upper-class members of the Government, a jibe at Fascism, or at Unity Mitford, such isolated squibs were all that passed for political views in the paper, and they were a minute speck. Much more often, news stories that were potentially exploitable in political terms (and which would unfailingly have been exploited in 1945) rested entirely on their human-interest value. 'Duke of Kent at Perfect Deb's Ball' headlined a front-page story in which the deb turned out to be the daughter of Sir Oswald Mosley. A picture of miners with, again, the Duke of Kent was titled: 'One Touch of Nature Makes Them Akin', but not so akin as to prevent a miner's wife being delighted by the Duke's gift to her of his button-hole: 'She triumphantly held aloft the button-hole and then kissed it.' It is not that the *Mirror* could have been expected then, or indeed in 1945 or any other time, to resist the appeal of royalty, but that common people at this time were pictured in sentimentally conservative colours (as they would be again after the 1940s). Underpaid charwomen, asking for a better deal, were pictured as the cheerful 'mop and bucket brigade' under the heading: 'Chars want a charter'. When 'secret penalties of the poor' were exposed in one feature, the facing feature no less clamantly tells us how 'Cupid runs riot'. Hitler may be a maniac and gangster on one page, but on another he is an amusing epithet—'Hitler mothers'—to describe bossy women. It is in the light of its own seriousness for a few years later on, not necessarily by some ideal standard of seriousness, that the *Mirror* looks politically superficial in these pre-war years.

In hindsight we can see how a view of society was being structured that made the political growth of the following years possible, though not at all probable: how, for instance, the columns of gossip about 'high society' were placing the upper classes as Them, though seldom with rancour: Them and Us rather than Them *v.* Us. Rancour was possible: in Henley week an Oxford rower was jovially identified as one of Them by the caption 'My Gorsh', but the same day's editorial more trenchantly commented that 'Manual labourers and weekly wage-earners may take part in the races if they can. But they can't because it costs too much ... so like democracy, votes without cash.' Yet so explicitly political a conclusion was very much the exception. The rule was that those in high society, places of power or privilege, were vaguely identified with the Conservative party and vaguely (except by Cassandra) expected to feel pompous indifference to the kind of men or women who read the *Mirror*. In most of its pages the *Mirror* was celebrating society as it was: a double spread of pictures on Derby day exulted about 'King and Commoner, Millionaire and Tramp' all jostling each other on their way to the races. When the goings-on of high society were a rich source of news matter, it would not have been easy to find a way of representing the same people as politically hostile to the assumedly engrossed readers, even if the paper had wanted to. When Emily Post was preaching the finer points of etiquette, it was not easy to attack those who most perfectly practised them. Such a paper need not have developed into one that deliberately located its readers as a force in politics, nor perhaps into such a best-selling one, without the powerful external stimulus of the war.

Yet that stimulus would not have been effective without some yeast already in the paper. The yeast that was later to swell in the *Mirror* was in its form rather than its content: a relationship with its readers rather than any precise view of what they were interested in, or whether they had any clear ideas about politics and social change. Hugh Cudlipp has described the relationship:

> Behind the barking and the tinsel, however, was a closely reasoned scheme. The plan which these young men evolved was simply this—to get under the reader's skin and to stay there. They were all, in their way, lay psychologists. Most of them had come from working-class or middle-class families in the provinces; they really knew and had personally experienced the aspirations and setbacks, the joys and heartaches of the millions of ordinary people whom they set out to entertain and instruct. The down to earth feature pages became more and

more like a letter home to the family, and that was their secret. Readers accustomed to ploughing through mild views of established authors were now expected to think and write for themselves ... It was soon apparent that readers considered that confession was good for the soul and were anxious to read the confessions of others.

It was confession, communion, for its own sake, not for the purpose of advancing real social knowledge. 'Scottish girls can knock spots off English ones' was a typical view sent back by a reporter on a missionary tour around the country to find out 'just what the young people of Britain are really thinking'. Cudlipp says that the *Mirror* set out to construct such a relationship with its readers with 'courage ... candour ... youthful vigour'; Cecil King,[8] however, describes it as, at first, a 'technical adventure in journalism', conceived in 'cynicism' that was only later 'dissipated by the waves of affection and loyalty which came welling up from the band of readers'. The effect, anyway, of the heavy emphasis on readers' contributions, and of the constant editorial use of the second person, was that the paper established a view of itself as a forum in continuous sitting, with chairmen, rather than a daily eavesdropping on high places. But until the war came, the *Mirror* and its readers were all dressed up with nowhere to go.

Two items from late in 1939 may serve to illustrate the *Mirror* in the process of ferment from a friendly relationship with its readers to acting as something more like a moral guide. The first is from an article called 'I confess to my unborn son' by Brian Murtough:

> For today, as I write we are living on the edge of the world—never quite certain that there will be a tomorrow.
>
> And I sometimes wonder if it is worth while fighting for a future that may never come. I grow afraid—for myself. Afraid at the thought of how everything I ever planned would be smashed if a certain German marches out of step.
>
> Then I think of millions of other young men and women in the same position. Millions who would lose everything. And I am not afraid any longer.
>
> I realise that only by carrying on with our plans and ambitions can we do our share in making the world a better place ...
>
> The moral of this is that you must co-operate. You must study other people and never forget that you are part of a nation, not a person on your own.

8 Ibid.

'You must co-operate', expressed in sentiment, might stand as a perfect emblem of what was to follow in the war-time *Mirror*. The other item is from a leader:

> Certain minor ministerial changes, announced this week, have passed almost unobserved by the great public.
>
> A shuffle of mediocrities from post to post does not convince vulgar outsiders that the result can be anything but a new combination of the mediocre.
>
> However, politicians are not like mathematicians. They think that a nobody in another's place makes a somebody; though nothing added to nothing does not mean more than it used to be.

The rancour is still only vaguely directed against authority, and seems to feel little solidarity with what it can refer to as 'the great public', but it was not a long step from the outright attacks on Chamberlain's government of the following year, or from the demotic tone that controlled the *Mirror* after 1940.

*   *   *

Since the *Mirror*'s paramount interest in the early days of the war was preparedness for fighting, abroad, at home, at Westminster and in the factory, it attacked Chamberlain, and the men around him, on those grounds (in unison, of course, with many M Ps). The *Mirror* did not now blame them for having led the country into war, only for having done so inefficiently. Associated with Chamberlain was anyone, at any level of command, who seemed to share his unpreparedness. Such people were characterized as 'old men'. Accepting that we had to fight, the *Mirror* strove to prepare the country itself. While it scolded authority into action, it enjoined upon its readers co-operation, sacrifice and vigilance. The news columns dwelt upon stories of heroism and tragedy, great and small.

The Old Codgers' personality became still more terse. They no longer solicited letters: the impression is that people wrote to the *Mirror* because they felt they must. Most of their letters concern war-time regulations and conditions, and are answered with brisk informativeness. A constant object of scorn was the mug caught holding naïve views, or asking silly questions. The reader who inquires how much it costs to post a letter to Northern Ireland is briskly told 'Why didn't you ask at the Post Office?' Another who wants to know how to separate yolks from whites is laughed away. People were impugned for gossiping, for not drying soap after use, for using valuable waste paper instead of rags for polishing. The

D*

Them/Us distinction is one purely of whether or not you are doing
all you can for the war effort. That is what you are judged by.
Communist and Conchie are dirty words. The nation's heroes are
the Battle of Britain pilots—'on wings of fire they ride the storms of
war in heaven's height' wrote Patience Strong—and Winston
Churchill, whom the *Mirror* praised for having urged armament
against Hitler since the early '30s. (He contributed a weekly article
to the *Mirror* for a time in 1939.) Churchill's 'we shall never sur-
render' speech was 'the greatest speech ever made by a Prime
Minister of Britain', the *Mirror* announced, and included him in their
'Thanks a lot' series for teaching Hitler a lesson in honesty, telling us
'the best and the worst'.

One page on May 11, 1940, the day following Churchill's accession to the premiership and Germany's attack on the Low Countries,
brings together a number of themes. It is headed: 'This Page Is
Dedicated To VICTORY!' and contains three articles, by
Cassandra, Tom Wintringham, and Conrad Phillips.

Wintringham's opening is typically informative: 'The main line
of the German attack on Holland and Belgium is through the centre
of these two countries . . .' and the whole of his article consists of
authoritative military analysis of the new offensive. He ends: 'The
nearness of our own forces will enable us to put up a good show.'
The tone of modesty and straight information, like an informal
briefing to troops, supposes a calm but keenly interested audience.

Cassandra and Conrad Phillips take different views of their
readers' state of mind. Each starts with a reveillé. Cassandra: 'We're
off! The Sitzkrieg and the Bore War have vanished. And the real
thing begins.' Phillips: 'today you wake up in a different world. It
is a world fraught with danger. You are not startled, because for
nearly eight months, this newspaper has told you what to expect.'
Now their paths divide.

Cassandra angrily surveys the depredations of 'the Boche' all over
Europe. 'I must admit that Holland's resistance was a relief. I
feared that the Dutch would capitulate. The place is rotten with fifth
columnists . . . only the treachery of the fat Judas of Rome has saved
his country of ravioli gulpers from the wrath of the Teuton.' The
epithets pile up. 'The Old Hun never changes. He just loves to be
legitimate . . . My God what a race!' The USA is an 'ostrich . . .
that flatulent bird.' The deposed Prime Minister is 'Jonah Chamberlain'. The article is a performance, a striking of articulate attitudes.
Cassandra's rhetoric is a model of how the *Mirror* expected men
would like to express themselves about these things. The ventriloquism is augmented by Cassandra's own pungency.

Conrad Phillips's article is something quite opposite, a civilian battle-cry. Having, as we have seen, begun by locating himself, and the *Mirror*, in a position of imperative command towards the readers, Phillips goes on to write an exhortation strongly reminiscent of Henry V before the walls of Harfleur:

> You are not frightened because you are part of a race that has lived dangerously for over one thousand years.
> You are on your toes ready to counteract any blow.
> Your jaw is set, your eyes narrowed with determination.
> The last wisp of illusion has vanished from your mind like mist in the morning sun . . .
> And from the remote depths of your soul come the muffled voices of your ancestors—those hosts of bygone warriors, who once marched through the leafy lanes of our glorious island home, determined to preserve the sanctity and honour of Britain.
> 'Stand firm and resolute', the voices say . . .
> The direct challenge will always induce the happy-go-lucky Britisher to take off his coat and fight . . .
> Our only regret is that we ever allowed the monster to rise after the licking we gave him in the last struggle . . .
> So this new world in which you find yourself this morning is a world of glorious opportunity!

The range of address, from Wintringham's 'good show' and Cassandra's pungent vernacular to the elevated sonority of Phillips's 'muffled voices of your ancestors', is very wide. If Wintringham takes a briefing session, Cassandra is a heightened version of an informal debate in the mess; and Phillips's tone, the unfamiliar one in the *Mirror*, is that of a very high-ranking officer, who never rubs shoulders with the other ranks he is addressing. Phillips can perhaps best be seen as seeking to supply in the *Mirror* the patriotic oratory with which Churchill was comforting and encouraging the nation in a time of peril. If that is so, it must be said that Phillips is a poor ventriloquist in comparison with the working-class ventriloquism we have heard elsewhere in the paper. After the solemn clichés about 'hosts of bygone warriors' in the reader's soul, it is a shock to find that he is also a 'happy-go-lucky Britisher' ready to hand out a 'licking'. A desperate strain can be felt in the final exclamation mark.

If Phillips's rhetoric were not so shoddy, one might understand the page as three didactic modes, each intended to give the reader confidence in his courage; though it is a matter for conjecture whether any reader could be expected to respond to all three modes,

even at a time of such peril. Wintringham exemplifies the courage
of the man who calmly takes stock of the actual situation and reckons
he has a good chance of winning through. Of the different roles the
Mirror apparently felt called upon to play on this page, Wintringham's is the one which most treats its audience as adult people, each
of them capable of privately forming his own judgement. Cassandra's
teaching has to do more with public behaviour, exemplifying the
courage of articulate defiance, the nonconformist tradition of the
unbowed head, ready to fling insults even when things are at their
blackest. Both Wintringham's and Cassandra's kinds of courage are
civilian as much as military, a kind that any man might one day
need in his private life. The kind of courage Phillips seeks to instil is,
in contrast, that of a special occasion, when the whole nation must
stand shoulder to shoulder. Any rhetorician, as good as Churchill
or as fustian as Phillips, must draw at such a time on the most widely
shared, deepest and scarcely conscious national sense of great
oratory: the Bible above all, Shakespeare for many, and non-
conformist chapel sermons or evangelistic trades-union speeches for
most of the working class.

Possibly the *Mirror* was still experimenting to find a tone of
address on which it could confidently settle. None of the three
exemplified on this page survived throughout the war. Cassandra
was called up, and no one took his place. Wintringham was succeeded by writers such as Garry Allighan, who adopted a more informal
tone with soldiers. Elevated rhetoric did crop up from time to time
in editorials, but nothing to match Phillips's sonorities.

A more likely explanation of the wide range of tone was that it
answered to the urgency of the war crisis in summer, 1940. On June
18, Bill Greig wrote:

> Today there can be only one question on the lips of each of us:
> 'How can I help Britain?' Let me answer that.
>   First must be blind, unreasoning response to the orders and
> advice of the Government and those set in authority over
> us.

By that statement Greig, of course, sets himself in authority over his
readers. 'Blind, unreasoning response' was certainly not the *Mirror*'s
attitude towards the Government from 1941 onwards. Only in the
few months around the Battle of Britain were tones so disparate,
and so distanced, heard in the *Mirror*. Peril bred urgency, and
urgency brooked no answering back.

A year later the war situation was still grim, amid the blitz, but
the urgency had lost its edge with the defeat of the Luftwaffe's

invasion plans. Although the *Mirror* described it as the gravest crisis since Dunkirk, its response to Government was anything but blind. Regretting that Parliament was in its summer recess, and would later return in secret session, a leader asserted:

> The nation ought to know who, in the House of Commons, has the strength and courage to speak up and speak boldly.
>
> Also, we ought to know what proportion of emotional back-benchers are ready to ride off in fatuously hysterical approval of blunders and delays—covered up with patriotic rant and futile assurances of ultimate victory some time before the end of this century.

The paper had returned to its place among the people. A little cameo story is worth quoting in full. The headline was 'They Call Her Mrs. Britannia'.

> 'Britannia' is the name by which Ma Shakesby is known in a poor Humberside district.
>
> Bomb raids have driven away her friends, but Ma refuses to quit.
>
> She is one of a family of ten, all of them serving the country.
>
> Her husband, George, is master of a defenceless lightship—favourite Nazi target.
>
> Her sons, Chris, Ernest, George and John are in the army. Sidney was too, until he was discharged to do special work. Tom is on a minesweeper.
>
> Daughter Ann is a warden, Lily a munition worker and Kathleen, Ma's daughter-in-law, works in a canteen.
>
> 'They're a grand lot,' Ma told the Daily Mirror.

Such an item clearly serves no news purpose. Its function is much the same as that of the *Good Morning* interviews: to sustain morale by showing how the rest of the country keeps going on cheerfully, with 'brave good humour', in a *Mirror* phrase. Many such items were scattered throughout the paper. Sometimes they were more overtly moralistic, or sentimental, as in this example of 1942, written by an ex-rear-gunner:

> To the happy band of travellers that share my bus with me in the mornings, I pay this small tribute.
>
> I admire your grit! You who are left behind to carry on while the others are away are playing your part with cheerfulness and courage.
>
> There are few young men among you, but many of you are

praying each day for someone whom you love who is in the
Services.

Housewives with 'the light of purpose in their eyes as they hugged
their baskets determinedly to their laps,' cripples who smile bravely,
'I like the crowd on our bus ... these are my people—and I am
proud of them'.

The Old Codgers remain a source of more humorous community.
A 'lady' wrote 'I want to go about without stockings, but my legs
are a purpley-red colour and go all gooseflesh. Can you tell me—?'
At which point the Old Codgers interrupted: 'For the love of Mike,
lady, DON'T DO IT. Have a heart.' The imperative mood is
still in evidence: 'Leave the wild flowers in beauty spots alone!'
they ticked off a reader.

By this time, June 1942, it is sometimes possible to perceive
specifically Labour sympathies in the *Mirror*, deriving directly from
the problems of the war. Dissatisfaction with the 'conditions under
which our men are serving' is identified as an issue that divides
Socialist MPs from the Government. On the vital issue of war-time
controls, the *Mirror* clearly ranged itself against the Tories: 'a big
section of the Conservative party is still determined to fight rationing to the last ditch'. Elsewhere, Bill Greig drops the comment: 'well,
it's a pleasant change to find the Midland group of Tory MPs on
the side of the workers for once'. Again, in the serious dispute at the
time over the miners' wages the *Mirror*, siding with the miners and
describing their plight at length, advocated that the mines should
be 'run as a *national* service. The result of such an experiment in
nationalisation would be most instructive.' A Live-letter pointed
out that the Ecclesiastical Commissioners drew the chief mining
royalties, and concluded that it was time to hand over to the workers;
the Old Codgers warmly agreed.

Those points of view were yet only hints of a loyalty to the Left;
but in the context of the whole paper—flanked, for instance, by
stories of war bravery and execrations of black marketeers—they
indicate a magnetic field. George Orwell[9] had detected a general
leftward shift in the popular press, and noticeably in the *Mirror*, a
year earlier. In a London Letter to the *Partisan Review* dated April 15,
1941 he remarked:

> The tone of the popular press has improved out of recognition
> during the last year. This is especially notable in the *Daily
> Mirror* and *Sunday Pictorial* ('tabloid' papers of vast circula-

9 *The Collected Essays, Journalism and Letters of George Orwell, vol. II*,
Secker & Warburg, 1968.

tion, read largely by the army), and the Beaverbrook papers, the *Daily Express, Sunday Express* and *Evening Standard* . . . they have all grown politically serious, while preserving their 'stunt' make-up, with screaming headlines, etc. All of them print articles which would have been considered hopelessly above their readers' heads a couple of years ago, and the *Mirror* and the *Standard* are noticeably 'left' . . . Nearly the whole of the press is now 'left' compared with what it was before Dunkirk . . . There is an element of eyewash in all this, but it is partly due to the fact that the decline in the trade in consumption goods has robbed the advertisers of much of their power over editorial policy . . . they are controlled by journalists rather than advertisers.

Orwell went on to say 'I think you can take it that there is a strong tendency to pipe down on labour friction and also on the discontent caused by billeting, evacuation, separation allowances for soldiers' wives, etc., etc.' The Government would presumably have excepted the *Mirror* from any tendency to pipe down, in view of Churchill's 'Fifth Column' remarks to Cecil King (quoted p. 82). It was Orwell's general belief, however, that 'this is the most truthful war that has been fought in modern times': he gave the radio chief credit for that.

The *Mirror* cautiously warned its readers in 1942 against too eager 'plans for a better world after this worst of all wars. Thousands of brave people seem to have convinced themselves that an earthly Paradise can be planned in Hell. But there must be an intervening Purgatory . . . the immediate post-war period, with its threat of chaos . . . we begin to fear that the second world war will be followed by another between the planners of the various Utopias.' That note of sombre unillusion was to be held all through the 1945 election.

According to Cudlipp, it was in 1943 that the *Mirror* decided to cast its lot for the Labour Party. It did so with misgivings about the party's sectionalism, which it raised in a spirit of concern, and hoped for unity. The leader column, newly taken over by 'BBB' (Bernard Buckham), described Labour as 'the nation's political hope' for a 'fundamental change in the political scene'.

Big political movements come from below. They manifest themselves in the thoughts and desires of the people. These thoughts and desires are clarified and interpreted by leaders who arise naturally through their own ability and passion for reform. Later the next general election will record the verdict of a new Britain. This election, when it comes, may bring surprises.

In 'a new Britain' is announced the war to win the peace, a new mission for the paper, which it deliberately developed during the next two years. The 'present tired obsolete House of Commons' would be 'replaced by one which bears some approximation to the country's real feelings, hopes and ambitions. The Labour party should prepare for that day . . .' and the electoral register should be revised in readiness. Cudlipp says that the *Mirror* was very much aware of the serious debates, in Nissen huts and air-raid shelters, about the social and political significance of the war. The hopes of 'a new Britain' had been definitively fired in late 1942 by the Beveridge Report, for the publication of which the *Mirror* pressed from November 1942 onwards, thus allying itself with the Parliamentary Labour Party in its only revolt against the war-time Government. 'Hands off the Beveridge Report' the *Mirror* warned 'certain quarters', 'the gentry', and 'vested, sectional or personal interests'—Them, in short. It is from this point that the paper's characteristic imperative mood, and its invitation to participate, are deliberately engaged in preparing for a General Election. Early 1943 is the moment when the *Mirror* began to cash the credit banked since the war's first weeks. It did so in terms of 'old' and 'new', and told its readers that they, the victors of war, would be the creators of a new world in peace. The *Mirror* had grown accustomed to enfolding its readers in a sense of purpose.

The sense of participation continued unabated in Live-lettters. The Old Codgers were settlers of friendly arguments, in the tradition of Northcliffe's *Tit-bits* (occasionally admitting to not knowing an answer). Did Shakespeare write 'a little bit of what you fancy does you good?'—'Our sainted aunt!' Who wrote . . .?—'That old warhorse, Voltaire.' What should be done about children who steal flowers from your garden?—'a workmanlike horsewhip. It's probably brats of incompetent parents'. The switch to solemnity was easily made. Where a man stationed far from his wife wrote to say that they both prayed at the same hour each day, the Old Codgers could 'commend this with all sincerity. It was John Aikman Wallace, we think, who wrote: "that power is Prayer, stupendous boon . . ."' A new Live-letters feature, which was to survive many years, asked for prayers on behalf of people it named as in distress.

By 1944, as we have already seen in the Forces and women's sections, the *Mirror* was actively rallying its readers in preparation for a General Election, chivvying them into registration and lectur-

ing them on the elementary principles of suffrage and democratic
responsibility, with the clear assumption that most of its readers were
apathetic, if not hostile, to politics, and ignorant of its machinery. A
regular page called 'Readers' Parliament' sought to make public
the debates of the Nissen huts and air-raid shelters. The topic
was proposed by the page's editor, who summarized the replies,
and in doing so helped to 'formulate the slogans of change', as
Maurice Edelman puts it. A discussion about war memorials, for
instance, could lead to very grand slogans (not to say echoes of
Horace):

> The job in hand is the war, which ordinary people believe to
> be the birth pains of a new and better world.
>   The work of winning it is to lead us to a new and better life,
> and the better life is to be the memorial more enduring than
> brass or stone.

By its syntax, the page has placed itself squarely among 'ordinary
people', for whom it is a spokesman more articulate than any
ordinary person might be: a spokesman, moreover, who is primarily
addressing his own group, more interested in encouraging them to
recognize themselves in his phrases than in being overheard by
outside parties, such as Parliament. A similar feeling of community
is lent to news reports by attributing them 'By Your Special Correspondent'. The Them/Us distinction is often explicit, as in a
leader which doubted 'whether the political heads of the various
countries which have made up the Alliance have come as close as
they ought to have done to the *peoples* of each other's nations. It is
the people's will on which democracy stands.' The 'fighting man' is
constantly remembered: his messages to old comrades are printed at
length, his low pay is a subject of rebuke to authority. General
Montgomery is praised for his 'at ease' relationship with his men.

The suffering and hopes of ordinary people are prominent in the
Live-letter Box. Pride of place is given to women who have struggled
to bring up their families in heartbreaking conditions: 'The courage
of this woman! And her philosophy' commented the paper—not for
her, or anyone like her, the 'last war's unkept promises of "Homes
for Heroes", the slogan which reached rock bottom of mockery and
became the chant expressing the disillusioned cynicism of the
between war years.' Other sorts of people appear in Live-letters as
social dramatizations of what the whole paper is saying:

> I read with disgust Lady Reading's speech to a thousand
> WVS last week—that the duty of the 1944 wife is to 'forget

your homes, leave beds unmade, leave the house dirty, don't
look after your husband's meals . . .'

The Old Codgers answered:

> Madam, the lady has never done these things, anyway, so it's
> no change for her. She has a staff of servants. You do as you
> have always done with your home. That's your duty; and don't
> listen to blah-blah!

Another woman, under the heading 'An Officer and No Gentleman', wrote:

> My mother, whose heart is in the right place, has been asked
> not to write any more as her son in law, a lieutenant in the
> Navy, feels he is being belittled by receiving letters with
> mistakes in spelling, etc. My mother is deeply hurt.

The answer:

> We are sorry, indeed, for your mother's daughter. We would
> sooner see her married to a gentlemanly chimneysweep.

And when the secretary of a women's guild wrote to protest against
'the nonsense presented in your notorious Live-letters column', the
Old Codgers immediately placed her for readers by retaining the
'Dear Sirs' at the start, normally omitted.

The *Mirror*, in sum, located its readers as a social grouping with
political potential by offering them an image in which they were to
recognize themselves, by assuring them that they above all others
deserved to benefit socially from the war, and by urging them to do
all that was in their power to effect the political change that would
be necessary. In parallel, it examined the political parties and found
that only Labour, although 'in some respects vague and mystically
platitudinous' and having too many 'old men' in its upper rank, had
'the temerity to indicate the road that should be taken' to 'a new
world', by way of rationing, nationalization, destruction of profiteers
and, in international affairs, the United Nations. Labour had 'ideas
and flair'; other parties were 'singularly barren of ideas'. Labour's
adoption of a clear and definite programme was 'more courageous
and more statesmanlike than tamely waiting to see which way the
electoral cat is likely to jump.'

II Into Peace

Hugh Cudlipp says that 'the Labour Party enjoyed the support of
the *Mirror* in the 1945 election because it incorporated or appeared
to incorporate in its programme more of the aspirations of the

Mirror's readers and writers than any other political group'. The confidence with which Cudlipp can identify and negotiate 'the aspirations of the *Mirror*'s readers' is striking; his explanation for it is that the *Mirror* in 1945 was the product of a 'new school of young journalists with an unorthodox outlook upon life and affairs in general as well as upon newspaper technique . . . new methods drew millions of working-class readers who were encouraged to express their views to their newspaper . . . the *Mirror* became an immense, permanent Gallup Poll survey of changing mass opinion'. Since Bartholomew's appointment as editorial director in 1934, the *Mirror* has always attended closely to what its 'survey' might reveal by summarily analysing the thousands of letters sent to the paper every week.[10]

This chapter has followed the dialogue by which that confidence was established over the war years. It remains to be shown how the dialogue, conducted in the same tone, was at the centre of the 1945 election *Mirror*s; how, that is, the *Mirror*'s view of its readers during the election was consistent with the sort of people it had envisaged as its war-time audience. Such consistency can be assessed from the two kinds of material—direct, imperative address, and reader feedback—that have been seen to be most representative of the 1939-44 *Mirror*'s peculiar immediacy: and that also serve to contrast the war-time *Mirror* most strikingly with the war-time *Express*, which adopted none of the *Mirror*'s imperative mode, and which printed, throughout the war in Europe, not a single reader's letter (that extensive sampling could find).

First, it should be made clear that the *Mirror* was not free of the ceremonious electoral rhetoric which was central to the *Express*. The 'Gestapo' line of the *Express* was echoed, though less resonantly, by the *Mirror*'s assertions on several occasions that the British Fascists were keenly assisting the Tories, and that 'German big businessmen are praying for a Conservative victory . . . their only hope'; and late in the campaign the *Mirror* picked up and amplified the word 'fuehrer' that had been applied to Churchill by Arthur Greenwood. What could be called the rhetoric of aspiration is not very different in either paper: the *Mirror* spoke of 'full opportunity for British enterprise to express its industrial genius', 'your hearths and homes', and 'the lusty youth of this great land'. 'Splits' and 'repudiations' were as rife in the *Mirror*'s view of the Tories as in the *Express*'s of Labour. The *Mirror* was not free of biblical sententiousness ('by their records

10 A fact confirmed by Michael Christiansen, editor of the *Sunday Mirror*, in a seminar at the Centre for Contemporary Cultural Studies in 1968.

shall ye judge them'), simple-minded antitheses ('vague promise or specific plan—which do you prefer?'), heavy irony and back-slapping ('wise voters will laugh off this nonsense'). An impartial examination of the parties' programmes, to let the reader judge for himself, was scarcely attempted in either paper: both represented the political process as the expression of preference for a stereotype (heroic leader versus Gestapo-bound puppet in the *Express*; unillusioned worker versus bloated profiteer in the *Mirror*). To the particular issue of Churchill's tour the *Mirror* gave, in all, only a few inches of news coverage, dwelling on his infirmity and mishaps.

The *Mirror* orchestrated its contents, from news of candidates' speeches to readers' letters, to represent a massive pro-Labour feeling in the country, which may well have been true among *Mirror* readers but was not an accurate picture of the whole, as the voting figures attest. There is no case to be made that the *Mirror* considered its readers as mature enough citizens to be told the socio-economic facts of the time and left to draw their own conclusions about how to vote. The absence of an explicit injunction to vote Labour is simply copy: a departing genuflection, perhaps, to the common sense of readers. (The *Daily Sketch* also avoided naming the party it expected its readers to prefer, though it, too, made its preference plain, extolling free choice in education and incentives for the small shopkeeper.) It is entirely consistent with the war-time *Mirror* that it should have chivvied its readers in this way. For years it had plainly believed them to be ill informed by other agencies about the realities of their social situation and the available resources. It had told them how to make corned beef tasty, how to stamp out gossip, how to demand play groups, and how to secure their welfare and political rights. The *Mirror* listened, and knew, and cared. To extend the advisory function to a General Election was only a short step farther.

But the heavy concentration upon actual social distress in the 1945 *Mirror*, and its continued dialogue with its readers, mediated the rhetoric, altered the assumed relationship between rhetorician and reader; so that the *Mirror*'s rhetoric seemed to be rousing an audience by telling them what they already knew, rather than, as in the *Express*, browbeating them into silence with inside revelations or authoritarian sermons. To readers two decades on, the critical effect is that in the *Mirror*, but almost never in the *Express*, one can sense the social feeling of the time, the same feeling that elected the Labour Government. It was, presumably, that sense which caused A. J. P. Taylor[11] to write that in the *Mirror* 'the English people at last found

11 op. cit.

their voice' and to propose the paper as the most authentic literary expression of World War II.

*   *   *

During the 1945 election period Garry Allighan's column for serving men carries a lot of advice about the problems left by the end of the war; about, for instance, the probable accommodation of the relatives of wounded men:

> In some towns appeals have already gone out to householders living near hospitals to provide the accommodation. The liaison officer provides the necessary ration cards for the household, and also a billeting allowance up to two guineas per week.

In the same column Allighan moved on to no less specific advice about registering as a voter:

> You fellows on home service, and you others overseas, should watch out that you don't lose the citizen's rights you are fighting to preserve.
>
> Go to your CO or Orderly Room at once—wherever you are—and ask for Army form B2626 (RAF form 2040 if you're an airman, and MNER1 if a merchant seaman).
>
> Fill this in and your vote is assured—whether the election takes place while you are in the services or not.

The first paragraph, in the buttonholing second person address seen often before, latches on to the tone and theme of the 'war to win the peace'—'watch out ... citizen's rights ... fighting to preserve'. What is being preserved is more than the mere idea of democracy; the serving reader is assumed to have a real personal interest in the war. He has to watch out at home, or in the offices of military bureaucracy, not only in the countries he is liberating. The stake is his own democratic voice; the implication, that he has *deserved* the citizen's right to have a say in the way the country is going to be run now.

Perhaps that is to read too much into one sentence, but that such implications lay behind it should be clear from the earlier examination of the 'war to win the peace'. They are more articulated elsewhere in the 1945 *Mirror*. A front page story reported an ex-serviceman's speech attacking the Government's inefficiency in making houses available for men coming home from the war. The ex-servicemen, he argued,

know pefectly well that if the houses had been military equipment needed to make England safe for Tories they would have
been produced quickly enough.

Soldiers are being talked for and, simultaneously, to; the Us/Them
theme is being converted into soldiers/Tories. From the contrast of
the wars to win the war and peace, an ironic grievance emerges.

'For the common soldier', wrote Barrie Pitt[12] in 1967, 'the world
is divided into "them" and "us". "They" inhabit the world from
which come all orders, circumstances and conditions which make
life unbearable and, in war time, often end it; "us" are all those in
like conditions to ourselves—including also the poor bastards on the
other side of the hill. "They" are unreasonable, omnipotent, and
above all, *invisible*; "us" are those we know, those we have seen—
above all those we have talked to or who have talked to us.'

That exactly fits the assumptions from which the *Mirror* talked to
its soldier readers from 1939 until the 1945 election. The trick, for
the *Mirror*, was to cash the distrust politically, a trick made easier,
of course, by the close identification of the war-time Government,
'Them', with the Tories now seeking re-election, and, presumably,
the soldiers' normal assumptions about the political loyalties of the
invisible higher command. As the *Mirror*, and many other people,
knew that the services (not only the ranks) were heavily pro-Labour,
the trick became that of getting the vote out—or, if not out, expressed in some other way. Hence, 'Vote for Him'.

In its 'Vote for Him' slogan the *Mirror* found a simple cry that
could be caught and re-echoed throughout the land. The deep
resonance was in the emotional content of the word 'Him': it could
invoke the war-weary husband abroad (its first ostensible reference),
the husband killed in the war ('some of them are going to vote for
those who will never come home, the men who died fighting'); and
it is hard to dissociate biblical overtones, too, from the way the word
was used. (The same slogan in the *Express* would, of course, have
had a single referent, Churchill, again with biblical associations.)

The electoral calculations behind the *Mirror*'s use of the slogan are
apparent. The Forces[13] were (rightly) thought to be very pro-
Labour. Many of them were disenfranchised, and this was an
indirect means of getting their vote out; and of the 2,867,836 who
were registered as service voters, some two-thirds had proxy votes,
the great majority of which would be cast by their womenfolk.

12 *Sunday Times*, September 10, 1967.
13 Information about Forces' voting is drawn from McCallum and
Readman, *The British General Election of 1945*, Oxford, 1947.

Furthermore, the slogan would encourage apathetic women to vote, many of them for the first time, and might diminish the Conservative majority among those women who needed no encouragement.

The slogan first appeared in a letter, printed on the front page, from a woman reader:

> My husband won't be home to vote. He is in the CMF. He has fought against the Fascist enemy in Italy and North Africa for a better Britain—now he is denied the chance of hearing candidates give their views for a better Britain.
>
> I shall vote for him. I know what he wants . . . I shall vote to ensure that he gets what he wants.
>
> He wants a good house with a bit of garden. He wants a job at a fair wage, however hard the work may be. He wants a good education for the children.
>
> He wants to feel they won't have to go through what he has gone through in this war. So he wants a Parliament that will be faithful to our alliance with Russia and America.
>
> Even if I had any doubts about the prospects of getting these things, I would still vote for him. Nobody has a better right to decide the future of our country than the men who fought for this country.
>
> Like my husband I believe in a better Britain. His letters to me have always been full of hope and courage—the courage that helped London to stand up to the blitz. The courage behind which we women hid our tears and troubles.
>
> How my husband would despise these politicians who are trying to scare us and stir up our fears.
>
> I can hear him laughing at those who think the world holds no promise for Great Britain unless we return to the bad old pre-war days.
>
> If he and his pals had not had the courage to laugh and have faith in each other after Dunkirk where would we be now?
>
> My husband would say, 'Vote for Courage'. I shall. I shall vote for him.

That the *Mirror* displayed this letter prominently, endorsed it as 'wise advice to all women', and based so much of the rest of their electoral campaign on it (it appeared on June 25) is not at all surprising. To a remarkable, perhaps suspicious, extent it embodies all the important themes, and some of the rhetoric, that the paper had been deploying for six years. The three kinds of war are explicit, and that seems to be the deepest calculation of all behind the coining of the slogan: the transition from fighting to win the war to fighting to win the peace. The franchise is extended by symbolic emotion to those who had died fighting. There is no need to emphasize the significance of such phrases as 'the men who have fought for this country', 'a better Britain' and 'the bad old pre-war days'. The rhetorical forms that the letter uses, with some sophistication, are reminiscent of the 'quiet strength . . . something restful and noble' enjoined by Janet Grey upon her women readers in the darkest days of the war, and reflected, as we have seen, in much of the *Mirror*'s own style at that time. Mrs. Gardiner, if she did write the letter unprompted, was no ordinary working-class letter writer; that is clear from the directness of the opening, the main-clause simplicity, and the controlled pressure of the argument. In the end, the letter's authenticity is less important than the use the *Mirror* made of it. Here we have the clearest possible picture of the sort of woman the *Mirror* wished to present as an ideal to its readers. That is not, of course, to say that it assumed them all to be like Mrs. Gardiner, or to aspire to be like her; the use the *Mirror* made of the letter was itself rhetorical, designed to chivvy women just as much as Cicely Fraser's bracing addresses. As rhetoric must in a mass medium, the *Mirror*'s electoral exhortations to women tended to disregard their diversity and seek a common multiple; elsewhere in the paper women were acknowledged as landgirls or politicians, but when they were to receive an appeal from the *Mirror* it was invariably in their role of 'wives, mothers, sweethearts'.

Although that letter first formulated the Vote for Him slogan, the idea had already been heard twelve days previously, in a June 13 report from a Forces correspondent abroad. The report spoke of 'bewilderment . . . indignation . . . anxiety . . . alarm . . . anger' among 'the men who won the war in Europe' that they might 'have no say in the choosing of the next Government'.

> Many of them . . . will write to their wives or parents or sweethearts, telling them how they want to vote, and asking them to vote the soldier's way. People at home can scarcely do less . . .

It is the reader's sense of common decency, fair play, that is aroused, not his democratic beliefs or his political loyalties. At root, the emotion that the *Mirror* is summoning is gratitude to the fighting man. Its front page on July 5, polling day, was devoted largely to reproducing the paper's VE day cartoon, by Zec, in which a wounded and weary soldier is handing over a wreath marked 'Victory and Peace in Europe' with the caption: 'Here you are—don't lose it again'. A leader beside it told readers to 'vote on behalf of the men who won the victory for you . . . who fought and died that their

homeland and yours might live . . . you failed to do so in 1918. The
result is known to all. The land "fit for heroes" did not come into
existence. The dole did . . . Make sure that history does not repeat
itself. Your vote gives you the power. Use it . . .'

In the ten days between Mrs. Gardiner's letter and polling day
the *Mirror* constantly screwed home its slogan, mounting towards
religiosity:

> I'll vote for *them*
> Voice of her dead boy will be heard

ran a June 30 headline, and the story below described the widespread response that the slogan had won in 'wives, mothers, sweethearts from all over Britain'. That day's leader described women as
'shouldering, with pride and religious fervour, the greatest responsibility now resting upon British electors . . . that the voice of the
fighting man will be heard'. Headlines elsewhere announced that the
church, up to bishop level, supported the slogan: 'Let us make
certain, is the cry from the pulpits, that the voice of the soldier, the
living and the dead, shall be heard in the land'. A clergyman was
quoted as describing Vote for Him as 'a challenge in the spirit of a
Mother Mary dreaming of the world her child would help to create
. . . the cry of Mother England, tired of the meanness, the pettiness
and squalor of partisan politics'. A great deal more than common
decency is being sought now in the *Mirror*'s readers. Just as the
Express was using messianic language about Churchill, so was the
Mirror summoning up the same sentiments of church-going on
behalf of the men who had made the sacrifice. To Vote for Him was
to join a crusade that transcended 'the squalor of partisan politics'.

Labour Party politicians were not slow to endorse that crusading
view. Herbert Morrison called the idea of Voting for Him 'a sacred
trust', a phrase that the *Mirror* in turn elevated into its leader headline on June 30. 'The patriotic women', said the paper, were 'insist-
ing' that the nation should keep the 'pledge' that 'every fighting
man' had a say in forming the next government; Churchill had
'broken' that pledge; but 'women will respond eagerly to Mr.
Morrison's patriotic plea,' the *Mirror* asserted with quiet assurance.
That use of the word 'will' is not far from such a phrase as 'platoons
will report to their sections at 0800 hours'; and the representation of
eagerness no less sentimental than the *Express*'s picture of Chelsea
pensioners 'awkwardly to attention' for Churchill's cavalcade.

As polling day grew close, the *Mirror* often reverted to that kind of
uplifting rhetoric, exploiting the courage of a nation recently at war,
that it had seldom found necessary, or appropriate, in the conditions

of war itself. (A rare example was Conrad Phillips's article of May 11, 1940, described on p. 107.) The front page of July 4 is a good example. Headed 'A message to the voters of Britain' and 'Why we'll Vote for Them', it addressed itself in toto (using ½-inch type and much white space, an extravagant gesture in those days of newsprint hunger) to 'you women' who 'must think of your men'. The nagging note of the women's pages can be heard in that phrase, but not in others, such as 'your hearths and homes', 'lusty youth of this great land' and 'march forward to a better and happier Britain', where the brisk but familiar, detailed persona of Cicely Fraser or Janet Grey has drawn a long way back and is making a speech, not confiding advice. The previous day's leader, headed 'Those dreams of youth!', had taken a similar view:

> The hopes of the rising generation are always much the same. Those who are no longer youthful may, before they cast their votes, turn back their minds to their own young days, and think what it was they most wanted from life. Nothing very grand. Nothing (they thought) very difficult to obtain. A job at a decent wage, a home, a little happiness, leisure and the means to enjoy it. A humble list. Yet what dreams were bound up in it. What rosy vistas stretched out before the young men and women as they set out bright eyed on their journey to the stars.
>
> And were those fond hopes realised? Did those dreams come true? Alas, in many cases there came the bitterness of disappointment and disillusion. Poverty and unemployment stalked the land.
>
> Thousands of little worlds went to pieces. Is that sorrowful history to repeat itself? Must once again youth's happy vision fade away and die?

Two idioms seem to be entwined there, both familiar to many working-class people (and the respectable lower-middle class: hence, perhaps, a faint resemblance to the *Express*).

The leader's home key is nonconformist rhetorical uplift. It is not hard to imagine a Welsh chapel voice delivering the pious cadences. A slight afflatus in the opening sentences prepares the way for an assertive switch to short, more challenging phrases ('Nothing very grand', etc.). The afflatus (or hwyl) returns ('rosy vistas . . . bright eyed', etc.) but has now been established, by the short limiting phrases, as a mode of mild, sad irony. Rhetorical questions raise the pitch of irony, which is suddenly dropped with a soft 'Alas', and home truths follow with a biblical cadence. There is no irony in the closing rhetorical questions, the curiously stumbling last sentence, but an uplifting adjuration to the departing congregation that they go and worry about these sorry matters, and feel determined they be put right.

The other distinguishable idiom is in the recurrent phrases evoking little humble folk in a big world: 'Nothing very grand. Nothing (they thought) very difficult to obtain. A job at a decent wage, a home, a little happiness . . . A humble list . . . fond hopes . . . little worlds.'

Together, the two idioms indicate that the *Mirror* is, for rhetorical persuasion, capable of taking a view of its readers rather different from the populist one implied in its imperative and public-forum moods. The assumption here is that they see themselves as little people with really quite small wants, up against a big, hard world. By taking the minister's place, the *Mirror* identifies itself as wiser and sadder in the ways of the world, and so perhaps able to help them by a cautionary sermon. The non-denominational minister in *Bleak House*, Mr. Chadband, expresses himself in similar cadences:

> 'I say, my friends,' pursues Mr. Chadband, utterly rejecting and obliterating Mr. Snagsby's suggestion, 'why can we not fly? It is because we are calculated to walk? It is. Could we walk, my friends, without strength? We could not. What should we do without strength, my friends? Our legs would refuse to bear us, our knees would double up, our ankles would turn over, and we should come to the ground. Then from whence, my friends, in a human point of view, do we derive the strength that is necessary to our limbs? Is it,' says Chadband, glancing over the table, 'from bread in various forms, from butter which is churned from the milk which is yielded unto us by the cow, from the eggs which are laid by the fowl, from ham, from tongue, from sausage, and from such like? It is. Then let us partake of the good things which are set before us!'

> The persecutors denied that there was any particular gift in Mr. Chadband's piling verbose flights of stairs, one upon another, after this fashion. But this can only be received as a proof of their determination to persecute, since it must be within everybody's experience, that the Chadband style of oratory is widely received and much admired.

Yet elsewhere in the *Mirror* the familiar dialogue continued. Perhaps the paper saw no disparity, or assumed that its readers were susceptible to both kinds of stimulus, the intimate imperative and the speech or sermon; and very likely the paper believed that its readers looked for fine phrases at a time of national decision, as they had indeed in the crisis of 1940. The facts remain that the *Mirror* seems to have had much less confidence in its readers, a much more blurred view of the sort of people it was talking to, when it reached for phrases; and that the weight of the paper, both proportionately and persuasively, remained on the dialogue conducted by Cicely Fraser, Garry Allighan, and others.

* * *

Cicely Fraser's relationship to her readers is never ambiguous. She began her column on June 18, 1945:

> 'Can't you *please do anything* to help me to get my vote?'
> That is the cry which has been coming to me from many of you this week. And my answer has had to be 'I'm afraid I can't.'

Her advisory position is still a firm one, but she speaks more protectively than in 1944. Instead of 'if you're too lazy to use your vote' we find 'if you possibly can—do use your vote'; instead of 'now's your chance—grab it!', 'the election gives you the chance you've been waiting for. Use it.' The imperative mood has taken on a more well-bred tone;

> The war has taught a lot of people to understand that we simply must pull together and do our bit in running the country.

The explanation may be that by this time it was too late to do any more chivvying of women into organizing themselves by ensuring their franchise; the voters' lists were fixed. The intention now was perhaps to consolidate her readers' confidence in their own actions, and keep them up to the mark: 'don't go back on the things you've been saying to me in your letters for so long'. The old enemy had been apathy in the readers; now they had to be protected against bureaucracy, big business, smugness, and injustice in authority:

> The really upsetting things about these letters . . . is that so many of you seem to be the victims of official bungling.

And again:

> Don't let them get away just with kissing your babies—find out what they intend to do for the *future* of those babies.

The enemy, in fact, was anyone who deprived ordinary people of their right to vote, find work near their home, have a home to live in, or who knew how to manipulate the system to their own advantage. 'Can candidates who make promises and then break them be prosecuted?' asked a reader. 'Well,' said Cicely Fraser,

> the answer is 'No'. But at least, you would think, nobody would trust them if they came forward again and asked for votes.
>
> Yet it looks as if a number of 1935 MPs are hoping that the public memory is short . . . if you have a good memory, use it, and disillusion them.

The nagging note can still be heard on occasion:

> I told you last week that nobody could threaten you about how you should vote. Now here's a woman who writes to me . . .

But the note is turned back on authority in the end; 'Well,' said Cicely Fraser,

> if that isn't a threat, I don't know what is. That landlord should be told where he gets off.

By issuing practical reassurance about how simple the voting procedure is in the same tone as the women's pages had used for tasty recipes for dried egg, Cicely Fraser, like the rest of the *Mirror*, was in a position to cash her credit with the readers by letting the detailed domestic advice shade into the specific political advice. Her avowed concern was to get the vote out: 'if you vote right and do your duty by your family and your workmates, the problems you have to send me won't be so hard to solve'. Her review of the Conservative manifesto left no doubt about how specific, beyond mobilizing the women's vote, her aim was: 'really, you'd think the Tories had never had a chance to prove themselves'. The attitudes she proffered to big business, bureaucracy and so on made the same point almost as clearly. A Zec cartoon buttressed her column, and Vote for Him, by picturing a soldier's wife smilingly disregarding the pamphlet pushed under the door, labelled 'Tory election scares'.

Another view of women, entirely compatible with Cicely Fraser's, was embodied in numerous articles about the victims of social problems, principally the housing shortage. The angry note, of people somehow coping though near the end of their endurance, is very frequent. The typical case of Mrs. Julie Summerhayes, inevitably (it seems) prompted by a letter from her to the *Mirror*, took up half the centre spread on June 13, under the headline 'She Only Wants A Home', and was illustrated by a very big picture of Mrs. Summerhayes, her three children, and a named cat. Subsidiary headlines were:

Mother-to-be tramps city for ten hours every day
Widow of Commando
Council's hand tied

The central article is the exceptionally long letter, about two columns, in which Mrs. Summerhayes describes her 'absolutely desperate' search for a home in Bristol. The style of the letter indicates that it has been printed without editing. It tells a distressing story, and is unquestionably a revealing document of the housing problem in the country at that time. Certain sentences must have recommended it particularly to the paper:

> I feel like ending it all, children as well, but that isn't what my husband fought and died for. He volunteered with a willing heart 5½ years ago to help save people like me from the evil that threatened.
>
> I ask you, is this a just reception after all I've given to be offered only the workhouse?

The letter ends:

> Hundreds of people have told me to write to 'The Daily Mirror' and make known the way I have been treated, so in desperation I have done so, hoping that it will make clerks of the Council realise that myself and perhaps other soldiers' wives and widows are human beings, and not public nuisances.
>
> Thanking you for all that you have done for the people in times gone by.

Two comments accompanied the letter. One was a statement by Bristol officials; the other was the *Mirror*'s introduction to the story:

> The 'Daily Mirror' believes that housing is the most serious domestic problem facing this country. And still there is no one really tackling it.

The letter, said the paper, 'presents the problem of bricks and mortar in terms of human misery and despair. Read it—and remember . . .' To make sure that they remembered, the *Mirror* printed news of similar cases (desperation/husband's sacrifice/letters to the *Mirror*) throughout the campaign. On polling day the paper described at length the plight of a woman who had asked if the *Mirror* could help her to have her third baby adopted. The husband had been invalided out of the Army after 'gallantry in action . . . if he had a home the citation would be framed, on the wall' said the *Mirror*. Elsewhere the paper, discussing housing, took care to remind its readers of the process of socio-political education it had engaged them in: 'Readers of the "Daily Mirror" know that this problem has reached a tragic stage.' They knew because the paper had constantly shown them particular instances before the generality, the example before the rule: readers of the *Mirror* were a forum, and the examples could be found among their own number. *Mirror* readers were a sectional interest in the country only in their opposition to those in high places; outside bureaucratic offices, they were the people, according to their newspaper. And the kind of people they were was very different from the kind of readers the *Express* envisaged. They were near the end of their long tolerance of a situation in which Julie Summerhayes could hopelessly tramp the streets of Bristol; they had supported it while their men were perforce engaged in war, but no longer. Things were going to be different now: different from the war, the pre-war, the 1919 post-war. And the difference was going to be determined by those who had made the sacrifices: the men who had fought, and the women who had waited. The final indignity, which would not be tolerated, would be if the serving man, who had put his faith in people at home, were robbed of the vote he had so richly deserved. Social justice demanded a decent recognition of his rights.

*　　*　　*

Apart from incorporating readers' letters in its news pages and signed columns, the *Mirror* also printed two separate daily features of letters throughout the election campaign. One such feature was Live-letters; the other was specifically devoted to electoral letters and entitled 'Labour and Liberal'. Their functions were different: in Live-letters the Old Codgers continued their familiar dialogue, now extended deeply into politics; Labour and Liberal made no individual replies to its correspondents, who testified to their voting intentions and briefly explained their reasons, but the column was introduced by a rubric that often stressed the great number of unprinted letters that the daily selection represented.

The sense in which the 1945 *Mirror* can be said to cash its wartime credit is particularly plain in Live-letters. The transition into specific political advice can be seen in every day's column, where electoral letters are mingled with both serious and flippant non-political ones. On polling day itself, for instance, the column, prefaced with the quotation 'be it never so humble, there's no place like home', began with a letter that asked 'you two dear old souls' why abandoned Army huts could not be used for emergency accommodation. 'We've raised the matter before', sighed the Old Codgers. The next letter complained of snobbery in a school, and elicited a characteristically terse reply: 'Send us the name and address of the school. We'll soon put a stopper on this.' The third quoted a baron: 'I would remind Mr. Attlee that the working class was created to do the work of the world not to rule it. Only gentlemen are fit to rule . . .' The next letter reverted to housing, and the Old Codgers took the opportunity to sneer at 'government propaganda'. The column went on to print and answer several trivial inquiries, to expose 'Red Tape brains', and to lament soft treatment of German prisoners. The 'mix' of plain political affiliation, social problems, social attitudes, lessons of the war and light back-chat ('and here, folks, is . . .') is successfully homogenized by the Old Codgers' persona into one more column of the kind that had held a very large audience throughout the war.

No pretence at political impartiality was seriously made during the campaign. A presumed convert from Tory to Labour was greeted with 'Goody, goody'. The Old Codgers freely gave their opinion that a government including 'vested interests opposed to the Soviets' would be detrimental to the country's foreign affairs. An opportunity to ridicule Beaverbrook and the *Express* was gladly accepted: 'always up a bloomin' tree is that paper. The boss must be Tarzan!' Churchill was more restrainedly mocked: 'You must excuse the Prime Minister, you know. He is, today, the leader of the Tory party, and must, of course, speak as the Tory party tells him'— there followed a quotation from an attack on the Tories made by Churchill in his Liberal days. Always, such items were surrounded by other, non-political ones that encased the whole column in the tones of paternalism. 'Peace, fearful', a worried lady was admonished; 'listen, gentlemen of the RAF' low flying pilots were threatened; 'well, paint us, here's Albert Perry, turned up again from Chelsea' an old contributor was greeted; and flowers were requested for crippled and aged people with 'we could make you cry if we told you the desperate methods they use to keep the flowers alive'. Readers, as they always had done, readily joined in the fun, joking, worrying, affectionate. Nothing in Live-letters was bland.

Something more than three-quarters of the letters in the Labour and Liberal column indicated an intention to vote Labour; the rest were Liberal except for a very rare Communist and a single Tory. A few of the Liberal letters criticized Labour's policy of 'control over all industry'. It was very seldom that a letter took up a point made by a previous correspondent. The predominant impression is of a series of voters marching up to the rostrum, delivering a brief testimony, and making way for the next. Assuming that the *Mirror*'s selection of the letters it printed was determined by considerations of rhetoric, not simply of representativeness, we can form an idea of the column's strategy. In general, the letters' themes corresponded to the tone of the news and editorial columns: with the important difference that letter writers were licensed to express their feelings, especially about the social flavour of the parties, more spontaneously than editorial writers, who at least nominally had to peg their feelings to news and facts.

> A Labour government will do more for the working people than the Tories.
>   Labour will study the masses rather than the few.
>   The Big Business party . . .
>   The Liberal policy . . . can be applied to all sections of our community.

Social flavour expressed itself through stereotypes: the ordinary working man, the top-hatted capitalist. The column could be seen in this respect as a living dramatization of the nation as it was mediated in the rest of the paper, acting as a daily touchstone for the editorial arguments. That view is confirmed by the propensity of the letter writers to look back on their political experience: these were the people who had been through it all, whom the *Mirror* sought to lead into a new politics ('let no one turn our gaze to the past' it wrote on polling day). And, of course, they were the people who had been attached to the *Mirror* all through the war and who now spoke in it as they might in their pub:

> The Chancellor of the Exchequer, Sir John Anderson, said on the wireless the other night the wonderful things that would be done if the 'National' government get another chance. Blimey, haven't they had their chance for years? And yet we have to be involved in a war before the Unemployment Exchanges start emptying under the lovely 'National' policy which we've been paddling with since 1931.
>   No, thank you, chums, my vote goes to Labour.

And again:

> Common sense has led me to decide that if the Conservatives were sincere, nothing could have prevented them, with their overwhelming superiority of numbers in Parliament during the past two decades, from leading us forward to the Utopia they still promise us, instead of pushing us down to the very depths of despair and misery. Instead—what a record!
>   No, never again.

Many other letters made similar points, about the Conservative record and public image, and scoffed at their electoral stunts, now and before the war. Occasionally a letter would modulate from that view into specifically recommending that Labour be given 'a fair chance' now, or into the War-to-win-the-Peace theme. Others dealt with the problem of Churchill's charisma by criticizing him as a politician (rather than a statesman) or more often representing him as an honourable but 'worn out, tired man' who should 'retire while he still has the respect of the people'.

Those two main themes—the social flavour of the parties, and personal testimony to the national political experience—are clearly consonant with the rest of the paper; what is particularly interesting, for determining the column's strategy, is the comparative rarity of letters that testified to immediate hardship (as Julie Summerhayes and others did on other pages), rather than taking the longer view. Housing, identified by the *Mirror* as the most vital issue of the election, was mentioned only three times. Other issues scored:

Social Security	12
Employment	10
State Planning	10
Foreign Affairs	5
Forces' Votes	3
Women's Role	3

The figures justify the view that in the Labour and Liberal column the *Mirror* was cashing its tradition of correspondence for a particular strategic purpose, testimony.

Before moving on from letters, it should be mentioned that in the last days of the campaign Zec regularly contributed a strip cartoon in which the war to win the peace was embodied in a soldier writing a letter to the folks at home, telling them about his social hopes for the future.

It is virtually impossible to find straight, actual reporting of the election in the *Mirror*. Apart from its own news stories, focused on *Mirror* readers in distress because of housing problems and so on, its coverage of the election consisted mostly in unashamedly biased reporting of politicians' speeches and acts that fed the themes current elsewhere in the paper. Speeches by non-politicians were welcome if they served an ulterior purpose, such as the *Mirror*'s image of voting for Labour as a holy crusade: 'Bishop denounces the evils of free enterprise'.

In the case of the *Express* it is necessary to analyse news reports because the paper's rhetoric was concentrated there. Apart from special cases, such as the social problem stories or the coverage of Churchill, separate analysis of the *Mirror*'s news pages would reveal no assumptions about readers that are not more plainly projected in those parts of the paper, principally feature columns, already chosen as uniquely representative. There are resemblances between *Mirror* and *Express* rhetoric:

> Socialist apologists have found during the weekend that voters all over the country have refused to accept the plea that the incident 'is only another Tory stunt'. (*Express*)

> 'Don't be vague' electors have cried to Conservative candidates—and refused to accept the stock answer, 'Ask for Churchill!' (*Mirror*)

And it seems irrelevant to describe in greater detail the form of slanging matches not particular to this election, such as those on unfair taxation or equal pay. Although the politics of between the wars was exploited principally in readers' letters, naturally the rest of the paper did not ignore them: 'appeasement' was used as a taunting word, and the bitterness of such memories as Jarrow was powerfully revived by the Political Correspondent who visited the town and wrote: 'You have to come back to know what the spectre of peace means'. That sentence is a contribution to the war-to-win-the-peace theme; and such thematic analysis is a more comprehensive approach to the 1945 *Mirror* than one which would consider parts of the paper, or topics, separately.

The paper's leader columns have already been touched on as tributaries to the main themes. It would be hard to find one that did not make such a contribution. Consider the leader of June 5, exactly a month before polling day. It discussed the 'spirit of anger' which, 'controlled and wisely directed, is a good thing' in that it might ensure that 'the selfish interests submerged in war' should not emerge again in peace time.

> What, then, is the cause of this *anger* of which the Brigadier speaks? It is due to a realisation by the fighting men of today that their fathers, who were the fighting men of yesterday, were tricked by political promises, and the signs have already appeared once again that the old game is on. Homes for heroes; jobs for all; peace and plenty with time to enjoy them. How those slogans come back to memory! *And it all began with a rush election.* That first cardinal error has been committed again, and there cannot be too much *anger* to rectify it.

Soldiers are not the only ones who feel this emotion of resentment. Civilians, too, are no less anxious. The question asked is:
*if so much can be done as a matter of war urgency, why can so little be
done as a matter of peace urgency?* In other words, if the houses
and other things which we so badly need had been a war
priority they would have been up by now. How long have we
to wait now that the 'blessings' of peace are returning? The
difference, of course, between peace and war is that so soon as
the common danger to our existence ends, sectional interests,
fighting again their former battles, appear. Back-woodsmen
man the ancient barricades of power and privilege. The old
days are back.

There is no need here to press the exploitation of themes that will
be familiar: especially the war to win the peace, and Vote for Him
(which had not yet been formulated as such). The feeling of Us/
Them is very strong: the 'fighting men', 'soldiers' and 'civilians' are
placed in contention with 'the old game', 'sectional interests',
'backwoodsmen' and 'the old days'. It is noteworthy that the
Brigadier is on the side of Us. The *Mirror* was anxious throughout
the campaign to welcome high-ranking officers to its cause. It gave
generous display to a letter from 'Colonel Brett Mackay Cloutman,
last man to win the VC in the last war' who wrote that 'the over-
whelming majority of the boys overseas are solid for Labour'; and
it welcomed the news that a General was standing as a Labour
candidate by deducing that 'the moral is plain' that a government
of the Left would not neglect defence. The tone of the leader moves,
like one of Cassandra's columns, easily between irony and forthrightness, ending in a passage of orotund irony. It is a property of
irony that it assumes an audience sensitive enough to follow it and
sympathetic enough to be willing to do so: that is, the leader is
another example of the *Mirror* counting on its easy familiarity with
its readers. The specific aim of the irony is to agitate the anger
postulated earlier. The last sentence, 'the old days are back', cannot
be read as the note of resignation; the ironic tone implicitly leaves it
to the reader to add 'but . . .'; or, as Cassandra might have said, 'are
they hell!' Thus, the leader is another example of the *Mirror*'s
injunction of solidarity upon its readers, with the implication that
we, the people, can get things done, our way. The whole leader
also has an educational purpose. In presuming that its readers
remembered the events and slogans of 27 years previously, it no
doubt flattered many of them, and in doing so persuaded them to
accept the conferred memory as, indeed, their own henceforth. At

the same time, the *Mirror* identified itself as not likely to forget anything pertinent.

In the weeks that followed, the *Mirror*'s leaders, as some examples have shown, seemed designed principally to be overheard by those in high places: the device of dialogue being used as a man might speak loudly to his companions with the intention of reaching the ears of a third party. At such times the *Mirror* was more prone to windy rhetoric. There is little of that in the leader quoted, which seems to be part of the more direct dialogue that the paper had conducted with its readers since 1939.

Because of the use to which the *Express* put Churchill, and in particular his election tour, it is interesting to examine briefly the *Mirror*'s treatment of him. Having urged his accession to the premiership in 1940 and welcomed it gratefully, the *Mirror* had subsequently criticized him on occasions but never questioned his supreme leadership. Neither public opinion nor its own record of him could allow the *Mirror* now to turn and rend him. Public opinion was not, in fact, as solidly for him as the *Express* implied—two important attitudes to Churchill are exemplified in the following entry in Sir Harold Nicolson's Diary,[14] dated February 7, 1944:

> In the station lavatory at Blackheath last week I found scrawled up, 'Winston Churchill is a bastard'. I pointed it out to the Wing Commander who was with me. 'Yes', he said, 'the tide has turned. We find it everywhere.' 'But how foul,' I said. 'How bloody foul.' 'Well, you see, if I may say so, the men hate politicians.' Winston a politician! Good God!

But now Winston was unequivocally a politician again, and the *Mirror* was quick to exploit its readers' feelings on that account: it suggested that there was something ignoble in Churchill's, and especially his party's, seeking political gain out of his war record. Further attitudes followed from that. First, by stressing the fighting man's ultimate responsibility, and suffering, in the war the paper reminded its readers that Churchill's role had been only one of millions, albeit the most important. From that, the paper inferred that Churchill must be a very tired man, if not actually ailing. Thus it offered the possibility of not voting for Churchill and yet not feeling ungrateful. It could almost be represented as a kindness not to ask him to carry on; by the same token, the Tory party was treating him crassly. Above all, the *Mirror* judged that its readers were in no mood to vouchsafe their destiny to one man: 'we reject entirely the

14 Sir Harold Nicolson, *Diaries and Letters 1939–1945*, Collins, 1967.

idea that the future of this country must, or should be, placed in the hands of one person. That is a matter which has caused much confusion in the present election.' Something of that set of attitudes can be heard in, for example, the *Mirror*'s report on Churchill's last election broadcast:

> He threatened Service voters that if they wanted him to carry on as Premier they would have to swallow his Tory supporters, though he didn't use the name. He did not refer to any of the big issues. The word 'housing' was not heard.

Herbert Morrison was quoted describing it as a '"be kind to me" broadcast'.

Churchill's first broadcast, in which he made the notorious 'gestapo' charge, was described as 'claptrap', and no doubt the *Mirror* subsequently felt licensed to attack him more confidently than they would have, alleging for instance that soldiers equated Churchill with the war. As the *Express* sought to place Attlee in Laski's shadow, so the *Mirror* identified Beaverbrook as the evil spirit leading Churchill astray: 'In what, no doubt, was a loyal effort not to let a colleague [i.e. Beaverbrook] down, Mr. Churchill let his Party down'.

To Churchill's tour, so lavishly covered by Beaverbrook's paper, the *Mirror* gave, on successive days, seven inches, fourteen inches, three inches, one-and-a-half inches of column space. Only the start of the longest report made the front page, and that was tucked in at the foot. The report dwelt upon organizational failures and delays, and Churchill's 'advanced age and tottering step', a phrase used by Churchill about himself. (The technique of lifting self-mockery out of context was shared with the *Express*.) Reports of his public addresses were cursory and processed: 'He would give no guarantees of the action to be taken in any particular time.' The paper sought to make capital of Churchill's electoral use of a train 'reserved for the Prime Minister's official duties'. It published a characteristic letter about his 'gallivanting around in it':

> I am leaving my washing because I must get this off my chest . . .
>
> I have two babies and less than a year ago I was queueing up for coke, and they calmly shovel six tons of coal into Mr. Churchill's train.
>
> Please will you publish this and remind the public that the world never stopped for one man yet. America didn't stop for Roosevelt and he was as good a man as Churchill.

The *Mirror*'s problem with Churchill turned on patriotism. Patriotism had won the war; converted into the war to win the peace, patriotism might give Socialists a 'tremendous lever', in Orwell's phrase (see p. 138). In 1940 the *Mirror* had demanded Churchill's leadership as the only patriotic hope. Since then, in representing the whole national war effort Churchill had been identified as the great patriot, and thus, in war's special circumstances, the great populist leader. Now the war was over, some of the old Them figures—the VC colonel, the general standing as a Labour candidate—had joined Us in patriotic populism; yet Churchill was now the leader of the Tories for the first time, and backed by the old upper class he had symbolically spurned in ousting Chamberlain in the national interest.

Ralph Miliband (see p. 140) asserts that the electorate had no difficulty in distinguishing Churchill the war leader from Churchill the Tory leader. It is, however, hard to see how the *Mirror* could easily have made that distinction without Churchill's 'gestapo' broadcast, which enabled the paper to dramatize the dissociation of Churchill's two roles early in the election campaign.

*   *   *

First servingman: Peace . . . makes men hate one another.
Third servingman: Reason: because they then less need one another.
                                            Coriolanus IV, 5.

Of the themes that were central to the *Mirror* in 1945, one—the sequence of three kinds of war: against Hitler, against bureaucracy and inefficiency, against the conditions that made war possible—represents an important and well established historical theory that, there is evidence, was consciously held by Cecil King during the war. The theory is that after a certain kind of war—a 'people's war', for short (the phrase was used by Bartholomew)—undertaken in conditions of social unrest the energy released in the military conflict can carry over into a struggle for social reform. (A Marxist thesis might propose, alternatively, that the external war was a necessary and inevitable trigger for the domestic conflict. Trotsky called war 'the locomotive of history'.) It is an open guess to what extent *Mirror* readers understood themselves to be motivated by war-surplus energy by virtue of the theoretical view offered to them in the *Mirror*'s three kinds of war. But because it is precisely on this question—whether to continue to struggle in a social context, or to return to things as they used to be—that the *Mirror* and the *Express* divide most sharply in 1945, it seems worthwhile to examine the theory more closely in its relation to Cecil King and the *Mirror*.

The briefest statement of the theory is Marshall McLuhan's: 'War is accelerated social change'. For most historians, the process is much more conditional. Both Churchill and Laski recognized it to be so. In *The Aftermath*[15] (1928) Churchill wrote that in World War I

> life had been raised to a strange intensity by the war spell . . . Unities and comradeship had become possible between men and classes and nations and grown stronger while the hostile pressure on the common cause endured . . . [but afterwards] Every victorious country subsided to its old levels and its previous arrangements; but these latter were found to have fallen into much disrepair, their fabric was weakened and disjointed, they seemed narrow and out of date . . . With the passing of the spell there passed also, just as the new difficulties were at their height, much of the exceptional powers of guidance and control . . . To the faithful, toil-burdened masses the victory was so complete that no further effort seemed required . . . A vast fatigue dominated collective action . . . revolutionary rage like every other form of psychic energy burnt low . . . Once the supreme incentive had disappeared, everyone became conscious of the severity of the strain. A vast and general relaxation and descent to the standards of ordinary life was imminent.

In *Revolution of Our Time*[16] (1944) Laski foresaw the possibility of a similar aftermath to World War II: many, he said, would feel 'a fatigue, a hunger for the ancient ways, which it will be difficult to resist'.

> The atmosphere of war permits, and even compels, innovations and experiments that are not possible when peace returns. The invasion of our wonted routine of life accustoms us to what William James called the vital habit of breaking habits . . . Common danger builds a basis for a new fellowship the future of which is dependent wholly upon whether its foundations are temporary or permanent. If they are temporary, then the end of the war sees the resumption of all our previous differences exacerbated tenfold by the grave problems it will have left . . . I am, therefore, arguing that the changes which we require we can make by consent in a period in which, as now,

15 Published by Butterworth.
16 Allen & Unwin.

conditions make men remember their identities and not their
differences . . . [but after the war] To insist, in the period of
pause, that we gird up our loins for a new and difficult journey,
above all for a journey into the unknown, is to ask the impossible . . . When hostilities against Nazism cease, men will want,
more than anything, a routine of thought and habit which
does not compel the painful adaptation of their minds to
disturbing excitement.

Laski accused Churchill of postponing 'controversial' official
issues exactly on the calculation of another 'vast fatigue' after the
war. He urged Attlee to introduce wide ranging Socialist measures
during the emergency: Attlee, according to Kingsley Martin,[17]
'with two fingers on his own typewriter at home, demolished the
whole idea.'
Another important treatment of the theory is George Orwell's,
in the essays begun in 1940 and collected in *England Your England*.[18]
The war, he said, destroyed 'the *privateness* of English life'. (Bevan's
sense of a 'universal desire for privacy and freedom of choice' in the
post war mood of reaction was quoted at the start of Chapter Two.)
Orwell believed:

Had any real leadership existed on the Left, there is little
doubt that the return of the troops from Dunkirk could have
been the beginning of the end of British Capitalism. It was a
moment at which the willingness for sacrifice and drastic
changes extended not only to the working class but nearly to the
whole of the middle class, whose patriotism, when it comes to
the pinch, is stronger than their self-interest. There was apparent, sometimes in the most unexpected people, a feeling of being on the edge of a new society in which much of the greed,
apathy, injustice and corruption of the past would have
disappeared.

For Orwell, as Stephen Lutman[19] has shown, patriotism—'the
impulse to defend one's country and to make it a place worth living
in', strongest in the common people and largely unconscious—
was an essential part of the complex of feelings through which war
might lead to radical social change. The war could not be won
without patriotism, and patriotism (not nationalism), Orwell
thought, must break down class differences and privileges in pursuit
of the common task; and 'to the vast majority of people Socialism

17 *Sunday Times*, October 15, 1967.
18 Secker & Warburg, 1953.
19 *Journal of Contemporary History*, Summer 1967.

E*

means a classless society, or it means nothing at all'. Consequently, 'Patriotism, against which the Socialists fought so long, has become a tremendous lever in their hands'. Lutman points out that Orwell's views altered later in the war, and he came to see the assumption that war was inseparable from 'revolution' as 'a trap': the trap, presumably, that Laski accused Churchill of preparing by the postponement of controversial issues in wartime (and, perhaps, Churchill's wish to postpone the General Election until Japan had been defeated).

In lineament, then, Churchill, Laski and Orwell accepted the theory that the war would breed a widespread desire for social change, but all three recognized that the desire would not of itself be decisive, or even articulate. It would require, in Churchill's phrase, 'exceptional powers of guidance and control'.

Philip Abrams[20] has described how the 1918 post-war coalition, which was committed to social reform, failed to solve the problems that faced it in bringing a better way of life to the people who had won the right to it. The principal problem then, as in 1945, was housing, and the principal issue that aroused was planning *versus* a free market. That war, says Abrams, was fought by groups 'with a very different sense of what participation meant to them': his conclusion is that social harmony would have had to be enforced for successful reform.

The essential difference, however, in 1939–45 was pointed out by Richard Titmuss[21]; far more than was necessary in the first war, the Government had to help the civilian population at home. The pressure of public opinion, said Professor Titmuss, forced the wartime Government to face the inadequacy of its social provision. Homeless people could not be left to live in tube stations for the duration. The immediacy of hardship, and its obvious causes (bombs could be understood, as the economic forces of the 1930s could not), protected the needy from social disparagement. Needs had to be dealt with humanely, not *en masse* at the dole counter, and privilege to give way to co-operation: 'self-control was easier when there was no awareness of injustice arising from the way in which primary needs were met'. The government machinery that had to be set up was far more geared to solving the post-war problems of reconstruction than any demanded in 1914–18.

As the war went on, other variously sized accumulators of patriotic participation began to be charged (some of them have been touched on): the overthrow in 1940 of Chamberlain, and of old-style generals,

20 *Past and Present*, April 1963.
21 *Problems of Social Policy*, HMSO, 1950.

the greater willingness than in the first war to put the soldiers, Britain's 'first national citizen army', in the picture, the introduction of battle dress for all ranks (Churchill's siren suit was an emblem of the same getting-stuck-in attitude), the social emulsifying that was encouraged by conscription, evacuation, postings abroad, the country's reliance on every civilian doing his or her bit in civil defence, the Home Guard, fire watching; and possibly the most important of these, the Beveridge Report, and the Army Bureau of Current Affairs' ready dissemination of the Report's ideas throughout the ranks. To this list must be added the *Mirror*; at a minimum estimate, it served as the house magazine of the millions of people most closely affected by the influences we have listed.

Ralph Miliband[22] has drawn together some of this argument and placed it in a context very like that of the *Mirror*'s three wars:

> For it was the experience of war which caused the emergence in Britain of a new popular radicalism ... submerged [in the first phase of the war] in the will to national survival, and in an intense national pride in Britain's lone struggle against the Axis powers. But once survival seemed assured, the men who had imperilled that survival were remembered, as well as the class to which they belonged, and the Party whose label they wore.
>
> The rhetoric of war was itself an important element in the fashioning of popular radicalism. That the conflict was ... against Fascism gave it powerful ideological overtones, with an emphasis on democratic values and a celebration of the 'common man' which entailed an implicit (and often explicit) condemnation of the manner in which Tory governments had treated him, and his family, in the inter-war years.
>
> ... It was also the war which was responsible for the setting in place of an elaborate system of State intervention and control ... a very successful exercise ... millions of people found themselves better fed than they had been in peace-time ... [he describes the State's promises of post-war employment, welfare, security and better education.] Nor were the millions of men and women who were winning the war disposed to regard these promises with the gratitude of the humble poor.

Miliband believes that the new radicalism, although not a 'formed Socialist ideology', resented the pre-war Tory readiness to co-operate with Fascism but not with Russia. He credits the popular mood with more Socialistic feeling than the Labour Party itself

22 *Parliamentary Socialism*, Merlin Press, 1964.

was willing to evince—the emphasis on Labour's Socialism was not the party's doing but the Tories'. The Laski stunt, he believes, simply 'strengthened the view, fatal to Conservative electoral fortunes, that the Tories had learned nothing and forgotten nothing'. The electors easily distinguished Churchill the war leader from Churchill the Conservative politician.

It is obvious how closely the *Mirror*, from 1940–45, fits the theory that the war itself generated a new popular radicalism. The paper clearly played an important part in disseminating the populist spirit, and probably in consolidating it: those of a similar mind could be encouraged by seeing, day after day, that many others shared their feelings, and that together they might add up to an authentic social power.

The *Mirror* was only one of many populist influences: there is little doubt that Labour would have won the 1945 election handsomely even without the paper's support; little doubt, too, that the *Mirror* could not have followed a populist line during the war had it not been reassured by the evidence, in its own postbag and through other channels, that popular feeling was already on its side. It is, however, interesting that as early as 1941 Cecil King[23] could say to Churchill that the war was a 'first step towards a new and better England' because 'loyalty to the future involves not only scanning the horizon for the new ideas and ideals which may shape the world, but also the discrediting of the men who made the period 1919–1939 such an ignoble page in English history'. King noted that 'Churchill *is* war-time England—England with all its age, its waning virility, its dogged courage, its natural assumption that instinct is more reliable than intellect'; but he predicted that a new leader, perhaps previously unknown in public life, would emerge after the war, and has more recently expressed his distrust of Churchill's judgement—'The eulogies of him have always seemed to me wildly exaggerated'.[24]

In 1966, King [25] described the *Mirror* of the period we have reviewed:

> Bartholomew's . . . formula was social realism though served up with buckets of sentiment. He was catering for people whose hopes for a better life depended on social change, without which their personal efforts could be of little avail . . . if the *Mirror* was sensational and sexy, it also had a nagging

23 Quoted by Edelman, op. cit.
24 Cecil King, *Strictly Personal*, Weidenfeld & Nicolson, 1969.
25 Granada Northern Lectures, October 1966.

social conscience. It was firmly on the side of the under-dog. It explored the seamy side of life, campaigned against the slums, against the vice, cruelty to children and animals, the mean treatment of servicemen, military red tape, the conventional honours list. To the *Mirror*, the world did not appear cosy, but harsh and unjust. Always it was necessary to attack the Establishment, to denounce blunders in high places, the selfishly complacent, the unimaginative and stupid old men who had too much power.

That is a great deal truer of the later war years than it is of the first six years of Bartholomew's control, 1934-40. Very little seems 'harsh and unjust' in the pre-war years, very little conception of 'social change' was in evidence. Miners' wives delightedly kissed dukes' buttonholes. The inference is that the *Mirror*'s later populism was as much the effect of war as it was in the population at large. Possibly the *Mirror* would have changed anyway during those years, without the war; but the war seems to have determined the direction of its change.

In the early days of the war King told Churchill that 'in a popular paper we were bound to write of politics in terms of persons not of principles'. By 1963 his views were not much changed: 'the popular press ... has taught ordinary people to question and to make up their own minds. They are still not very good at it. They still come to decisions emotionally rather than by reason.'[26] In 1960 he had expressed himself even more disobligingly about his readers:

> It is only the people who conduct newspapers and similar organisations who have any idea quite how indifferent, quite how stupid, quite how uninterested in education of any kind the great bulk of the British public are ... surely the amount of uplift you can fit into any popular medium has got to be kept pretty low ... if you are dealing with masses of people you are dealing in emotional terms most of the time.[27]

It is not impossible to equate those opinions with the *Mirror* of 1945; but it is very hard indeed to imagine that the *Mirror*, holding them, could have developed so confident a political rhetoric, as it did from 1940 to 1945, had it not been that the war was, through other channels (including the *Mirror*'s postbag), indicating that the audience was already prepared for it. Perhaps the largest claim that

26 *Twentieth Century*, Spring 1963.
27 NUT conference on Popular Culture and Personal Responsibility, October 1960.

can be made for the *Mirror* in 1945 is that it managed to avoid underestimating its audience's intelligence. In the light of King's opinions, too, it is plain how much ventriloquism Cudlipp had in mind when he described the *Mirror* under Bartholomew as having 'embarked upon a mission to ensure that the voice of the people was heard in the land'.

Yet the fact is that the voice of the people *was* heard in the land in 1945, as it had not been after 1918: more precisely, the voice of 1945 was the same one as the war-time voice, whereas the voice of the first war soon succumbed to the 'vast fatigue' of which Churchill wrote. The vote of 1918 was a gesture of confidence in 'the man who had won the war', Lloyd George. In 1945 Churchill was rejected, along with the 'ancient ways' and 'competitive life of nature' that the *Express* promoted; and the country accepted, in some measure, the idea of planned change that the war seemed to have proved possible. Beveridge and the ABCA may have been partly responsible, and the idea was supported in 1945 by, among others, *The Times* and several bishops. But the demand for social justice, and the call of popular radicalism for 'exceptional powers of guidance and control', found its loudest voice in the *Mirror*.

4

TRANSITION TO 'AFFLUENCE'

DURING the 1950s, the belief grew up that the working class was being 'decomposed' by affluence, the increase of white-collar and semi-skilled jobs, and the Welfare State. Society was on the way to being classless. Embourgeoisement would lead to a contented apathy in politics.

Before considering what the *Express* and the *Mirror* made of the belief, it needs to be said that it has been radically questioned more recently.[1] That the 1950s were visibly prosperous years in Britain is incontestable, but the extent of prosperity was exaggerated at the time. Poverty has since been rediscovered on a large scale. Income redistribution has been marginal. The proportion of manual workers in the labour force has declined only from 70 per cent to 60 per cent, and they still enjoy few of the privileges of non-manual workers. The middle class, although often resenting the National Health Service because it gave manual workers 'something for nothing' and 'a corresponding gain, of maintenance of position, was being denied to non-manual workers',[2] have in fact benefited more than the working class from the Welfare State and educational reforms. The stereotypes of class are still derived from the Bad Old Days, an epoch from which the new prosperity was supposed to have marked us off absolutely; but class patterns persist, in new clothes. Politically, it is still the case that

> The understanding of contemporary working class politics is to be found, first and foremost, in the structure of the worker's group attachments and not, as many have suggested, in the extent of his income and possessions.[3]

For working-class Labour voters those group attachments will express themselves politically as 'instrumental collectivism'. There

1 The introductory section draws on a critique of 'affluence' specially written for the project by Alan Shuttleworth, a sociologist at the Centre for Contemporary Cultural Studies.

2 W. G. Runciman, *Relative Deprivation and Social Justice*, Routledge & Kegan Paul, 1966. See also Richard Titmuss, *Essays on the Welfare State*, Allen & Unwin, 1963.

3 Goldthorpe *et al*, *The Affluent Worker: Political Attitudes and Behaviour*, Cambridge University Press, 1968.

is evidence from McKenzie and Silver[4] that working-class voters recognize instrumental collectivism as distinguishing Labour voters from Tory:

> Almost all the working class Conservatives who were interviewed indicated a preference for individual over collective action for personal betterment ... Working class Labour voters ... much more frequently expressed the desirability or the need for collective working-class action.

The Labour voters 'tended overwhelmingly' to describe the two main parties as differing in class interests, whereas working-class Conservatives 'very rarely describe their own party in class terms', but stressed its service to the 'national interest', its patriotism, its 'ability to insure prosperity', and the 'personal qualities' of its leaders, in contrast to the 'sectional' interests of Labour.

The basis of the belief in affluence, and the associated myth of embourgeoisement, lay in social, economic and educational changes that began during the Attlee administration, but did not deliver a visible prosperity until after the return of Churchill in 1951, and the important complex of events, notably the Coronation, in 1953. To see the *Mirror* and *Express* in perspective during the 'affluent' years, then, it will be helpful—as with the *Mirror* in 1945—to start by considering, briefly, their response to the incubation period, the later 1940s.

* * *

The most significant fruit of the trust that, in 1945, the country planted in the Labour Party was Bevan's introduction, three years later, of the National Health Service and National Insurance. Both the *Mirror* and the *Express* warned their readers that full social security 'must be earned' by hard work to increase the national income. Beyond that point of agreement, the papers diverged down the lines set out in 1945.

The *Mirror* greeted the NHS on July 5, 1948 thus:

> THE DAY IS HERE! For years reformers of all the Parties have tried to safeguard the aged, the poor and the sick. Much has been done—much more than in any other large country. But always *you* wanted fuller protection against misfortune. You wanted the State to accept larger responsibility for the individual citizen who served it faithfully. *You wanted social security. From this day hence, you have it.*

4 R. McKenzie and A. Silver, *Angels in Marble: Working Class Conservatism in Urban England*, Heinemann, 1968.

The second-person address, enjoining solidarity, was familiar to those who had read the war-time *Mirror*; and, although the leader does not refer to the war, phrases such as 'for years' and 'served it faithfully' have behind them the weight of the *Mirror*'s memory of the war and of the 1945 General Election. The war is felt as a watershed in our social history (as it was in the *Mirror*'s own internal history): elsewhere the paper was talking of the days when the country had 'tolerated poverty, disease, unemployment. In it some people had a good time. Many more had a very bad time.' The 1948 leader moves easily on to reinvoke the Us/Them structure of feeling:

> Of course there are critics of social security. They are the same sort of people who, when the first five shillings was paid to the first old age pensioner, declared that the country could not afford it and that social services would lead to bankruptcy. You know better than that. You know that social security means a fairer and better distribution of the National Income and that no country can be too poor to guarantee its people a fair share of the essentials of life.

Among the critics of social security the *Mirror*, earlier in the debate, had attacked the British Medical Association for opposing the Bill 'from motives of self-interest as opposed to the interests of the community as a whole ... Few individual doctors will, we feel, accept the BMA's interpretation of where their social duty lies.'

In none of its war-time and 1945 election leaders had the *Mirror* ever pretended that easy times were just around the corner, and its mood in 1948 is as much of a piece with its earlier analysis as the Us/Them orchestration of society is. In the middle years of the war the paper had called social security 'an investment ... designed to keep men and women fit for producing the wealth in which they will share'. The Beveridge Report itself was 'no revolutionary document ... It is a beginning, not an end.' There was 'a depth of feeling in the country which has made the Beveridge Report, in itself of no paramount importance, into a symbol of the new Britain'. Social security, said the *Mirror* in 1946, should be regarded as 'a springboard for enterprise'. Enterprise would have as its object 'fairer shares all round in the prosperity for which everyone hopes tomorrow'. Enterprise would take the form of 'cleaning up' essential industries—'agriculture, cotton and brick making'—in which conditions were poor, and of teaching people that 'work in these industries is proud service to the community'. Enterprise was also defined as the rapid introduction of modern equipment, maximum

operation of it—'twenty-four hours a day if necessary'—the refusal
of 'trade union or other restrictions', direction of labour, increase of
skill. All such enterprise was recommended in terms of benefiting
'the community'. 'Here is your incentive—to work for your country
and a larger, more social security!'

The *Mirror*, knowing that a long slog still lay ahead, reflected a
tiredness in the national mood, now that the cold war had succeeded
the first optimism of 1945. Bread was to be rationed for years, and
circuses were depleted. Consequently, when prosperity did begin to
seep back, the *Mirror* was all the more eager to celebrate it.

The *Express*'s contrary connotation of enterprise is well known and
sincerely defended by the paper. In 1943, concerning Beveridge, the
Express had asserted that 'to an incurable degree the British people
in the main look to their own individual enterprise and exertion as
the guarantee of their future'. In 1946, opposing the nationalization
of the coal industry, the paper explained that: 'State monopoly is
less efficient than private ownership ... It evades the harsh discipline of free enterprise, which provides sharp punishments for
inefficiency and waste ... [Nationalization] provides jobs for talkers
rather than for the men of shrewdness and skill ... State monopoly
encourages nepotism, favouritism, privilege.'

A year later the *Express* argued that 'nothing like prosperity and
happiness can reign in Britain until taxes are savagely cut'. The
middle classes were being 'filleted financially', a reader complained.
William Barkley set out a credo which, in view of his position on the
paper, can reasonably be taken as representative of the *Express*.
'Equality means stagnation. Inequality means progress ... It is
wicked to regard the rich with envy, at least where wealth has been
accumulated by successful exertion', even when 'we are engaged on
a holy war against poverty'. 'Look at the success of this Daily
Express, of which almost every director began as a cub.'

> Why, for example, is this dead level of sugar rationing main-
> tained?
> There is plenty of sugar. But its price is subsidised. The
> Government cannot allow people to buy as much as they can
> afford except at the market price of 6*d*. a pound. If that were
> done, the cost would be heavy on the lowest paid. So everybody
> is held down.
> It is a harsh but true doctrine that incentive operates at the
> point where a man sees the chance to get more sugar in his tea.

One remembers Barkley's 1945 phrase about 'the competitive life of
nature'.

In a 1947 leader, the *Express* said:

> The people will respond, as they always have done, most lavishly to the mood of the happy warrior, the stir and the throb of daring, the electric air of risk. In short, the energies of the British are most abundantly generated by an example of energy and individuality in their rulers.

The slogan over that leader was 'Set the People Free'. Its predecessor had been 'We are all Empire Free Traders now'. In 1945, we have seen, the *Express* had converted 'freedom', for which we had fought the war, into 'free enterprise'.

During the NHS debate the *Express* supported the British Medical Association's Defiance Fund against 'regimentation'. 'Can the Minister,' the paper asked, 'be induced to take the advice and benefit by the experience of a great profession in its own affairs?' It warned that the proposed NHS 'squeezes and reduces the private practice of medicine and surgery, with its confidential and unique relationship between doctor and patient'.

> Doctors . . . bitterly resent the attempt to manoeuvre them into becoming civil servants. They ask, 'What have we done to deserve this?' They sense a reflection on their calling, a suggestion that they have failed in their duty to the public.
>
> They feel that a great deal of the incentive which has always inspired their efforts must wither.

What the *Express* assumed that incentive, that unique relationship, to be was spelled out by William Barkley on January 9, 1947. Pointing out that in private practice a patient's death meant a termination of his fees to the doctor, he asked:

> Remove the risk of loss if the doctor is careless, remove the opportunity of profit if he is clever and successful, and which of us will take with safety to our beds?

By early 1948 the *Express* had apparently warmed a little to the NHS bill:

> Now is the ideal of Social Security presented to the lawmakers.
>
> Now comes the effort to translate the glowing phrases of the politicians, the patient thoughts and calculations of the economist, into a practical scheme . . .
>
> The nation welcomes the effort wholeheartedly and warmly.
>
> Most of all does it welcome that part of the Social Insurance scheme which at last offers dignity and modest comfort to old age . . .

These proposals wipe out a stigma and a reproach from our social life.

As in 1945, the *Express* nowhere attempts, as the *Mirror* constantly did, to assure readers that it was their doing, by their solidarity and determination, that the scheme is being put into practice. The whole policy is presented as being the product of 'lawmakers', 'politicians', 'economists'. The nation's part is simply that of welcoming the result; as, in a leader already quoted, 'the energies of the British' are said to be 'generated by an example ... in their rulers'. The *Express* went on to warn its readers against premature jubilation, in terms that hint, as the *Mirror* never does, that the scheme may be ill conceived: 'must be subjected to careful scrutiny ... may be welcomed for what it is'; and the paper emphasized that, to the citizen, it would not be a free service but 'will cost a great deal ... that fact should be faced squarely at the outset.'

It is not surprising, then, that where the *Mirror* greeted the start of the NHS with 'THE DAY IS HERE!', the *Express* that day thought the scheme worth only a second leader, which began:

> Doctors and people collaborate today in a tremendous social experiment. The new National Health scheme is launched. Wish it success.
>
> The public should be mindful of the sacrifices and difficulties of the doctors.
>
> Their personal skill, knowledge, and in certain cases genius, are being nationalised.

By the steep declension from 'tremendous social experiment' to sympathizing with individuals whose private enterprise is being restricted, we are propelled into feeling in the word 'nationalized' only a sense of loss. Sacrifices are to be made by doctors; there is no acknowledgement of sacrifices enforced on patients in the past.

In an adjacent feature the *Express* plays yet another variation on 'free'. A report on the start of the scheme is headed 'Midnight—and the Free for All began'. The pun is brilliant and, in the *Express*'s context, telling. A socialist slogan is converted into an image of aggressive selfishness.

*   *   *

During the Attlee administration the *Mirror* and the *Express* seem to have retained the same webs of values and assumptions about their readers as each had deployed in the 1945 election. In 1951 the Conservatives were returned to power, and the period of post-war reconstruction shaded into growing prosperity.

To the *Express* prosperity under Churchill was simply the ful-
filment of what it had been saying since the war. Its vocabulary
required no change to make sense of the new period; nor, therefore,
did its view of the social process need to alter. Although a series in
1953 entitled 'The New Poor' represented the middle class as so
oppressively taxed that their 'struggle to keep up appearances' was
desperate, still the middle class was seen to be clinging on to its
entirely distinctive style of life, and no tide of classlessness threatened to wash away the divide from the working class. 'The abiding
ambition of any person in the middle class is to get out of it, upwards,' wrote William Barkley; 'those who depend on their own
efforts know a keen pleasure in success which is denied to what are
called the organised workers ... the middle class has everything
on its side in the struggle—standards, ambitions, self-discipline,
education, and immense adaptability.' In the same series Frank
Tilsley made another crucial class-distinction: middle-class surplus
income before the war had been responsible for 'deciding ... the
quality of our cultural life', but now 'new people' had a 'state-
subsidized' surplus and 'Alas, we know only too well where the
greater part of it goes: on tobacco, drink and gambling: in that
order.'

In contrast, the *Mirror* could not comprehend the new state of
affairs within the language it had forged during the war. That
language, however ventriloquistic, had reflected the solidarity of a
readership that shared a sense of social purpose. But now the last
of the three wars, 'to win the peace', was apparently won. Prosperity
was on the way in. Certainly, some pockets of poverty could still be
found when the *Mirror* needed them for its rhetoric, but to have gone
on talking about poverty in a period marked by rising consumption
might have seemed like dismal harping. Unable or unwilling, for
whatever reason, to discern the persistence of a class structure below
the glitter of affluence, the *Mirror* could offer its readers no purpose
now which would distinguish Us against Them. The result was a
relapse into discontinuity of language, sometimes from page to
page. Cassandra could write a column about 'the Middle Classes'
that might as well have appeared in the *Express*:

> These are the people who never strike. These are the people
> who, by their own efforts, try harder to improve themselves
> than any other class and who most frequently succeed; the
> people who strive to give their children a better chance than
> they themselves ever had. But they are being wiped out by
> murderous taxation.

Elsewhere the paper was blaming workers as much as bosses for industrial relationships 'corroded by bitterness'.

Effectively, the *Mirror* conceded that affluence was eroding the old divisions and solidarities, and that society was no longer to be discussed in terms of class inequalities. Instead, it increasingly tried to explain social change in terms of those whose style of life appeared most conspicuously decorated by affluence, young people. There was a particular emphasis on styles of dress, but the less apparent, moral changes in attitudes to the family, sex and marriage also preoccupied the paper.

*   *   *

The conservative confidence of the *Express* in a time of prosperity, and the incoherence of the *Mirror*, were plain to see during the 1955 General Election.

The *Express* sang a psalm of prosperity, 'an outward and visible sign of an inward financial grace'. News from abroad, where great-power conflict was abating, and from at home, where rationing had been ended in 1954, alike blended into an image of booming Britain. 'The British people never had it so good,' said the *Express* in a phrase that Macmillan would make famous in the following election. 'They would not risk losing these things in a hurry.' Such a risk would, of course, be run by those who voted against the Conservatives. 'Who would change governments in the midst of this prosperous stream?' William Barkey demanded.

Since Labour had governed in the years of post-war hardship, it was easy for the *Express* to identify them as a party actually committed to austerity. The Socialists 'loved rationing', and

> sneered at freedom to buy as you please. Now the Socialists have found out that rationing is unpopular. They have discovered that the people enjoy freedom. So now they say that rationing is not in their policy after all.

In other respects, the *Express*'s picture of Labour strikingly resembled the one it had painted ten years earlier, a party of unfreedom, where secret hands controlled the levers of power, and behind the decoy-duck of Attlee waited a figure that threatened violence if necessary: only by now 'the authentic voice of Socialism—a threat, naked, cold and sinister' was not Laski but 'Comrade Bevan'. The isolation of Bevan, and his 'faction', was facilitated by the Parliamentary Labour Party itself, which had withdrawn the whip from Bevan two months before the election. Like Laski, Bevan was given far more coverage in the *Express* than Attlee, and presented as larger than life, aloof but irascible, unamenable, extremist. Bevan it is who hungers for more nationalization, a 'grab plan', 'planned smash and grab', that 'bludgeons . . . a fine and enterprising organization out of existence,' and invariably replaces it with the controls and inefficiency that reduce our freedom and prosperity. It is Bevan, too, who hints at violent revenge: when he accused the Tories of gerry-mandering with constituency boundaries, his speech was head-lined 'If the Tories get power by a trick people may resort to other methods of getting their own way'. And Bevan is also a threat to the improving international climate, for he might well be foreign secre-tary in a Labour administration.

Peace was an important theme in the *Express*'s campaign, not only because it filled out the area of optimism but also because Eden, who had just succeeded Churchill as Tory leader, was identified by his career in foreign affairs. His negotiation of the Cold War was greeted with pulpit imperatives:

> Rejoice in the news that Eisenhower has given the green light to a 'parley at the Summit' with Sir Anthony Eden, Marshal Bulganin, and M. Faure. Look on this dramatic turn of events as the happiest international development for years.

Churchill was bound to remain an active ingredient in the *Express*'s image of the Tories, a grand old man, benevolent but still barbed. Answering Bevan's allegation that he had been reluctant to resign in favour of Eden, Churchill 'had fun last night'; his speech was punctuated by 'loud laughter' as he mocked Bevan, 'looked over his spectacles' with 'raised eyebrows and hands upstretched'. Churchill is the man who can still draw the crowds; a cloakroom attendant is found to testify that he had to stand in sleet to hear Churchill, but it was 'worth it'.

Broader than the *Express*'s directly political tactics, however, was the strategic assurance that prosperity was coloured blue. On election day itself the main feature article ostensibly took up no political topic. Instead, an Australian, Russell Braddon, offered a pen-picture of Epsom Downs the previous day, when the Derby had been run. He remembers the British,

> as I first saw them in 1949. Badly dressed, haunted by queues, pushed about by a Government of regimental sergeant-majors and at the bottom of the ladder in every sport because they had spent too long winning a war in which they alone had fought from beginning to end. They were badly fed, badly housed and poor.

But now, the picture is one of cars, nylons, butter, fivers, and people
who 'ladled four teaspoonsful of sugar into their cuppa.' We hear
of 'a gaggle of chauffeurs, neatly uniformed, huddled together
eating whelks', reminiscent of the Chelsea Pensioners 'awkwardly to
attention' in 1945. People are content with their fixed roles in the
tapestry, if they are kept well fed and amused, as this Epsom crowd
is seen to be. Their voices readily articulate, with some British
understatement, the prosperity they are enjoying, and—in consequence—their carelessness about the election. 'He was a Socialist
supporter and not going to vote. Why? "Because I am happy as I
am, so why should I change it? And anyway I'd only be backing
another loser."'

A similar carelessness had been reported by William Hickey in
his gossip column on May Day, the day when 'the workers . . .
rattle their chains in Hyde Park and Red Square'.

> I remember pre-war May Days in Hyde Park. There would be
> 100,000 or more workers marching along with their banners.
>   It was a brave sight. There were bands and bowler hats.
> Slogans about the workers of the world uniting . . .
>   Ah! They were brave days!
>   But now times have changed. You cannot have giant
> demonstrations when the battle has been won.
>   You cannot sing the Red Flag when one union is fighting
> another about wage differentials . . .
>   And the rain dissipated what little ardour may still be left to
> destroy the capitalist system . . .
>   This is, essentially, a satisfied country.
>   The basic problems of sharing wealth in an industrial com-
> munity have been solved.
>   The working class—to use an antiquated phrase—doesn't
> march in Hyde Park in the rain.
>   In the comfort of their home they watch politicians arguing
> on TV for their favour. Watch with the amused contempt of
> men looking at performing fleas in a circus side-show.

The column moves into a minor key with doubts whether we have
'kept faith with the ideals we had in 1945 . . . the struggle for life of
the ex-Servicemen has been so hard that they have done little to
make their voices heard. And now we have muted our judgements
and accept the compromises of the wordly wise.' But this vague
gesture, perhaps of remorse at the earlier smugness, is left unresolved.
The fact is, times have changed. The battle has been won. We are
all satisfied and comfortable now. Only trivial intra-class conflict

persists. The working class is just an embarrassing memory. 'As a nation we are all a little snobbish at heart' we learn from a later Hickey column. The 'better paid artisan', surrounded by his consumer goods, may 'secretly express the feeling that he is middle class' by voting Tory.

So, only two years after the middle class were labelled 'The New Poor' (and still the paper expresses concern for the plight of clerks), we are all one class now, and embourgeoisement by affluence has taken place? Not really. The phrase 'working class' is 'antiquated' because it evokes the poverty of the pre-war years, and the lowest-placed are no longer (as far as the *Express* knows) in such plight; yet they remain lower-placed, only the 'better paid artisan' aspiring—daring—to think himself middle class. The social pyramid still stands, though it has shifted upwards in its economic entirety. The little men at Epsom still speak in their cockney voices to us, and proud of it; great figures still watch benignly over the progress of the nation. What the Conservatives have produced, by removing the 'bitterness and frustration of the Socialist regime' and rendering the old political battle-lines meaningless, is not embourgeoisement but apathy.

Apathy, the *Express* suggests, is really very British. 'It takes a crisis to make an Englishman think and change.' Hickey reported a pre-election speech:

> I am sure the company at lunch felt there was wisdom in his order of importance . . . flowers; racing; and a bad third, politics. I suppose that is what foreigners mean when they talk with envy of the political genius of the British people.

The Opinion column made the same point that day, although the previous day it had declared that 'the people are not bored at all', and summoned politicians to 'get the hustings going before it is too late.'

But it was always too late. Television, prominent in an election for the first time, had contributed to the apathy; early fears of glamorous politicians mesmerising the electorate soon gave way to (relieved?) comments on the great TV 'flop'. *Express* readers were invited to estimate politicians' television 'impact', with the aid of a check-list, on which all the offered responses had to do with image, not argument, performance rather than policy. Politicians, as Hickey wrote in his May Day column, merely performed to keep us 'amused'. The election was not even much of a circus any more.

The *Mirror* in the 1955 election was in striking contrast not so

much with the *Express* as with itself ten years before. Hardly a trace
remained of the confident exchange between the paper and its
readers then. Whereas readers' contributions had accounted for
30 per cent of the 1945 election material, in 1955 the figure was 3
per cent; and of that 3 per cent only one-sixth expressed partisan
views—six pro-Labour letters and one pro-Tory, to be exact. As for
the imperative mode of address that was marked in the earlier
Mirror, that had been reduced in ten years to a quaint bidding by
Cassandra: 'Madam, go you, and Sir, go you to the polls this very
day'.

In 1945 the 'Vote for Him' campaign may have been a stunt, in
that it was orchestrated rhetoric, but it was a stunt with deep roots
in the social beliefs of the time. The *Mirror* ran two campaigns
in 1955. It is hard to relate either to social reality.

The first was a demand for youth in politics:

> The Mirror has more readers under 35 than any other daily
> newspaper in the world. So we are going to bang the drum for
> youth.
>
> What are the under-35s to expect from the coming election?
> Are the old men coming back to tell them what to do?
> Whichever party wins ... will it be the return of the Old
> Boys' Brigade? ...
> THIS IS NOT A PARTY ISSUE. WE ARE LIVING
> IN THE FASTEST AND YOUNGEST AGE IN THE
> HISTORY OF MANKIND.
> Let's speed things up in politics, too.

In accord with its campaign, throughout the period the *Mirror*
constantly mentioned the age of politicians, even foreign ones, to
which it referred. So obsessive was the habit that the paper's own
cartoonist parodied it by signing himself 'Vicky (aged 98)'. By
claiming youth as its constituency, however, the *Mirror* ran into the
problem that the Labour Party's leader was 72, and Labour
MPs were on average five years older than the Tory members.
Although the paper's enthusiasm for Labour was tepid, it certainly
did not wish to run a pro-Tory campaign. It attempted to cash the
campaign in favour of Labour firstly by characterizing the party's
original founders as 'young pioneers' (historically questionable),
secondly by describing its original spirit as 'youthful, questing and
restless', and thirdly by appealing to Attlee for a declaration that,
if elected, he would form 'the youngest Cabinet since Adam ruled
in Eden'.

Nothing could be more exhilarating for Labour supporters than to know that at last—*at last*—AT LAST—the Labour Party intends to call upon the young in heart, mind and spirit.

Seeking to structure society in Us/Them terms, the *Mirror* had chosen a distinction that, electorally, was at best meaningless. As it said itself, 'This is not a party issue'.

Its second campaign, in the last three days before the election, was couched in the tones of retreat. The opening headlines were:

Keep the Tories Tame
The Daily Mirror's Election Policy

The article below, in heavy type, praised Labour's record—'a square deal and a better life'—and argued that such achievements had survived the 1951–55 Tory administration only because of the government's small majority in the Commons; but 'the return to power of the Tory Party with a bloated majority . . . would be an open invitation to the most sinister and reactionary section of the Tory Party to grab power and to attack and destroy the Welfare State'. Readers were urged to vote Labour in order to restrict the Tory majority.

This defeatist campaign might be defended as *realpolitik*. That it incorporated no more of the issues actually being argued in the election than the Youth campaign had might be defended on the grounds that the protection of the Welfare State was the paramount, though unargued, issue. It seems, however, defeatist in a more profound sense when contrasted with the 1945 *Mirror*. Not only are the election issues absent—and any boom of the prosperity so loud in the *Express*—but so are the electors. Nowhere does the 1955 *Mirror* offer a coherent picture of what We are like. The nearest it got to identifying Us were references to children and pensioners, neither of whom were part of its 'under-35s' constituency of voters. Likewise crude was the image of Them—'the Stone Age Tories in Eden's Party', who had 'fought to keep the world of 1939—THEIR world of profit and privilege'. There were a number of pictures of Eden posed, dressed and smiling with an elegance that would distance him from the ordinary *Mirror* reader; in one case an adjacent headline put the question 'Trust *Us*, say the Tories'; with another, of Eden aged 13 in an Eton suit, was juxtaposed the contemporary picture of a 13-year-old boy, Alan Smith, at a secondary school.

The relationship that these images bore to the election issues in 1955, or even to the rest of the *Mirror*'s campaign, was no more than the sudden images of publicity bear to a product, discounting rational choice by appealing more totally to semi-conscious fantasy. The explanation may have been that the *Mirror* saw no rational argument for voting Labour. It went to some lengths to avoid identifying itself with the party. Discussing the Conservative manifesto, for instance, the paper wrote that Labour 'will say that it is smug. They will say that it is full of fine words—but short of hard and fast plans ... On peace, the Tories say ... Labour will certainly reply ... Labour will demand ... Labour will say ...' The effect of the future predictive tense is to ritualize the election, and separate the *Mirror* itself from the ritual.

The *Mirror* itself was, indeed, the product chiefly promoted by the factitious images of publicity—the 'pack-shot', in TV-advert jargon. The paper repeatedly presented itself as informed enough to talk familiarly to politicians, and respected enough to have them anxiously waiting for what it would say. Thus an article was headlined 'The Tories, The H-Bomb and The Mirror', drawing on its 'Whose finger on the trigger?' reputation (of 1951), and quoted references to the *Mirror* in several other papers while spreading across the centre pages a text in which it referred 15 times to itself: 'The Mirror declared ... The Mirror still holds to this view ... The Mirror says ... The Mirror believes ... The Mirror will take no part in scare campaigns one way or the other', and so on. Particularly relevant among many similar examples are those in which the paper stresses its independence of Labour and its own autonomous political experience: 'In the past three elections, the Mirror has supported Labour. What is our advice to our readers this time? It is this: The Mirror again says: VOTE LABOUR'; and again, 'For ten years the Daily Mirror has warned the Labour Party about ...' It should be added that the Mirror's self-importance was not restricted to the election. A front page was devoted to a story headlined 'Mirror agrees to new Royal plan for Prince Charles'. The *Express*, in contrast, gave the story six inches the next day.

The distance of the 1955 *Mirror* from its 1945 character may be summed up by considering a letter printed in Live-letters, with the headline 'Who is for Peace?'

'YOUNG MOTHER' writes from Romford (Essex)
My husband and I are both in our early twenties. We have two children and live in a council house.
    This will be the first time we have been eligible to vote in a General Election.

> We were children during the war. We don't remember mourning the men killed at Dunkirk and we were not inspired by fiery speeches of 'Blood, sweat and tears'.
>
> We fought our battles in wet streets with evacuees' tickets pinned to our coats, and our battle cry was: 'How many children can you take in?'
>
> We remember the wail of sirens, the scream of bombs, and the terror of cowering under the blankets while the world fell to pieces.
>
> We do not want our children to lose their youth as we lost ours.
>
> Therefore we will vote for the party that puts forward the most constructive plan for world peace.
>
> Which one is it?

The Old Codgers answered:

> During the coming days we will all be subjected to *the usual political smokescreen*—food subsidies, housing, inflation, Bevanism, pensions, taxation, nationalization and the rest.
>
> But this smokescreen can't hide the stark, stupendous truth which 'Young Mother' puts so well.
>
> We'd like to think that EVERY candidate—of whatever party—will read her letter.
>
> Why not cut it out and send it to yours?

The language of the letter is as direct (and as dubiously authentic) as the 'Vote for Him' letter ten years previously. In reply the *Mirror* does not choose to bring out the latent connection between youth and peace, nor to echo the deflation of Dunkirk and Churchill, nor to mesh the letter into the paper's prevailing rhetoric, as it would have in 1945. Rather, the political process is seen as an evasion of the real issues—more, a deliberate cover-up. In 1945 this cry for peace would have been taken to have meaning within the immediate issues of the election, but now food subsidies, housing, inflation, pensions, are all a 'usual political smokescreen'. No answer is given to the woman's inquiry.

The thematic continuity of the *Express* from 1945 to 1955 is apparent. Its notions of freedom, tradition, and a hierarchical society in which individual enterprise, not class conflict, is the principle of progress, served the *Express* as an ideology in which the prosperity of 1955 was as readily comprehended as the war's meaning and the post-war's tasks. Even in the details of its rhetoric, the paper was remarkably constant: Bevan was cast in the part Laski had played, television performance—not content—succeeded Churchill's performance on tour, and such turns of phrase as 'so now they say' and what we have called 'pulpit imperatives' recur.

Clive Irving[5] has written that in the 1930s 'The affluent society was still in its incubator, but Christiansen saw it coming and decided that the *Express* was to be its bible . . . at the peak of the Christiansen age the *Express* gave the feeling that it had all been written by the same man, whose style had the distinct ring of New Brunswick staccato.' Irving does not date the peak, but the early 1950s, and perhaps the 1955 election in particular, seem to have been a moment in the *Express*'s history when the whole paper was able to articulate that optimism for which Christiansen, on his own evidence,[6] had striven, just as the war and the 1945 election had been the moment of creation for the *Mirror*. In 1955 the *Express* could present Britain as a land no longer rent by the deprivations and struggles that had thrown people together without precedent, a land where life is good for everyone, and the great figures of the past smile down benignly upon their worthy successors. It is an essentially private land, where 'every man his own garage' represents a proper aspiration and reward for 'the habit of hard work and thrift', a land typically inhabited by 'the young couple who do not possess their own home or their own car, but have the ambition to do so at the earliest date,' in Christiansen's phrase. It is prosperity, oil on social friction, which has brought Britain into the *Express*'s fixed focus; now the paper can, as a coherent whole, address its readers in the confident imperatives of the protestant ethic.

And it is prosperity which has dislocated the rhetoric of the *Mirror*. In the 1940s it had been able to count on collectivist feeling in the public sphere. Now the sphere of progress looked distinctly private. Like the Labour Party itself, the *Mirror* sensed that social developments such as the growth in consumer spending and youth culture had political relevance, but it had not developed a political language in which to articulate them. The paper followed the party in abandoning the search for radical language and programmes, in to what the New Left called 'revisionism'.[7] Cudlipp's comment on the

5 Article in *The Spectator*, October 4, 1963.
6 Arthur Christiansen, *Headlines All My Life*, Heinemann, 1961.
7 The thesis that affluence had undermined the Labour Party's traditional position can be fully documented in the period before and after the 1959 election. See, for example, Crosland's *The Future of Socialism*, Mark Abrams's *Must Labour Lose?*, and articles in *Socialist Commentary* and *Encounter*. For a classic statement, see Hugh Gaitskell's speech to the Labour Conference at Blackpool after the loss of the 1959 election. For a

1959 election would have been apt in 1955 too: 'It was clear to the Mirror that, for a period, party politics were not going to be a live issue.'[8]

The *Mirror* was in a dilemma typical of mass media, having to find the highest common factor among its audience. It dared not 'genuinely disturb or call in question the *status quo*' or 'inspire distinctions and so create minorities'.[9] John Beavan, Political Adviser to the *Mirror* group, wrote in 1961: 'The popular newspapers have been described as a federation of minorities and the first instinct of those who conduct such newspapers must be to keep the federation intact'. The highest common factor in 1945 was high indeed: the *Mirror*'s readers were the war victors, aiming to win the peace. But who were its readers now? What united them as Us? The *Mirror* had no answer. Its appeal to 'Keep the Tories Tame' was based, thinly, on what remained of action in the public sphere. Coming as late in the election as it did, it sounds like a despairing gesture towards what had once been the centre of the *Mirror*'s understanding, the things it did know about in the past. But a discourse with its readers on the 1945 scale could not return. Prosecuted as thoroughly as then, it would inspire distinctions.

Nervous of dividing its readers, nervous of criticizing prosperity and seeming killjoy, nervous of the Labour Party and its Tory-fostered association with austerity, the *Mirror* retreated from imperatives of collectivist action, and conducted a campaign of consensual images. Its appeal for Youth derived from the highest common factor of *Mirror* readers, that they were predominantly under 35, but it also sought resonance in the novelty, the youth, of the cycle of prosperity. A new-look country could be expected, as another common factor, to require new-look leaders. Even further removed from real political thought were the *Mirror*'s self-conscious appeals to its own identity and importance, drawing on its own mythology. It assumed that its readers would acknowledge the paper as a repository of experience and wisdom irrespective of what it actually had to say about the election. The implication is that newspapers have a role in the democratic process beyond that of articulating their readers' voices, which, in striking contrast to 1945, were scarcely heard at all in the *Mirror*. The paper will still be drawing on exactly the same mythology—'Whose finger on the trigger?'—nine

8 Hugh Cudlipp, *At Your Peril*, Weidenfeld & Nicolson, 1962.
9 Richard Hoggart, 'Mass Communications in Britain', *The Modern Age*, ed. Ford, Pelican Guide to English Literature, vol. 7, 1961.

critique of the position, see articles in *Universities and Left Review* and the *New Left Review*, 1958–61.

years later. Meanwhile, its fears of 'inspiring distinctions' were aggravated when its circulation dropped, in 1956, after its opposition to Eden's intervention in Suez.[10]

*   *   *

Although the *Mirror*'s accent on youth was incoherent during the 1955 election, it was a growing theme in the paper throughout the 'affluent' years. The demand for youth in politics had been heard some months before the election; discussing the diplomatic service in South-East Asia, an editorial asked, 'Let us have youngsters there who can think of the future—not "sahibs" who are living in the past'. At home, the world of the young is described as

> Loud. Violent. Unpredictable. Sizzlingly ALIVE. And that's what grips the vibrant youngster of 1955.

There was a series on how young people were developing a language of their own, particularly through jazz clubs, and behind the language different social attitudes. Beat music has 'become the symbol of hostility between two generations.' Older readers are found, however, who wish to overcome the hostility, and have developed a taste themselves for the music. 'A grandmother' writes that she is 'anxious to catch up with the times'. And the vibrant youngsters' hostility does not extend to the fundamental moral values of their parents. The *Mirror* reproached a magistrate: 'Is Sir Leonard suggesting that youngsters who are lively enough to dance are TOO LIVELY to settle down in happy marriages? THAT WOULD BE NONSENSE'. The traditional 'good scout' image of clean, helpful youth is still dominant in much of the paper.

Towards the end of the 1950s, intimations can be found in the *Mirror* of a teenage subculture independent enough to contradict established values, transmitting itself most powerfully through pop. Even then, a weekly Teen Page hedged its bet with a subtitle, 'for the young of all ages', and a 59-year-old granny was a 'typical teenager'. Elsewhere, articles on fashions in clothes, exotic food, new cars and other goods, leisure, and investments, witnessed the paper's acceptance, in the Macmillenium, of an unprecedentedly affluent society. The *Mirror* was not going to be left behind by the pace of change. Its front page lead on October 12, 1959, was headed: 'Here's the Mirror . . . sparkling NEW ideas, NEW features, NEW

10 Another analysis of 'The Popular Press in the British General Election of 1955', by A. H. Birch and others, was published in the journal *Political Studies*, vol. IV, No. 3, 1956.

contests, NEW writers . . . THE RACE INTO THE NEW YEAR'.
The text began with the imperative of a television age: 'Sit back
folks. Just look—and listen'. The *Mirror* is 'gay . . . buoyant . . .
moves with the times,' full of 'the fun of the newspaper that loves to
bristle and gurgle and bubble with Bright New Ideas . . . The
Accent is on Youth.' A new strip cartoon introduces Patti: 'Brudders-
field, this dump I live in, is for the birds. I've got a sister in London.
So, look out! HERE COMES PATTI!' The paper used a wealth of
phrases to define Now against Before (the new Us/Them): the jet
age, this nuclear age, the new trend, just a generation ago, the pace
at which life now tears along in Britain, and many more.

The *Mirror*'s portrait of a new, youthful, buoyant, racy, mobile
society is now and then brushed with doubt, on three grounds. The
first is a doubt whether those in power are geared to the pace of the
young. (The War to win the War translates as the Race to win the
Now.) The Tories are old-fashioned, of course, but too often so are
Labour politicians. During the 1959 election a special feature of
letters from young readers was summarized: 'There is a rocket from
you under-25s for any politician, Labour or Tory, who "quotes the
past too much". You all want your politicians to look forward.'
The white coat *versus* bowler hat style of government, later exploited
by Harold Wilson, was an argument pioneered in the *Mirror*.
Strikers, too, were seen as selfishly out of gear with the tearing pace
of a technological way of life.

The second doubt concerned the effect that affluence was having
on moral and social standards. The doubt was to peak in the
'permissiveness' argument of the 1960s. Earlier, it was sometimes
heard in the *Mirror* in reports such as one that a health inspector,
surveying 200 houses in an industrial town, found three baths, four
toilets, and 125 television sets. More often, the doubt was expressed
by denial. For instance, a letter from an under-25 declares that his
generation likes 'roughing it' all over Europe, and 'can't be bought
for the price of a new fridge . . . This is what the Tories are trying to
do. "London's streets are paved with washing-machines", they say.
"Forget Hola, Nyasaland, Suez."'

Only the third ground of doubt, reports of deprivation or poverty,
actually questioned whether prosperity was being 'shared out justly',
and they were rare, except as election rhetoric in 1959. Old-age
pensioners and teachers were the only groups consistently seen as
deprived. A striking account of 'Life on the Dole', in January 1959,
described the hardship of over half a million unemployed; but their
misfortune is analysed as local, a condition of the place they live in
—they might do better if they could move to 'another part of the

country'. In their isolation from the general prosperity, they are as
discontinuous, just unlucky, as the lucky pools winners who grin
from other pages.

Such doubts seldom assailed the *Express* in the late 1950s. A branch
treasurer of the Miners' Union was reported to have torn up his
invitation to a £6-a-head union dinner, protesting that:

> Every fortnight, as treasurer, I have to pay out to 86 old age
> pensioners. They get 8s.—the price of a bag of coal. To qualify
> for that they have had to work for 25 consecutive years in the
> mines. They are living in poverty—yet the Union can spend
> £3000 on a dinner.

The Opinion column told him he was 'well behind the times . . .
The Trade Unionist is one of the most influential persons in the land.
They are valuable members of the community, who have a right to
celebrate, if they wish to do so, in the same way as doctors, school-
masters and any other body of professional men.' That was hardly
the point the branch treasurer was contesting. The oiled view of
industrial relations was often heard in the *Express*, even during a
national bus strike: 'Britain is fortunate in her industrial and trade
union leaders. They have shown common sense and a broad understanding of the nation's necessities . . . And the transport workers'
leader, Mr. Frank Cousins, has conducted himself quite reasonably.
He has made no inflammatory speeches.'

Competitive enterprise by individuals, not by groups or classes,
was always the only fuel for the social engine. Groups were seldom
seen as deprived: exceptions were clerks, who were indeed worse off,
and farm workers, whom the *Express* supported against 'privileged
farm landlords.' The enemy of enterprise was high taxation, from
which the middle class suffered so much that some were unable to
put their talented children through university.

Middle-class *mores* were, anyway, changing, to judge from an
ironic feature on the BBC's threat to end Mrs. Dale's Diary. The
article described the ambiance of the serial as an 'endless, placid
summer', 'genteel thraldom in the suburb,' and Mrs. Dale herself
as 'the nation's dispenser of tea, sherry and small talk . . . pillar of
international middle class society.' End it?—'the idea is outrageous,
they will say in the polished parlours of Badminton and Barnes
Common.' The paper is apparently operating a dual model of the
middle-class life: the traditional one of Mrs. Dale, to which the
Express had often enough addressed itself, now invaded by a more
abrasive, probably self-made new generation, the new Elizabethan
buccaneers, as impatient of gentility as of socialist controls.

In the 1959 election campaign, Tory prosperity was once more compared with the austere past:

> Anyone who wants to work can have a job.
> Fortunate is the land where such a situation prevails in industry. Fortunate is Britain where during long years for two generations or more men strove to produce these happy conditions.

Which men strove is not said. The happiness was reflected in social life. 'There is a boom on,' wrote Ann Scott-James, 'social life is bounding, parties pile up, and society thrives.' In the advertising and fashion columns, consumption was conspicuous. An emblematic hero, given an entire feature article, was a Tory-voting bus conductor who was buying his own house and was unpopular with his council-housed colleagues because he had criticized their complaints about rising council rents.

Godfrey Winn went to Lancashire to find three families who modelled the vision of affluence, 'the new aristocrats of Britain'. Obligingly, with polite fervour, they display to Winn their range of new consumer goods, produce colour snaps of their holidays abroad, marvel at the attractive careers their children are successfully pursuing, and explicitly contrast it all with how things had been only a decade before. 'It was good to see the upsurge of their fortunes, so typical of thousands of other members of the new aristocracy.'

> I thought how Mr. Hartland with his ruddy skin, his craftsman hands, sitting there in his shirt sleeves, would have laughed aloud had I labelled him there and then a member of the aristocracy. All the same, unconsciously he agreed when, stressing frankly how much higher the family standard of living was than a decade ago, he volunteered: 'What I don't understand about the Labour programme is their determination to have more nationalisation. It just doesn't make sense to me.'

In the voice of another, Mr. Sagar,

> there was glory . . . when he said: 'At the works, where I am a foreman, they call me The Capitalist, because of the car, but some of them don't understand you have to decide what you want in life and make the sacrifices to get it.'

Home-centred, accumulating goods, launching their children, identifying with the middle class, these people, once the Old Poor, symbolize bourgeoisification at every point. With no worries about income, employment or housing, and profiting from their leisure, they are seen to model the full-blown fruits of affluence. It is as such, as advertisements, that Winn, with oriental reverence, presents them. But, crucially, we are kept aware that only those who 'make the sacrifices' can attain to the 'new aristocracy'. Darker, less aristocratic figures hover in the background, as in a Morality play: the Tory bus conductor's colleagues, for instance, and the men at Mr. Sagar's works who 'don't understand' the importance of being ambitious. Although opportunities are now there for all, *Express* affluence does not fall like rain, upon all those beneath, but like nuts, to be garnered by those who know what they want in life. Affluence alone is not flattening the social pyramid, just smoothing the way for individuals who are ambitious to improve their private status.

*   *   *

While the Tories continued to govern in the early 1960s, neither the *Mirror* nor the *Express* changed its song. In December 1962, for instance, a government report on Britain's progress since 1951 was hailed in the *Express* as 'an amazing picture of Merrie England'. Everyone was better off, especially manual workers, whose wages had almost caught up with those of clerical workers, from which the paper concluded that we were all 'increasingly middle class'. Family life had been strengthened, although crime and sexual licence were much increased among the young. 'Booming Britain', the *Express* announced. Three days later it was to describe unemployment as 'one of Macmillan's grimmest difficulties'. Finding the picture less merrie, the *Mirror* expressed its doubts about what affluence was doing to social morality. 'Nation of affluent debtors' was the headline; a 'basic discontent' was 'expressing itself in a grasping after unearned wealth' through hire-purchase debts and gambling. What was family-centredness in the *Express* comes through as 'staring at the television' in the *Mirror*. Still, there was no denying that living standards had risen. In a later article the *Mirror* was fretting over 'the ordeal of the housewife who has to work in a cramped kitchen . . . She may even have to choose between a washing machine and a refrigerator—because there isn't room for both.'

The papers were similarly divided over the major reports on education that were published in this period. The Crowther Report filled the *Mirror*'s front page: 'A revolution in our schools . . . the most vital Report ever written on education . . . SOCIAL, EDUCATIONAL AND POLITICAL DYNAMITE . . . the sensational Crowther Report proves that BRITAIN IS LETTING HER

TEENAGERS DOWN.' The *Express* did not mention the report on its front page, nor in its Opinion column. A brief summary was buried deep inside the paper. A simple difference in the papers' assessments of the report's news-value can hardly account for such a striking disparity. The *Mirror*'s hope that 'political dynamite' would explode under the government obviously had much to do with it, and so did the paper's assumption that its readership, being on average younger and worse educated than the *Express*'s, would have the keener interest of the relatively deprived, of those whom Britain has 'let down'. As at all moments of political controversy, but seldom at other, 'buoyant' times, the *Mirror* had its Us/Them awareness ready, like an old uniform kept in the attic; whereas Crowther's concern with class distinction in education did not interest the *Express*, or surprise it. Private enterprise, not state provision, was what mattered in education, and after.

The Newsom Report went the same way. 'One of the most important reports ever written on education,' the *Mirror* exclaimed. 'Bang up-to-date. That's the Newsom Report . . . Too much young talent is being wasted in the classrooms . . . the sense of failure must be banished from the secondary modern schools . . . All this adds up to educational justice and a fair start in life for EVERY CHILD. Instead of a fairer start for some than for others.' The affluence that, elsewhere in the *Mirror*, has liberated young people is suddenly found to be haunted by a sense of failure. The *Express* again buried the report, being moved in Opinion only to endorse the 'wise words' about 'firm guidance on sexual morality based on chastity before marriage and fidelity within it.'

Splashing the Robbins Report, the *Mirror* attacked *The Times* and *Daily Telegraph*, who had made criticisms. 'Is this the old outlook that college education is only for the privileged few?' There is a ventriloquistic ring in 'college education'., the *Mirror* finding the old-fashioned working-class phrase it assumed would be recognized by readers perhaps overawed by universities. (The *Mirror*, in fact, has a very high proportion of graduates on its staff.) The *Express* took a slightly warmer interest than it had in the earlier reports, arguably because university entry has more to do with freedom of choice than the state school system has.

The Plowden Report, finally, again led the *Mirror*'s front page: 'The classroom revolution . . . one of the most reforming documents in the history of English education . . . It is no good lavishing millions on super secondary schools and super universities if large numbers of children are doomed to begin life in poverty-stricken primary schools in poverty-stricken areas.' This time the report made the front page of the *Express*, but only in an article that said the country could not afford to implement it. With a Labour government now in power (it was 1967), education was again a political weapon for the *Express*. The recruitment of more teachers, the paper told Crosland, the Minister for Education, was far more fundamental than 'messing about with the superstructure . . . Let him take a long holiday from political meddling.'

The 'messing' and 'meddling' referred, of course, to the issue of forced comprehensive schools, a move that the *Express* detested because it infringed freedom of choice (for those who were free to choose), and diminished the opportunities for competition between schoolchildren and between parents. The paper was as loquacious against comprehensives—'teaching factories where uniformity will be the highest achievement'—as it had been taciturn on Crowther and Newsom. 'It is a theory,' John Braine wrote in a main feature, 'that exalts mediocrity, when what we should be concerned about in Britain are the brightest children'. 'Competition, diversity, pace-setting,' said the Express, '—*that* should be the pattern for education.' A report of 'a secret plan' which 'Tory chiefs will challenge' deployed all the armoury of rhetoric familiar from 1945. Suggestion by reported denial was not missed: 'Last night Mr. Crosland denied that his plans represented a totalitarian attempt . . . denied that there had been any watering down of the Government's determination . . .' In a leader it is said that 'tens of thousands of quiet, responsible citizens are forming themselves into protest movements . . . When such schools can command so much fervent loyalty it is not only wrong that they should be destroyed: it is wicked.' Wicked too, we remember, was it to 'regard the rich with envy' in 1947; and only wickedness, we now understand, could move 'quiet, responsible citizens' to unaccustomed collective activity.

The disparity between the *Express* and the *Mirror* on comprehensive schools is as striking as the reverse disparity over the education reports during the Tory administration. To the *Mirror*, Crosland's policy was one of 'friendly persuasion', seldom meriting more than a mention inside the paper.

It was in 1967, too, that a moment occurred which crystallized the two papers' attitudes to youth: the 'hippie summer', and in particular the Legalize Pot rally in Hyde Park. The view of hippies as exhibitionist parasites was loudly put by Robert Pitman in the *Express*, and attacks on drug-taking were frequently reported, but in two long articles the *Express* examined seriously, and with some sympathy, the significance of the 'alternative subculture' in America and England. Hippies were 'a highly colourful manifestation of the

tremendous forces of change which are present in California', and
their politics of love and freedom were echoed from Amsterdam to
Peking. Drugs, too, were discussed unhysterically—users were 'in
search of an awareness and breadth of experience they do not believe
they can achieve under normal circumstances'—and the cultural
connections with pop and poetry were touched in. The articles
ended by judging that the hippies were a negative phenomenon.
They certainly had style, though, and it was for that that the *Express*
was usually interested in them. The spillover from hippie culture
into the world of fashion and the fashionable allowed William
Hickey to link the aristocracy of pop with the pop of his more
conventional champagne acquaintances.

The *Mirror* did not try to make sense of the hippies. By 1964, with
confident gossip about the Top 30 and mod styles, it had embraced
the commercial image of youth culture (though Cassandra could not
stomach the 'furry twanging' of the Beatles, 'as unskilled as a quartet
of chimps tarring a back fence'). The events of 1967, however, numb-
ed the *Mirror*, cutting right across its theme that the lively independence of young people served to revitalize the old moral values. The
paper gave prominence to such statements as Alice Bacon's attack on
the Beatles:

> Today there are those who see in society's attitude to drug-
> taking the opportunity for questioning traditional values and
> social judgments of all kinds.

The questions the hippies asked were isolated in the *Mirror* as potty
or criminal.

5

EXPRESS AND MIRROR, 1964

THE issue which dominated the 1964 election, economic growth, was one particularly associated with the Labour leader, Harold Wilson. (Wilson was a professional economist; the Tory leader and Prime Minister, Sir Alec Douglas-Home, had, in contrast, been widely caricatured as calculating the national economy with the aid of matchsticks.) The only leading Tory issue that, during the campaign, rose in salience was the nuclear deterrent, particularly associated with Douglas-Home, a former Foreign Secretary.[1] The fact that issues associated with each party leader were those that appear to have made most impact on the voters supports the opinion of Butler and King[2] that there was a greater emphasis on political personalities than in any recent election.

To television had been added the custom of daily press conferences at party headquarters. Douglas-Home was generally thought to be most confident on foreign affairs, and to lack conviction when talking of 'full employment and rising standards of living'. His most publicized remarks were his 'menu without prices' accusation that Labour dared not reveal the cost of their proposed programme, his televised description of pensions as 'donations', and an accusation that Labour was 'hiring' the hecklers who confused many of his meetings. The Tory who gained most publicity, however, was Quintin Hogg, first with a vehement rebuke to hecklers—'If you can tell me there are no adulterers on the front bench of the Labour party you can talk to me about Profumo'—and, in the last week of the campaign, with the remark that anyone who voted Labour must be 'stark, staring bonkers'. R. A. Butler also attracted sudden attention with a notably unoptimistic interview with George Gale of the *Express* (it won Gale the Interview of the Year Award). As a personality, Wilson scored heavily over Douglas-Home; reservations were often made, however, that Labour was a 'one-man band'. Wilson's most successful speaking, it was thought, was about a 'purposive new Britain' which would replace the 'tired philosophy

1 Data on the salience of issues in 1964 can be found in Jay G. Blumler and Denis McQuail, *Television in Politics: Its Uses and Influences*, Faber, 1968.

2 D. E. Butler and Anthony King, *The British General Election of 1964*, Macmillan, 1965.

of a day that is gone' and oust the 'closed and privileged circle' that had 'condemned so many of our ablest young people to frustration'. The need for a change of government was an obvious issue after thirteen years of Tory rule. Wilson's most controversial remark was that serious strikes seemed to coincide uncannily with general elections (thus tarnishing Labour's image)—the strike in question was at the Birmingham car components firm of Hardy Spicer, and another occurred towards the close of the campaign, among London Underground workers. George Brown also raised a passing storm by commenting that mortgage rates might be brought as low as 3 per cent. Other issues that figured with only local (in place or time) intensity were immigration, restrictive practices, the Common Market and the Commonwealth. Perhaps the single most influential news fact during the period before polling day, on October 15, was the September 30 announcement of seriously worsened balance of payments figures.

One other sort of election reporting was prominent, that which dwelt upon the process of the campaign itself, as a news event. Much attention was given to opinion polls, and to the new incidence of betting on the result: both polls and betting suggested a gradual shift to Labour. Another aspect of the process was heckling, which was thought to have reached unparalleled unruliness.

*   *   *

Neither of the main parties specially recommended itself to the *Express* in 1964. The outgoing Conservative government was eager to enter the Common Market; as that would mean abandoning Commonwealth preference, and weakened links with the USA, the paper found its traditional Tory-Empire-Atlantic policy drifting apart. Labour, on the other hand, was critical of the Common Market. Remarks such as one by Arthur Greenwood, the party's chairman, who attacked the Tories for being 'prepared to sell the Commonwealth down the river in the vain hope of getting into the closed shop of the Common Market' were given prominence in the *Express*, which, moreover, seems to have found Wilson more impressive than any leading Tory figure. In the final analysis, on election day, the choice was unambiguously put, between 'a single individual, the apostle of an unpopular creed, and a party which can appeal to its record'; but until then the paper's reservations about the Tories were weightier than its usual opposition to nationalization and other Labour policies.

The dilemma was rationalized by asserting that there was 'no difference of principle' between the parties, that on domestic

F*

isues especially they were 'like Tweedledum and Tweedledee'. Calling it 'The Inscrutable Election', George Gale wrote on election day that 'great tracts of each side's speeches could as well have been uttered by the other side,' and Cummings's cartoon represented twin Tory and Labour politicians shouting hot air, while between them stood a gagged 'Goddess of Truth'. A few days earlier, Beach-comber wrote:

> Election week. With a frankness and lucidity which beggar description nearly all the issues of importance, with the exception of nearly all the important issues, have been ex-plained to the electorate in words of many syllables.
>
> Yet a discordant note, nay, a cacophony has marred the charming music of the pre-election concert. Here and there the raucous voice of gross and unashamed materialism has been heard, asking the impudent and irrelevant question: 'Who is going to put up the money for building Utopia in Cloud-Cuckooland?'

Outside its leader column, the *Express* consistently aimed to sound the note of plain scepticism. An example was an article on October 5, by Jill Butterfield (pictured with pursed lips and a sidelong glance), headed:

> Women and the election with ten days to polling
> I know what we will vote for!

It opens on a tough note:

> This year will go down in political history as the year when the baby-kissing had to stop. The year when the wool that has been pulled over women's eyes by generations of soft-soaping politicians just wouldn't wash.
>
> The year when women, the most unpolitical animals God ever created, finally got into the game. And were responsible for the result.
>
> For this is the year when women are at last thinking for them-selves about who should govern them.
>
> And, dear prospective Prime Ministers, you can't afford to ignore us.

No explanation is offered why 'women are *at last* thinking for them-selves', as not before. The opening is simply a gambit to arrest our attention by dangling before us the promise of something new and uncompromising, to be reckoned with. In the popular press, news-values put a premium on discontinuity.

'Whoever wins this election has got to win the women first.' True;

and had been for years. Miss Butterfield goes on to locate herself as the qualified spokeswoman promised by the headline:

> From the cross-section of women I have spoken to I have found that we have become very cautious and very concerned.

It has taken her almost half-way through her article to present these credentials of serious attention to the 'dear prospective Prime Ministers'. The trick of being 'overheard' addressing authority is familiar; Marjorie Proops used it in the *Mirror* two days later.

Now Miss Butterfield comes to the cautious concerns she has found:

> Most of all about prices.
> Of course, every politician says he is going to bring them down. But *we* will vote only for the one who can tell us how in terms of loaves and fishes and not just give us loads of figures.

Politicians are identified with rhetoric, soft soap, loads of figures. Men, it seems just possible, might be prone to fall for all that; but we, *we* women:

> will be interested in the kind of candidate who realises that, while there is only one woman in a hundred who cares whether Blue Streaks are in the hair or the air, the things we DO care about we want to know all about.
> So we will not be very impressed by the platform orator who is not prepared to listen afterwards, in private perhaps, to the kind of question that cowardice, self-consciousness, or incoherence prevents us asking publicly.

In the TV age we look askance at oratory, the hustings, the public performance, then; and, again, there is the implication that such things are best left to men, who are more likely to get, slightly ridiculously perhaps, worked up about remote questions such as Blue Streaks, but who, as a possible result, might be weak at seeing just how politics affects their own daily, domestic lives. Education, for example—women are concerned about:

> State nursery schools . . . NOT very interested in the rights and wrongs of the public school system.

Practical concerns, loaves and fishes, not abstract principles, rights and wrongs, are what bother *Express* women, and what politicians, unless you watch them closely, are given to skating over. Women are unlikely to have feelings about social justice except when it touches them directly, in their own homes.

We want to air that very dangerous thing, our little knowledge on the question of tax reform.

Why, for all your screams for married teachers, married
technicians to return to work, do you politicians penalise us
with joint taxation?

'Screams . . . you politicians . . .': the sceptical gulf is very wide.

In its disenchantment with the politicians' arguments, and perhaps also in response to the certainty that television would be first
with the news, the *Express*'s main election reports concentrated on
leading politicians' performances. Both scepticism and curiosity
about performance always were ingredients in *Express* elections:
William Barkley's barking in 1945 of 'Walk up, walk up, to the
greatest circus' implies both. The difference before 1964 was that
Tory performances easily transcended *Express* scepticism and invited
its complement, fulsome acquiescence, whereas Labour performances were exposed as such. Now, politicians of both parties are seen
as having more in common—they are all just politicians in the end—
than they have in contention about policies. The unusual incidence
of heckling accounts for some of the stress on the election as a public
event, for consumption, rather than a national debate involving
the voters. But heckling is not mentioned in roughly half the reports
in which a politician's performance is the chief interest.

Wilson's performances, as well as his statements of policy, were
given more attention than Douglas-Home's. Sometimes the *Express*'s
old devices were levelled at him—'Mr. Harold Wilson has committed
his biggest blunder yet'—but more often a note of respect, even
warmth, was heard. One report, from Bradford, tells how the
'Yorkshire lad' made jokes about heckling at Douglas-Home's
expense, then attacked the Government's economic management, the
'faceless men' who ran the steel industry, 'the coterie of class
privilege' in the Tory party, and 'with supreme confidence' said
'vote for your children's future'.

Attlee, now in the Lords, played some part in the election,
rebuking Hogg for his 'adulterers' remark. The *Express* devoted a
short leader to the 'deeply respected veteran . . . A bonny man to
have on your side!' A far cry from the decoy-duck of previous
elections, this Attlee. His 'reputation is impeccable . . . He has always
been a stickler for propriety,' wrote Trevor Evans (billed as reporting 'with the personal touch', as opposed to the 'human drama',
George Gale's prerogative on the facing page). George Brown was
said, in a quoted Tory remark, to have 'brought that fine element
of comedy to the election that it so badly needs'. Even Jack Dash,

the unofficial leader of the dockers, was profiled with an objectivity far from what the Express in earlier elections would have made of his Communism in relation to the Labour image.

Some Labour performances were regarded with scepticism, but it was at least as keen when Tories were performing. Evans reported:

> Very discreetly, officials at party headquarters were compiling their assessments yesterday of the leaders who have performed best during this campaign ... More from courtesy than conviction, Sir Alec Douglas-Home was thought to have done a good job.

Scepticism could be winsomely suspended, as by Gale: 'they all know that Sir Alec was an earl, and therefore not in it for power and glory, and therefore to be liked and trusted.' But it could also be suspended for outright attack, as by Robert Pitman on Douglas-Home's intention, if re-elected, to apply again for Common Market membership. (Pitman was polemically licensed as Cassandra was in the *Mirror*. On this occasion he went on to attack Roy Jenkins and Aubrey Jones for saying that immigrants were needed to fill 'jobs that wouldn't be done by other people ... precisely the Cotton Fields argument once used to justify bringing slaves into the Southern States.') Hogg was cast as roughly the Tory equivalent to George Brown, volatile, outspoken, a potential embarrassment. In reports of his speeches there was a particular stress on performance, through such scenarios as casting him as a Wild Westminster gunman.

Perhaps more revealing than these examples, which deal with single politicians, was reporting like the front-page lead on October 12. It was headed 'Let's be realistic', overlined 'Tories all-out for Liberal vote', and began:

> The Tories broke their 'never on Sundays' campaign rule yesterday to reveal their final election tactic—a fight to the death for the Liberal vote ...
>
> Tonight, 19 Ministers are being dispatched to meetings in the biggest Tory blitz of the campaign. They will make co-ordinated speeches, stressing Sir Alec Douglas-Home's two bull points ...
>
> And everywhere they will be hoping to work-up Liberal fears of Socialism, to produce Tory votes ...
>
> Tory tacticians have obviously been affected by public opinion polls ...
>
> Lord Blakenham, a former Eighth Army colonel, was positively Monty-like at yesterday's conference.

The detached disclosure of tactics, the hint of panic, and the defusing use of the future predictive tense are all reminiscent of the *Express*'s attitude to Labour two decades earlier.

Officially, however, the *Express* could not allow that no vital issues were at stake, even though both parties were skirting them. There is an unbridged gulf between the tone in which politicians' performances are reported and the paper's own leading articles on the election. On October 1 Opinion complained, 'In this election far too much time, far too many words, are being spent on trifling issues,' a complaint that was heard again.

On October 7 the *Express* laid out its leader much more boldly than usual, displaying it with generous white space across the top of seven columns of the page, under a prominent 'Opinion' block. The presentation and the headline, 'The Express and the Election', made it plain that the article would be an official statement of policy. It began:

> The Daily Express is an independent, classless newspaper. It holds strong views about national policy and expresses them with vehemence and consistency.
>
> What is its duty toward the public in the General Election? First, to give each of the parties in the contest a fair show in the news.
>
> The Daily Express has the further duty to single out what it believes to be the main issues before the electorate and to refuse to have its judgment blurred by petty incidents in the party dog-fight.
>
> What *really* matters in Britain today? What *are* the vital issues before the people and what is the relative importance to be assigned to them?
>
> In answering these questions, the Daily Express speaks as a newspaper with fierce and immovable principles.

The assertiveness, extraordinary even in the *Express*, seems intended to negate the one phrase in the passage where the tone descends for a moment from its elevation, 'petty incidents in the party dog-fight'. While devoting almost all its election space to willingly reporting that sort of pettiness, the paper wished to assure us that at heart the *Express*, at least, preserved a respect for the traditional dignities and wisdoms, the tried and trusted ways, the ancient freedoms of British political history. It reserved for itself a position above the petty fray, whence issues were discernible; and when occupying that position it assumed that its readers would respect its maintained integrity, authority, and right to speak on their behalf.

Almost half the article, which runs to barely 400 words, and all the weight of presentation affirm the self-assigned place of the *Express* itself in the election. It goes on to list its principles:

1. The Daily Express believes in the greatness of Britain, in her continuing and essential role in world affairs. This means that Britain must be strong in weapons and independent in policy.

2. It means too that Britain should continue to maintain her positive role as the heart of a world-spanning Commonwealth.

3. The conception of full employment is inextricably bound up with the philosophy of the newspaper.

4. A steady and constant expansion of the national economy is something that must be attained. It can best be sought through the well-tried and self-regulating mechanism of free enterprise.

We trust to the individual, to the man prepared to take risks in business.

5. One particular section of the economy has always engaged the special interest and enthusiasm of this newspaper—Agriculture.

The Daily Express looks with pride and satisfaction on the prosperity which British farming enjoys, and on the enhanced sense of national self-sufficiency which its increased production brings to all our people.

The ring of phrases 'pride and satisfaction . . . all our people' condenses the magisterial, not to say regal, attitude which has already been implanted by the paper's repeated references to itself in the third person, a habit broken only once in the article, 'We trust . . .' The whole message is credential, rather like a prospectus, seeking to convince us that what the *Express* thinks is importantly relevant to our thinking about this election. It could, however, hardly be said that we are invited to join a democratic debate on the issues. The mode of address unflinchingly puts us in our place, sitting and meditating on what those of 'strong views . . . fierce and immovable principles' have to say about it all.

The article ends:

With this philosophy to guide it, the Daily Express seeks out the real issues before the people in the election.

Between now and polling day, the Opinion column will be devoted to the discussion of these questions.

The newspaper will give its free and frank opinion on the grave matters which the public must determine in eight days' time.

There are, then, 'main issues', 'real issues', 'grave matters' at stake in this election. The dog-fight will not blur our judgement of them if we attend to the *Express*, which refers to itself by title seven times and by phrase some dozen times more.

A later editorial will illustrate the persistent function of that official tone, to inject a sense of ancient wisdom even into the contingent pettiness of the daily dog-fight. It was headed 'How fierce is their will to win!' and began:

> The British are the most dangerous animals in the world when they have their backs to the wall.
> History demonstrates its. And every man's inner knowledge of his own nature supports it.
> So Labour, beware!
> The Tories feel that they have their backs to the wall now.
> Be sure that they will fight with renewed fury . . .

and ended:

> Mr. Wilson, you are fighting against a shrewd and doughty foe.
> A foe who is now at his most dangerous.

The actual subject of this article may seem to be very like 'petty incidents in the party dog-fight'. It is couched entirely in terms of combat (intrinsic in the British character, like 'the competitive life of nature' in 1945) and deals entirely with the tactics of an election campaign. But by assertion, imperative and warning, the *Express* assumes for itself a privileged position in the affray, from which it is able to direct our minds to British history and character. Even in a dog-fight, traditions will out.

A similar example occurred with the publication of the balance of payments figures. In its front-page lead, the *Express*'s angle was the effect of these 'highly embarrassing statistics' on the election campaign, but Opinion declared that they 'must not be exploited for political gain . . . Let the politicians argue fiercely about the best way to conduct the economy. But let them remain united about the aim: prosperity through continued expansion.'

There, in that assumed consensus over what the nation is aiming at, is the root of the *Express*'s scepticism about the election. The matter is really no more grave than a choice between rival stage-managers of the prosperity the paper had hymned since 1951. 'Why do they sneer at affluence?' wondered the headline on an article by Macmillan. Another headline spoke of 'the race to make money': it is institutionalized by the *Express*'s definite article, a permanent part of the scene, along with investment hedging or betting against the election result, pools winners, *Express* competitions for cars, and the 'confident young' who, a series tells us, 'are revolutionizing the business thinking of this country'. Attlee might be reported as blaming 'the "low ideals" of the Government for contributing to the rise in crime . . . "Big business gives the lead in getting rich quick"' ; but Labour's 'menacing statement' about nationalisation, 'State meddling', is identified by Opinion as the 'fundamental issue':

> Competition yields far happier results . . .
> And who are the pace-setters? The innovators. The thrusting, zestful men with ideas and the capacity to develop them.
> In the free enterprise system, they benefit the community by advancing their own interests.
> But if they are denied rewards, weighed down by regulations, and badgered by officialdom they will cease to spark. Their projects will wither on the Whitehall grapevine. And that restless urge to experiment, to risk, to dare will peter out.
> With disastrous results for the nation.

Personal success through cleverness is advertised everywhere in the paper. 'It's thinking girls who get the man,' the women's page confided. 'All the really clever girls are playing it cool on the intellectual beat. Suddenly it's smart to be brainy. Suddenly it's sexy to look intellectual . . . The brainer breed can struggle through Kafka.'

Meanwhile, the election is a performance, and not a very entertaining one at that. Maudie tells Littlehampton, who is gazing at television, 'You can wake me up, darling, when you're quite sure we're through with the Westminster commercials'. Election night would be not quite so boring, with 'swing charts' and other psephological kit to 'make you an Armchair General at tonight's election battle'. Conflicting opinion polls, mocked by Beachcomber and Pitman, nevertheless frequently served to spotlight the dog-fight. 'Something horrible is coming over General Elections,' lamented William Barkley, the old circus barker. 'They are becoming computer business.'

In the good old elections Barkley remembered, his paper had woven the stuff of its reporting into the pattern of its own views. Now, there is scarcely any party angle on the news; and as for the voter, who was never prominent in *Express* elections, he is an Armchair General bemusedly watching the politicians yap. It needs the assertive editorial drum to stir us from our consumer contentment. The news will not be hard enough.

Beachcomber spoke for the *Express* when he wrote:

A forecast I made some months ago has proved fairly accurate. The Tories promise a happy and prosperous country, with increased production and economic expansion. The Socialists, on the other hand, promise a prosperous and happy country, with economic expansion and increased production. Each party uses the magic word 'modernisation' to put a spell on the apathetic. The acting of both casts would disgrace an amateur company in a small town.

*   *   *

The *Mirror* did not concentrate on the election in its early weeks. It printed summaries of all three party manifestoes, but with an unequivocal preference for Labour's 'bright and sizzling' programme, a preference that also influenced the news pages. It was, however, largely content to do no more than shape and emphasize the politicians' own campaign.

But on September 28 it devoted its front page to its own question 'Whose finger on the tranquillizer?', subtitled 'Mirror enters the election', and subsequently gave 9 per cent of its total space, including ten of its fifteen front-page leads, to a patently anti-Tory coverage of the election. (The *Express* gave the election only 6 per cent of its space.) Nearly half (45 per cent) of the *Mirror*'s coverage consisted in special splashes, that depended on no immediate news-event but appeared to be a series of shots planned irrespective of the course of the external campaign. The *Mirror*'s entry into the election, that is, was made not in its capacity as a news medium but as a daily advertisement of its opinions.

It offered no evidence that its opinions were shared by its readers, no sense of the paper/reader dialogue which had permeated it in 1945. In the sixteen issues before polling day only six letters referred to the election, and in only three of them could a party preference be discerned (unless teaching a budgerigar to say 'Labour' can be counted): one was from a Conservative MP, one complained of Tory canvassing methods, and one was from a woman in difficulties with finding a house who had inadvertently appeared in a buoyant Tory television advertisement.

The *Mirror*'s own privileged personality is repeatedly to the fore. It is hardly to be distinguished from a type of commercial advertisement in that, or in its other modes: a tendency to write in slogans, to create images (Tory images, the subsequent destruction of which is in itself another image), to hammer home a single message by multiple assertion without argument, to appeal to emulative emotion rather than reason, to adopt inflexible attitudes of praise or

condemnation; and also, in the larger sense, to follow what seemed
to be an overall campaign strategy, an attack on the Conservative
record and ministers, with hardly any recommendation of Labour's
alternatives. The stylized rhetoric and selective attack suggest a
fear of that scepticism about both parties which the *Express*
endorsed. The *Mirror* set itself up as a model of strong political feeling, which its readers could emulate instead of gliding from scepticism into apathy.

Some explanation is in Cecil King's memoirs:[3]

> I was not particularly impressed by the prospect of a Labour
> Government but quite convinced that it was time for a change.
> It seemed to me that if we supported Sir Alec Douglas-Home, a
> difficult manoeuvre but possible, he would win. If we went
> flat-out for Labour, they might win. It would be a close-run
> thing and the attitude of the Mirror would be decisive.

Butler and King,[4] too, noting that the *Mirror* was read by a third of
the voters, believe that the paper's strategy may have been decisive:

> It was the *Daily Mirror* rather than Mr. Wilson which sus-
> tained the Labour campaign to a polling day climax. It was also
> the *Mirror* which almost by itself tried to remind voters of why
> they had turned against the Conservatives during the previous
> two or three years.

The Tories were pictured as an ageing clique hoping to hush up their
record of incompetence. Labour's claim, by inference (almost wholly
by inference), rested upon a complementary picture of the forces of
youth, who saw through the Tories' evasions and clamoured for a
change of government. It is one more manifestation of Us v. Them,
the most persistent structure in the *Mirror*. The social composition of
Us and Them might alter a little from election to election, but the
vertical structure of social conflict seems to have been permanently
necessary to the *Mirror*'s orchestration of political feeling. It can, in
that, be crucially distinguished from the *Express*, where the structure
of political choice (hardly present in 1964) was typically based on
levels of political wisdom arranged in a continuous hierarchy, at
every level of which the chief loyalty is to the nation.

Traces of the *Mirror*'s earlier Us—servicemen, and their womenfolk at home struggling to make ends meet; the young and under-
privileged—are present in the Us of 1964; traces, too, of the earlier
Them, entrepreneurs and High Tories. But the vertical conflict can

3 Cecil King, *Strictly Personal*, Weidenfeld & Nicolson, 1969.
4 op. cit.

now be primarily read as the ruled *v.* the incompetent rulers. The first group just wants efficient government for all, the second just wants to cling on to power. The first has no social identity other than its position of being ruled; the second is narrowly identified as a specific number of government ministers. No room is found in this structure for two other elements, the Labour Party and the *Mirror* itself. The party is a vague alternative group of prospective rulers; in the news pages they appear as dynamic personalities, but in the splash features, which dominate the paper's presentation of politics, they hardly figure at all. As for the *Mirror*, it identifies itself with the ruled in shouting loudest for the removal of the incompetents, but gives no further evidence of belonging with them, offers no further reason for political action, nor any consistent definition of its readers in terms of a particular, socially-based interest they might collectively have in the outcome of the election.

It is not hard to suggest explanations of the change from 1955. It was easier to represent a 13-year-old administration as outmoded than a 4-year-old one. Developments of the early 1960s supported the 'time for a change' cry: the pay pause, trade difficulties, rising unemployment, Macmillan's purge of ministers, the Profumo scandal. The point is that the *Mirror* took them as symptoms of a tired government, not necessarily of one with wrong priorities. It might be that the notion of affluence, which seems to have dazzled the *Mirror* in 1955, had lost its shine in nine years. Certainly in 1964 the *Mirror* set out to publicize areas of conspicuous inaffluence as it had barely done in 1955, and more than once held up the word 'affluence' to mockery, but with the implication that we weren't all affluent yet, not that affluence was perhaps a misleading ideal.

The splash features were as follows:

September 28; Front page and turn, 'Whose finger on the tranquilliser?'—an exposure of a Tory plot to 'keep the election quiet'.

September 29; Centres, 'The deathbed repentance'—an attack on Tory pretensions to continue in government.

October 1: Centres, 'The end of the dynasties?'—an exposure of family relationships among Tory ministers.

October 5: Centres, 'This election is about people'—the plight of old age pensioners, with their portraits.

October 7: Centres, 'So Alec thinks I'm his secret weapon!'— Marjorie Proops attacks the Tories' appeal to 'the weaker sex'.

October 8: Centres, 'Top people, too, are voting Labour'—a photo-feature in which celebrities explained their voting reasons.

October 9: Centres, 'My case for the Tories', by Edward Heath, a 'dynamic and progressive personality in the Tory party of today', who, said the *Mirror*, was likely to become his party's leader, in time.

October 12: Centres, 'Why should Britain be run by "chaps" mourning for George the Third?'—an exposure of old school ties in the Tory government.

October 13: Centres, 'The Tory record'—a montage of headlines from national newspapers of the previous 13 years, charting government failures, with brief comments by the *Mirror*. (For this splash and the next, the three columns of advertisements normally on the centre pages were cleared.)

October 14: Front, centres, four other whole pages and a three-column item, 'Election shock issue: Is this the Promised Land?'—a widely cast, generously illustrated attack on inadequate social provision.

October 15: Front, 'Let's *all* vote today'—with a large portrait of Harold Wilson, no text, some lesser injunctions all of headline size.

That schematic evidence already lends substance to two points made earlier. First, the weight of the campaign is anti-Tory, not pro-Labour. Of the eleven splashes, eight attack the Tory record or personalities; of the two that support Labour, one does so by photographically representing a section of the community, top people, as being pro-Labour instead of advancing arguments, and the other is simply an election-day poster. Second, none of the splashes depends on an immediate news peg. That is not to ignore that the October 14 splash, easily the biggest, is lavishly documented with photographs of the social deprivation on which the paper's anti-Tory case on this day rests; such evidence could justly be said to be far more important to the election than any immediate news of the politician's day. Yet the sense of discontinuity remains—the implication is either that the *Mirror* had not exposed such social conditions until the day before the election, or that it did not trust its readers to remember them (as Butler and King suggest in the remark quoted earlier). The discontinuity, apart from merely seeking to shock, indicates that the *Mirror* felt called on to behave during a general election differently from normal, to play a special part as a newspaper, *this* part, exposure. Its manners of exposure may be studied in the first splash, on September 28.

The headline, 'Whose finger on the tranquilliser?', deliberately draws on the *Mirror*'s own myth, referring, as the paper did in 1955 also, to its celebrated, and litigious, headline during the 1951 election, 'Whose finger on the trigger?' 'Tranquillizer' is an

alliterative substitute, and brings a flavour of the 1960s; it is set in
capital letters nearly two inches deep, and underscored with a black
12pt. rule. A subordinate reverse block places the feature: 'Mirror
enters the election'.

The contemporary flavour is enriched by a big portrait of Honor
Blackman, her finger on the trigger of a pistol, with this caption:

> ●Here is Miss Pussy Galore in person—pointing a real gun (the
> sort that kills) at Bond in the new film 'Goldfinger'.
>   But it was the Tranquilliser Gun that foxed Bond. It sent him
> to sleep for twelve hours.
> ●The brainy boys of the Tory Party had a similarly ingenious
> idea.
>   They were hoping that the British public would remain
> sunburnt and 'tranquillised' until the election was over . . .

The sequence of 'finger' in the headline, the pictured finger on the
trigger, and the title 'Goldfinger' in the caption thus associates the
Mirror's own personality with the celebrity of the Bond films, and
achieves a transition from 'trigger' to 'tranquillizer' by mixing the
modes of popular fiction, political-journalistic memory and alliterative association. The thrust of the complicated technique is towards
establishing the word and concept of tranquillizer for coinage in the
article; that the *Mirror* felt such preparation necessary is indicated
by its heavy setting of the word in its headline and yet placing self-
conscious inverted commas round it in the caption. The caption
also sets up another theme that the article will develop, a disparaging contrast between the 'brainy boys', 'ingenious' and 'hoping'
Tories, and the possibly 'sunburnt' and 'tranquillized' British
public. The chief message of the feature will be the *Mirror*'s role of
mediator between the two, underpinned perhaps by worry that the
public was indeed too sunburnt, apathetic, for an election.

Here is the text of the article:

> From today on it will be known as The Tory Plot That Failed.
>   The idea was not flattering to the electorate, but it was
> ingenious enough.
>   With a certain amount of winking and nose-tapping, the
> order ('the word') was put around Cabinet Ministers and
> principal Tory Party speakers to—
>   'Keep the election quiet. Play it down, chaps. Don't rouse
> the sunburnt public. Let them wake up quietly on October 16
> to find that we're snugly back in office for the fourth time run-
> ning.'

Yesterday's Sunday Express said that 'over the Tory camp there hangs a most eerie silence. Their party headquarters is an armed fortress. As difficult to get into it as into Fort Knox.'

Some attribute the idea to Mr. Julian Amery, the Aviation Minister. He attended the first night of 'Goldfinger', in which Fort Knox actually is raided. In that riotous film starring Miss Pussy Galore (Honor Blackman) he saw a tranquilliser gun used on James Bond to send him to sleep for twelve hours.

In fact, the Tory plot—Operation Apathy Galore, designed to send us all to sleep until after the election—was cooked up by cleverer men than Mr. Amery.

Chancellor Maudling, Sir Alec's chosen mouthpiece for the election conferences, would be a shrewder guess—thus making him the first spokesman in political history to applaud a conspiracy of silence.

There was always the risk that Mr. Quintin Hogg, the ebullient Minister for Science and Education, might blow his top and say something wild and unscientific.

But what the Tories did not anticipate was that the Daily Mirror would today bust the plot to keep-it-dark wide open.

There will be no Apathy Galore in this newspaper, Sir Alec.

●The Mirror is going into the election right now with all guns firing.

●We're going to make it our business to alert the British public to the peril of 'leaving things as they are'.

●We're going to wake up the politicians, too, so that this becomes the toughest-fought election of the century.

Sorry, Alec. There's going to be no choir of yes-men and yes-women singing
All things bright and beautiful
The Tories made them all . . .
Let there be no doubt, none at all, about where stands the Mirror in this election.

WE BELIEVE
Britain desperately needs new men at the top with new ideas.

WE BELIEVE
a fourth term of office for Westminister's weary willies, with the die-hards even more firmly in the saddle, would not only be *BAD* for the country but fatal for the Tory Party itself.

WE BELIEVE

a victory for Labour will not only be *GOOD* for the country *but essential if we are to maintain in Britain the basis of a two-Party democracy with an alternative Government.*

Thirteen years in power have reduced the Tories to confusion and exhaustion, with much of their available talent—men of the calibre of Iain Macleod—outside the Cabinet because of the bitter quarrels over the leadership within.

The Conservative Party needs a period in the wilderness to re-discover its soul, shed its old-hat leaders and build a new philosophy with relevance to the hurrying years in which we live. And the more thoughtful of the top Tories know it.

Tory policy has become a circus of rash contradictions. The Party has about-turned on the Common Market. About-turned on the Commonwealth. And turned its Colonial attitudes inside out.

The casting, miscasting, re-casting and down-casting of the principal performers has been farcical.

Selwyn Lloyd—the most notorious example—was sacked by Macmillan as Chancellor in 1962 because he was 'a tired man'. Alec Home brought Selwyn back as Leader of the House in 1963 because he found the others were even wearier.

Nevertheless, the present Government's leading men have been there, muddling along, ever since the time when the new voters of 1964 were getting ready to face their 11-plus. All the time they have been growing from primary school children to adult citizens, Sir Alec Home, Rab Butler, Duncan Sandys and Reg Maudling have been in some Government office or other.

Henry Brooke is not quite the veteran he seems. The Home Secretary has done only ten years' hard. But that is enough—for us, if not for him.

It is too long. Ten, eleven, twelve, thirteen continuous years in the corridors of power.

The Victorian big-time politicians such as Gladstone and Disraeli never served stretches of this length—and life was much easier for Ministers in the age of the hansom cab.

Now these Ministers, gluttons for punishment as well as for power, are asking to be sent back for another five years.

The Tories need a rest

The country, well aware of the perils of a one-Party State, needs a rest from the Tories.

The Labour Party has fresh men with new ideas and the energy to carry them out. After thirteen frustrating years in opposition they are eager for the spur and challenge of power.

It is time for a change. And on Thursday, October 15—for the *FIRST* time for five years and the *LAST* time for yet another five years—the power will be in the hands of the people for one day only to bring that change about.

The Mirror will be fighting for change and action.

Operation Apathy Galore ends today.

Half of the people in this country are now aged under 35, and we believe they want to know the facts.

The opening repays close attention. The first sentence seeks the impact of news, a substantial development in public affairs, by compressing words and tenses denoting sudden and irreversible change. 'From today on'—what is special about today is indicated by the near-by block, 'Mirror enters the election'; 'it'—the pronoun without antecedent invites us to consider what will follow as something whole, objectively separate from us, and open to our thorough scrutiny; 'will be known as' places the subject as something finished, now sufficiently dated to be labelled; 'The Tory Plot'—a plot made public is no longer a plot and therefore no longer effective (try substituting 'Plan'); both definite article and capital initials reinforce the objectification started at 'it'—something so officially labelled is sealed off from us; 'That Failed'—the ineffectiveness foreshadowed by 'Plot' is flatly asserted, and the tense relegates it to mere history; the failure has been implied all through the sentence and comes as no surprise; the phrase refers us back to the sentence's beginning—When did it fail?—'From today'—Why?—because 'Mirror enters the election'. Thus the article starts with two statements. The surface one is that the Tories have been plotting, the sign of a party both devious and worried; the latent, stronger one is that the plot has been foiled by the entry of the *Mirror* into the arena. From any pretence to beguiling us the Tories have been removed, set as an object against our picture of ourselves; in that picture the *Mirror* occupies not a participant position (as in 1945) but that of holding the ring for us.

The second sentence is less urgent. The *Mirror* has claimed its role, now it can relax a bit and articulate an urbane character. It is one of barely concealed amusement: by its tone we understand again that there is no call for alarm at the plot, or even indignation, since it is not only clearly fixed in the perfect tense but is also fit for supercilious mockery: 'not flattering to the electorate, but . . .

ingenious enough'. We have already heard 'ingenious' in the caption, and by now understand that 'brainy boys' have no place in a General Election; we may infer that honest feeling and plain speaking are the proper currency. The 'electorate' is firmly distanced from the Tories who, having misprised ('not flattering') the people, are now in for a dose of their own medicine of patronization.

Next the *Mirror* confirms itself as an inside dopester. It knows the ways of these men ('a certain amount of winking and nose-tapping') and their vocabulary: 'the order ("the word") was put around . . . "Play it down, chaps".' Readers are expected to recognize the caricature of traditional Tory demeanour, and to respond as they would to a cartoon, laughter reinforcing the recognition of essential, not literal, truth, and affording them a feeling of superiority.

The quotation from the *Sunday Express* serves two purposes. Initially it lends authenticity to the *Mirror*'s picture by providing corroboratory evidence—evidence, moreover, which some readers will know comes from a usually Tory witness. The reference to Fort Knox allows the *Mirror* to introduce the Bond metaphor.

The next paragraph is a digressive joke to substantiate the use of Bond, but its first words ('Some attribute the idea . . .') prepare us for a more serious turn in the tone, when the following paragraph begins 'In fact . . .', and so can lead to more inside-dopster phrases: 'cleverer men than Mr. Amery . . . Sir Alec's chosen mouthpiece . . . a shrewder guess'. The movement to 'the first spokesman in political history to applaud a conspiracy of silence' seems a flabby piece of word-spinning at odds in thought, though not tone, with the self-assuredness elsewhere.

'There was always the risk . . .' carries on the note of patronizing inside dope, but the meaning of the paragraph is a departure from what it follows, has no initial logic of argument. Its oblique function, preparing in the word 'risk' for another rhetorical shift (as 'Some attribute . . .' did), becomes clear when 'But . . .' heralds our approach to the major turning point of the article: 'what the Tories did not anticipate . . .'—they too are apt to gang agley. Not so the *Mirror*, which 'today'—the pseudonews emphasis recurs—can 'bust the plot . . . wide open'. That was the real risk with which the Tories should have reckoned.

The first movement has been completed by a bold statement of the main subject, the *Mirror*'s role in the election, and now the key has to shift to accommodate a new sort of material. The mode used for exposure will not serve for statements of political intention. It is worth pausing to ask why: why is it necessary for the *Mirror* to deploy its apparatus of supercilious tone, caricature, and an extraordinarily extended metaphor from popular fiction, to put across the surface message, 'The Tories have been trying to keep the election quiet but the *Daily Mirror* will not let them get away with it'? What are all the rest of the words doing there? Two answers suggest themselves: tactical—the *Mirror* is inflating a small perception and is not confident of its readers' unsweetened attentiveness or assent; strategic—it needs an occasion for the rhetoric of self-assertion to allow it to carry on its campaign henceforth at a higher pitch ('Mirror enters the election'). Both answers may stand, but the strategic one is surely more important, and it carries an assumption by the *Mirror* that neither itself nor politics is, in the normal, continuous run of things, influential enough on readers to serve during a General Election.

Now the *Mirror* has the centre of the floor it can appear to address the Prime Minister with pride ('There will be no Apathy Galore in this newspaper, Sir Alec') and arrogance ('Sorry, Alec'). The bold, blobbed paragraphs in between affirm that the *Mirror* is the uniquely active principal in this election, no less: 'all guns firing . . . make it *our* business to alert the British public . . . we're going to wake up the politicians, too, *so that* . . .' Still it feels a need to digress into caricature ('choir of yes-men') and, again, to revert to piling menacing emphasis on its own credentials: 'Let there be no doubt, none at all . . .' The grandiose inversion, 'where stands the Mirror', is a new and odd tone here, perhaps felt necessary to usher in the first statement of solemn principles, all before having been manoeuvres. It is a grandioseness that was very occasionally heard in the *Mirror* as 1945 election day approached; again, perhaps the *Mirror* assumed that readers expected a few notes of high pomp at a time of national decision.

Three beliefs are now set forth, serving the theme of the ruled (young in spirit) *v.* the rulers (the tired must make way). The tone, which the preceding grandiose credentials have built up to, seems to wobble: the grandiloquence of 'WE BELIEVE' thrice repeated and of the closing phrases about 'if we are to maintain in Britain . . .' is deflated by the pedagogic stress on 'BAD' and 'GOOD'. It is as though the *Mirror* feared its peroration might be lost on its readers unless it gave them a wink behind its hand, as if to say 'This is the way you have to talk to politicians, but it's all matter of brass tacks really'. The concern for the future welfare of the Tory party, lest 'two-Party democracy' atrophy, plainly indicates that the *Mirror* was not bothered, nor expected its readers to be bothered, about the parties' policies, only about their efficiency. Neither Labour nor Tories, here nor often elsewhere in these *Mirror*s, are identified as representing a sectional social interest in *policy*, but only in the question of present zest *v.* present tiredness. The *Mirror* is 'fighting for change and action', as it says at the end of this splash, for a change in the rulers' style, not their philosophies. Even when, on October 1 and 12, the paper attacked family and educational privilege in the outgoing administration, it aimed at named ministers, and did not argue, as it had in 1945 and 1955, that the whole Tory party might stand for privileges not shared by most *Mirror* readers. In the present article, when Tories are enjoined to 'build a new philosophy' the phrase is left without meaning, merely 'with relevance to the hurrying years in which we live'. In personnel, not philosophy, is where the *Mirror* locates the Tory malaise on its own evidence; there is nothing philosophically wrong with Edward Heath on October 9, that 'dynamic and progressive personality in the Tory party of today'.

In the repetitious paragraphs describing the onset of 'confusion and exhaustion' in the Government is heard again the note of the shrewd inside dopester: 'men of the calibre of . . . the more thoughtful of the top Tories know it . . . The Victorian big-time politicians never . . .' The phrases 'ever since the time . . . all the time . . . too long . . . need a rest' are further demands for change, change for its own sake: we are just plain bored with the same old faces, not particularly critical of them. The *Mirror* appeals to the taste for novelty in the 'new voters of 1964' and to traditional British grumbling about incumbent politicians in older voters. No more than that. There is nowhere the *Mirror* wants to go, but it wants to go anywhere faster.

The passage quickens its tone to end on 'eager for the spur and challenge of power'. The word 'power' hangs with us for a moment, while the article is punctuated with a lead and drop capital. It is a word we have heard twice before in the last 100 words. Is that what the *Mirror*'s aspirations for Labour amount to: power, not justice? If the question seems trifling, and we are told that power is the prerequisite of justice in parliament, we may nevertheless ask why the *Mirror*, which has always thought so much elementary political education necessary for its readers, took that for granted. And the word 'power' is used again, more questionably, in the next paragraph, where the context is precisely that of a little political instruction to the reader, the pedagogic 'FIRST . . . LAST' recalling 'BAD . . . GOOD'. After the litany of 'It is time for a change' the *Mirror* assures us that 'power will be in the hands of the people *for one day only*' (an advertising slogan). That may be realistic, but it is a disobliging definition of parliamentary democracy from the most

popular newspaper in the country, and is at least open to the interpretation that elections are about politicians and power, not
policies and social justice.

The last sentence of the feature, underlined for emphasis, touches
again on the theme of youth and the *Mirror*'s vow to serve them. (Is
it, incidentally, unusual for half of a nation to be 'now aged under
35'?) An immediate service is promised at the foot of the article by
a block that reads, 'TOMORROW: The deathbed repentance'.

'From today on' the *Mirror*'s own performance is what it will
expect to interest readers most. The 'tranquillizer plot' is adventi-
tious, a convenient occasion; the intentions and beliefs are expressed
in such a way ('WE BELIEVE ... WE BELIEVE ... WE BE-
LIEVE') as continually to return our attention to the holder of the
beliefs rather than the beliefs themselves; and the description of
Tory tiredness is at least in part an opportunity for the display of
inside dope. It is not necessary to deny all political intention in the
article to conclude that, starting from a headline that trades on the
paper's own myth, the syllogism of the *Mirror*'s primacy is the heart
of the feature.

The splashes that followed that first one shared its rhetoric, and
its elaboration of an image that, like Guy Fawkes, will at once be
destroyed, so that the destruction becomes the message. Question
marks proliferate over the days—Is this the Promised land? Just
how mad are we? Are you going to be taken for a ride *AGAIN*? The
Mirror answers itself in slogans—Time for a change. This election
is about people. Give your verdict! It is a sealed and self-fulfilling
model of communication.

Only a few of the splashes (except of course the one by Heath)
departed from the model. 'This election is about people,' on October
5, was illustrated by pictures of pensioners captioned with such
phrases as 'Still smiling at 73', 'Ain't she neat?', 'Knitting for some-
body', 'Takes a lot to get Walter Bacon down.' These are some of the
'men and women who are on everybody's conscience during this
election campaign. The 6,000,000 old age pensioners.'

> Their plight is a scandal and a national shame. How can
> anybody whose living standards have improved over the years
> have an easy mind while the pensioners remain deprived?
> *How dare any Government babble about an 'affluent society' while*
> *more than a million pensioners are forced to exist on National Assistance;*
> *and while probably a million more are on the bread-line, but too proud*
> *to apply for National Assistance?*

The Tory record is assailed, and particularly Douglas-Home's televised reference to a possible increase in the pension as 'a donation'. 'The Prime Minister, cold as charity . . . What is this haughty aristocrat yattering about? . . . It is wretched and revealing.' Labour's promise of action on pensions is welcomed. What is striking about the short text, compared with the other splashes, is that at every point its rhetoric is spliced with facts and figures. The *Mirror* felt no need to invent fantastic conversations, reach for remote and colourful names or pompously label its facts 'Fact No. 1', etc. Consequently it has a drive, a pressure of indignation, that the others never have, and which is dissipated only in the manipulating sentiment of the captions. The reason may chiefly be that the plight of old age pensioners was widely acknowledged to be shameful. A lesser, but significant, reason may be that the *Mirror* was considering an identifiable section of the community, which had a clearly defined collective interest in politics. For once the communication model was not sealed, and needed no hard-sell technique; at least six million people were known already to be interested, and they could be addressed accordingly. (Any explanation that accepted the *Mirror* as the unquestioning champion of the socially deprived would have to explain why other large sections of the community, such as coloured immigrants, were given no coverage at any time in the election: although earlier the paper had attacked the 'outrageous' Immigration Act of 1961.) Support for this reason is available in the October 14 'Election Shock Issue' where, among pages typically modelled on selective advertisement, certain features stand out in their unostentatious confidence.

'Top people, too, are voting Labour' on October 8 is a straight exploitation of what a sociologist would consider as reference-group theory. The top people are A. J. Ayer, Alan Sillitoe, Iris Murdoch, Humphrey Lyttelton, Lewis Cohen, Annie Ross, Michael Ayrton. Sir Jock Campbell and (the largest portrait) Dame Peggy Ashcroft. Each is briefly labelled: 'Top jazzman', 'Our greatest Shakespearean actress', 'Wykeham Professor of Logic', 'Painter and critic (you've seen him on the TV programme "Monitor").' The thinking of each is expressed in quotations of between four words ('I will vote Labour' —Iris Murdoch) and forty. 'THEIR REASONS ARE INTRIGU-ING' says a subordinate headline, and many of the reasons are repeated in large type. Of all the splashes it comes nearest to arguing the case *for* Labour, and it cannot be said to come very near. Six artists, two businessmen and one of our better-known professors: it is not the sort of reference group one would have predicted for *Mirror* readers, to authenticate their inclination to vote Labour by showing them that it is socially all right, or possibly to tap the old working-

class respect for 'brains'. The same use of reference groups was made
in a non-splash feature on October 14, which began, 'One of the
remarkable aspects of this election is the support Labour is drawing
from journals and from famous people the public would not expect
to be on Harold Wilson's side.' Exactly: although the subsequent list
includes such men as the Bishop of Woolwich and Richard Hoggart,
both of whom would surely have been rated Labour in 1964 by, say,
readers of *The Times* or *Guardian*, the *Mirror*'s structure of society did
not allow its readers to expect 'famous people' to be politically like
us, the readers. Political views were assumed to be a function of class
or status. Fitzgerald: 'The rich are different from us.' Hemingway:
'Yes. They have more money.' The *Mirror*, except Cassandra, would
have been on Fitzgerald's side.

Marjorie Proops's article is the straightest, most pugnacious
eloquence in all the splashes.

> But when I contemplate the three or four million who still,
> in 1964, have to trudge down backyards, or share squalid out-
> side lavatories with countless other citizens—I am over-
> whelmed with scorn for you [Sir Alec] and the rest of the never-
> had-it-so-good brigade.
>
> *Has your Lady, Sir Alec, ever had to lug hot water to a tub in the*
> *kitchen to bath her young? Or herself? Or you come to that? Ever had*
> *your back scrubbed in a bath in the kitchen? . . .*
>
> The trouble with you, Alec, is you've seen too many Tory
> ladies in flossy hats beaming at you and clapping their hands at
> your patronising little jokes.
>
> Of course, these ladies love you. You are good for *them*.

None of the gentility of Jill Butterfield's address on behalf of *Express*
women is present here. Clearly, such forthright appeals to prejudiced
images of class are not available to a paper with the range of readership the *Express* presumes to represent. The *Express*'s scepticism about
both parties would in any case have forbidden an outright attack on
either party leader. Proops's article is distinguished from the other
splashes, too, by a postscript which describes, in impersonal prose,
'What Labour will do for women'.

Neither that splash nor any other felt able to talk straight *to* the
readers, as the *Mirror* did in 1945. The 'you women' tone of two
decades earlier implied a confidence in a known audience, with an
understanding about shared experience and values, that was perhaps not available to any national paper in 1964's open society. All
the 1964 splashes sought to be overheard giving a performance,
all seemed to assume that you have to shout, colourfully and

repetitiously, to make yourself heard and understood by such as read the *Mirror*. Political language, like political views, is taken to be a function of social class. It was only a year earlier that Cecil King had written:

> the popular press ... has taught ordinary people to question and to make up their own minds. They are still not very good at it. They still come to decisions emotionally rather than by reason.[5]

*   *   *

On October 2 Cassandra wrote:

> A cynical view of the traditional British General Election is that the Conservatives will not really vote Tory. They will vote anti-Labour.
> And the Socialists will not really vote Labour. They will vote anti-Tory.

By that definition, the entire *Mirror* campaign must be judged to have taken the cynical view. Nor did Cassandra himself diverge much from his paper's line. He too spent his time attacking the Tories, on the grounds of boredom. His rhetoric had an easy certainty denied to the editorial splashes, but often he repeated arguments first made a few days earlier by one of them. Like Pitman and Beachcomber in the *Express*, he disapproved of the opinion polls that his paper gladly headlined on the front page; but otherwise, although the external and internal evidence is that Cassandra had a free hand in what he chose to write, he generally fought in line with the rest of the *Mirror* battery.

What was his function within it? Consider the following item. It is as angry a comment as any that Cassandra made in this period, and happened to be the last in his column on election day itself. It was headed 'Senseless Selfishness'.

> Of all the idiotic strikes, that of the Underground crews was outstanding in its senseless selfishness.
> Hundreds of thousands of Londoners were compelled to hang about in long bus queues or to go on enforced marches.
> I hope these misguided railwaymen got their full measure of warped satisfaction at seeing their fellow workers put to such discomfort and inconvenience.
> These wretched, reckless men defied their own union and by association blackened the Labour Party. They have earned the distaste and contempt of the whole community.

5 Cecil King, article in *Twentieth Century* magazine, Spring issue, 1963.

Because the pressure of feeling is particularly strong, perhaps the item informs us particularly clearly about Cassandra's tone. The first thing we notice is the aggregation of words of condemnation. Within the space of only eighty-five words we read 'idiotic . . . outstanding in its senseless selfishness . . . compelled . . . long bus queues . . . enforced marches . . . misguided . . . full measure of warped satisfaction . . . such discomfort and inconvenience . . . wretched, reckless . . . blackened . . . distaste and contempt.' Cassandra's grievances seem to be: (i) any strikes are idiotic; (ii) this one has brought about unusual inconvenience; (iii) the crews were motivated by malice; (iv) they may prejudice Labour's election chances. It is, in fact, a view characteristic of many Labour voters, including a substantial proportion of union members. And although Cassandra exonerates the men's 'own union', he neither differentiates 'all the idiotic strikes' from those he might think sensible, nor does he mention the men's grievances in this case; apart from the reference to the Labour Party, the item's views are consonant with that large body of the population, especially represented in the *Express*, who distrusted the trades unions at all times. The point, with or without the implied allegiance to Labour, is that Cassandra represented the views of a wide section of the community, perhaps the majority view in most instances. It is an error to depict him as essentially his own man, a non-conforming gadfly.

It was, surely, his tone that created the reputation of nonconformity. He was a brilliant exponent of a traditional tone in English life, that populist eloquence which has at least one root in the non-conformist movement. It is essentially a public voice, one that enjoys a good barney; the most admired exponent has a rich but narrow vocabulary of cajoling irony, sarcastic adjectives, and a ready range of historical instances. Though radical in expression, it may not be so in effect. It is British grumbling raised to an art; no matter what changes may come about it will, like grumbling, always find an object, because its function *is*, as an art, to be enjoyed in itself, and not necessarily demanding actual change. If it is hard to imagine anyone opposed to Labour enjoying Cassandra, it is no less hard to imagine Labour voters provoked to constructive political *thought* by his ready-made indignation. His function in the *Mirror* is that of a proposed everyman, an emblem of that majority of the community the *Mirror* sought to represent. He is the *Mirror*'s saint, quirks and all.

A few more quotations may confirm the description. Supporting George Brown on lowering mortgage rates, Cassandra called the current rates 'usury on a Merchant of Venice scale . . . the cost of setting up a decent home is kept artificially and profitably high by the Tory Government'. Laughing at a series of mishaps endured by Douglas-Home, Cassandra concluded, 'The noble Duke of York marched his men up and down the hill, but at least he hadn't disarmed himself, been late on parade, or mistaken them for someone else.' 'What is wrong with the Tory contenders who seek power next Thursday is that the system has given them the short cut to office and that any Government they may form is flabby and inbred and does not understand a world where unkind hearts and coronets are symbols of impotence, and objects of contempt. Soon they will know.' His constant distaste for humbug was often in evidence. On the Hardy Spicer chairman's remarks about his employees, Cassandra commented 'There is not a lot of difference between being called of "low mentality" or "not of very high intelligence". It is like describing a glass of water as (a) half empty or (b) half full.' In an item about *The Times*'s election leaders, Cassandra wrote, 'It is hard for any hen to lay an egg while sitting on the fence'. Equally, he deplored 'mods-and-rockers heckling'. His view of what behaviour is proper to an election is easy to infer, and Cassandra himself embodies it.

The *Mirror*'s other features can be quickly described. All its cartoons were anti-Tory, and all made use of invented symbols (not just caricature): 'Alec's Ancient Ark', Hogg as an uncontrollable rhinoceros, the octopus of the credit squeeze. Such symbolism may be equated with prose devices like Apathy Galore. Non-governmental Tories were still pictured, as in 1945, as whiskered profiteers, with wives in flossy hats; Us wore caps and headscarves. The cartoonist's use of rhetorical images is, of course, of ancient journalistic lineage, but it is no less the technique of advertisement for all that. Another practice reminiscent of 1945 is that of printing brief Election Profiles, a portrait of a candidate and about 100 words about him; Labour candidates predominated, but a few Tories appeared, usually young ones whose chances of election were in the balance. By such a selection the *Mirror* preserved the semblance of fairness alongside its contention that the top Tories, the old and tired ones, were to blame for the state of government. A weekly column, deep inside the paper, put the Liberal case. Formal editorials appeared seldom, and were used only for non-political comment, about the electoral process: one deplored hooligan heckling, another complained that party television broadcasts were 'DULL', and encouraged boredom among the voters. On October 7, a book by Cassandra about George Brown was reviewed: 'A kindly, likeable, endearing man.' Most of the back page on election day was given to a photograph of Wilson at the age of eight wearing a big cap outside 10 Downing Street; a long caption reported Wilson's father's memories of that trip to London in 1924.

*   *   *

Once it has been said that the *Mirror*'s news pages were unashamedly biased against the Tories, little more needs saying, except on the special topic of Quintin Hogg. The bias is plain on every page, and closer analysis does not reveal any assumptions beneath the bias, beyond the obvious ones: that the *Mirror* desired a Labour victory and did not expect its readers to mind about bias in presentation. The tactics and techniques are familiar ones; the *Express* in 1945 had used the same ones, as well as some uniquely its own. Broadly they were as follows.

Labour politicians, whether advancing policies or attacking the Tories, were given generous space. Any editorializing was aimed at sharpening the impact of the politician's own performance. In headlines and opening paragraphs especially, verbs and adjectives denoting aggression and success were preferred:

> Wilson hits at land highwaymen
> Wilson slams into Amery
> Wilson lashes the faceless ones
> Brown hits back
> Tax scare is exposed

The party spirit was always represented as buoyant. The only note of caution in all these news pages was a single comment in a constituency survey that 'the affluent age is taking a toll of some traditional Labour support'.

Tory politicians were given less space overall (with the exception of Hogg) and were typically represented as defending themselves unconvincingly against Labour accusations, failing to dominate hecklers, or worried by organizational failures or mishaps. Heavy editorializing sought to emphasize those traits, and quite often took leave to doubt or deny the truth or efficacy of what the Tories were reported to have said or done:

> the Tories tried to put over the most blatant commercial . . .
> gave a false impression that . . .
> pretended that . . .
> Tory leaders were severely embarrassed by . . .
> four severe shocks sapped the declining confidence of . . .
> The Tories are becoming appalled at the Prime Minister's
>   failure to make a favourable impact . . .

Headlines sought the same effect:

> Squire Alec is rapped
> Tories looking rattled
> Sir Alec admits it: The economy is in trouble
> 'Slipping' Butler changes tune
> Tory bid to stir up loans row
> Premier backs the wrong man—'Oh dear . . .'
> 10,000 in uproar but Sir Alec talks on
> It's all unreal, says Sir Alec

The Tories were pictured as trying on tactics which the *Mirror* saw through (as in the use of 'bid' above):

> The Conservatives yesterday produced their expected pre-election nationalisation 'scare' . . .
>
> It's out at last . . . that eleventh-hour Tory 'scare' [about tax and insurance] which Labour leader Harold Wilson foresaw a week ago . . .
>
> Tory leaders yesterday were desperately searching for some way to snatch victory. . . . They will heighten their attack on Mr. Wilson and try to convince people . . .

Particular stress was laid on Douglas-Home's lack of impact, compared with Wilson's dominating image. Some examples have been given. Others included:

> Sir Alec is plainly out of his depth . . .
>
> 'Sir Alec is such a pleasant sort of bloke', one Labour supporter told me, 'that it will be a shame to see him disappointed . . .'

On an occasion when Douglas-Home favourably compared his appearance in person against his unprepossessing 'TV "face"', 'A voice cracked back: "I see no improvement."' Even in its splashes the *Mirror*'s presentation of Douglas-Home varied oddly, from the patronization of 'Sorry, Alec' and (on October 12) 'There's something about him that appeals to the Mirror's maternal instinct', to the 'haughty aristocrat, cold as charity' of October 5. Possibly the differing images were calculated to blur his impact.

The election was represented as 'hotting up', despite the Tories' 'Apathy Galore' plot. It may have been true, but it was interpreted as an advantage to Labour:

> *When the campaign opened, Labour's big fear was an atmosphere of boredom—which usually produces a low poll that damages Labour more than the Conservatives.*

But now, with only five days to polling day, there is no doubt that the election is very much alive.

Popular feeling was represented as moving in favour of Labour; again, it may have been true, but it certainly sought the 'bandwagon' effect, which troubled Cassandra among others. All favourable indications were reported, in opinion polls, bookmakers' odds, share movements.

Only a small minority of election news was not perceptibly biased, including news about the electoral process. The *Mirror*'s equivalent to the *Express*'s 'Armchair General' was a computer called Ringo, which merited several descriptions, and the news that red, blue and yellow rockets would be fired from the *Mirror*'s roof during election night to signal constituency gains and losses.

*   *   *

Easily the most salient news story, occupying one-sixth of all the *Mirror*'s election news space in the 16 days before polling, was provoked by Quintin Hogg's remark about 'adulterers on the Front Bench of the Labour Party'. It led four of the *Mirror*'s sixteen front pages in this period, was referred to in a front-page slogan on election day, and was also the subject of lesser articles and a cartoon. The *Mirror* gave the whole story splash treatment, and in a number of other ways too it resembled the splash features.

Essentially, this was the course of the story:

October 7: The front-page headline was 'Hogg blows his top/ He makes a fantastic smear against Labour Front Bench'. The main headline will be recognized as fulfilling an earlier *Mirror* prediction: 'There was always the risk that Mr. Quintin Hogg . . . might blow his top' the *Mirror* had said in its 'Apathy Galore' splash nine days previously. The story reported the relevant passage in Hogg's speech at Plymouth, and his comments afterwards to the *Mirror*'s reporter.

October 8: The front page was led by 'Home must rebuke Hogg, says Attlee'. The story began with a long excerpt from Attlee's 'stern' speech, continued with brief quotations from Wilson's and Lord Blakenham's (Tory Party chairman) reactions to Hogg's Plymouth speech, and ended with a very long excerpt (over 700 words) from another speech Hogg had made in Dulwich the previous evening, in which he defended his own ethical interpretation of his original remark and made a lengthy charge of misrepresentation against the *Mirror*.

October 9: Again leading the front page with it, the *Mirror* headlined the story ' "Halo" Hogg versus the wicked, wicked Mirror', with a caricature of Hogg and his halo. The paper replied to Hogg's charge against it by recalling the facts, recording the reactions of the reporter and the audience at Plymouth, of Attlee, Wilson, and of other newspapers, describing Hogg's political character, and finally rejecting his charge. Stories elsewhere in the paper reported continuing controversy over the original Plymouth remark.

October 12: Half the front page was occupied by a facsimile of a short letter from Hogg to the *Mirror*, under the headline 'Now Quintin Hogg writes to the Mirror and says: "Let's call it a day!" ' Beneath the facsimile was a brief reply to the letter. The halo caricature was repeated.

October 13: On page 2 the headline was 'Hogg blows his top again!/ This time he is insulting the voters'. The report described how Hogg, at a Tory press conference, had remarked that anyone who voted Labour would be 'stark, staring bonkers'. A repetition of the remark was reported the following day.

October 15: A single-column panel on the front page reprinted the halo caricature, with the slogan 'Let us show "Halo" Hogg just how many of us are "Stark, staring bonkers!" Mr. Hogg will be surprised . . .'

Opinions may vary about the ethical and party-political issues raised by the entire incident, but it seems clear that the *Mirror*'s use of it fluctuated well beyond its immediate relevance to the election. After the first report, and the next day's reaction by Attlee, the main story became the *Mirror*'s own bout *versus* Hogg. The paper's tone changed abruptly. On the first day it found the remark a 'fantastic smear'. The next day began no less gravely:

> Speaking with all the authority of a former Prime Minister, Lord Attlee last night sternly reprimanded Mr. Quintin Hogg for his smearing remarks about the morals of the Labour Front Bench.
>
> And Lord Attlee called on Sir Alec Douglas-Home to rebuke his Minister for Education.

Attlee went on to call the remark 'an impulse of a lower school-boy', to comment that 'Public Office used to be considered an honour'—both phrases were echoed in subordinate headlines—and to draw the moral that 'the Conservatives have debased the standard of public life in this country . . . One sees the effect of this attitude throughout our national life right down to the prevalence of crime.' Hogg's charge against the *Mirror* was also serious in tone:

They put that misleading headline on the report knowing that there was nothing in the report to suggest it, and knowing it was the opposite to what I was saying, for the worst possible reasons—to smear my character and try to destroy the chances of the Conservative Party.

I say this to them: They are a millionaire corporation— I am only a man with a limited amount of means, with a family of five to keep.

Let them not rest on their wealth and try to take my character away, and let them come out in the open and fight.

He went on to challenge the *Mirror* to confess its record on libel actions.

But the *Mirror*'s reply to 'Halo' Hogg the next day, starting with the 'wicked, wicked Mirror' headline, put a quite different, much lighter gloss on the affair. It began:

Pleasing all the people all the time is mighty difficult. Pleasing Mr. Quintin Hogg any of the time is impossible.

But the Mirror tries to be a fair newspaper.

THAT is why it published yesterday, at length, the curious attack made upon it by Mr. Hogg ... But now that we have printed HOGG AT LENGTH, the Mirror proposes to reply to his wildest and most vituperative charge—that this newspaper deliberately put a headline on a report of his Tuesday speech to suggest 'exactly the opposite of what they knew I was intending to say.'

Later in the article it had this to say:

Mr. Hogg is a barrister, trained to select his words with care. Lord Attlee, also a barrister, denounced what Mr. Hogg said as a railing accusation made by a man who had lost his temper, an outburst that calls for an appropriate rebuke.

Basically, Mr. Quintin Hogg is a sincere and serious person with academic qualities of great distinction. But there are, regrettably, moments when he *DOES* blow his top. Just as clowns yearn to play Hamlet so Quintin McGarel Hogg occasionally plays the clown.

Examples of Hogg's public 'clowning' followed. Finally, the *Mirror* gave its answer to Hogg's challenge about libel costs, which 'will woefully disappoint Mr. Hogg.'

The October 12 front page was still further removed from gravity. Hogg's letter is friendly and informal, ending 'Shall we call it a day?

There are more important issues to discuss. Anyhow, it's my birth-day.' By printing the letter in facsimile, the *Mirror* adds to the levity, and its reply ends:

> The Mirror is happy to CALL IT A DAY—and wishes Mr. Hogg a happy 57th birthday! The Mirror will, of course, con-tinue to deal with the 'more important issues' every day until Polling Day.

The apparent loss of gravity in the incident over less than a week is striking. Whether the 'fantastic smear' view or the closing friendli-ness is thought more appropriate, they can hardly both be. It is one thing to start an argument in righteous anger and end by shaking hands; it is surely another publicly to raise issues of politicians' morals and end in arch birthday messages on the front page and the promise 'of course' to continue to deal with the 'more important issues'. Either the *Mirror* did feel as shocked as Lord Attlee, whose speech it used to lead its ethical criticism, in which case its climb down to mutual joking with Hogg was very abrupt forgiveness; or it recognized from the outset that in the hurly-burly of an election a volatile character like Hogg was prone to make ill-advised ripostes, which were fair game for creating a stunt. If the latter was true, the *Mirror* was hiding behind Attlee's stern figure, not taking him seriously but only looking for polemical advantage in embarrassing the Tories. By adopting first one posture, then the other, perhaps playing it by ear from day to day, it seems that the *Mirror*'s real interest was that its role in the election could be aggrandized. The aggrandizement was initiated by Hogg's challenge, but there were other means of answering the challenge than the treatment chosen by the *Mirror*. The emphasis on the paper's own performance in the bout elaborates its claim to a privileged role in the election: as a chivalrous defender of public ethics it will not fail to tell the people all they ought to know, but as a basically good-natured and mature paper it knows that politicians are not to be taken too seriously.

*   *   *

There are superficial continuities in each paper from 1955 to 1964. The *Express* again assumed in its readers a consensus of opinion that the maintenance of private prosperity was the main issue and, albeit marginally, opted for the Tories. The *Mirror* again assumed its readers were impatient to see new, younger blood in the govern-ment, and represented the Tories as too attached to privilege and Old-Boyism to supply it. The *Express* felt that the most impressive leader was not in the Tory party. The *Mirror*, which had sought to 'tame' the Tories in 1955, now concentrated on their 'tiredness'. Put in those terms, both papers can be seen to have conducted in 1964, as in 1955, a debate about Conservatism. Socialist policies as an alternative were not more than passingly considered in either paper in either election.

That arresting consensus about aims, leaving only men and methods—or style—as a field for debate, may well have closely reflected the politicians' own views. Economic growth, which Blumler and McQuail[6] suggest was 'virtually what the 1964 campaign had been about', was not, certainly, the sort of issue to arouse ideological dispute between the Tory and Labour parties in the 1960s; Wilson's campaign slogans about 'purposive' government were free of socialist nuance. To describe the papers' attitudes to their readers, then, may in effect be to describe the politicians' own 'pragmatism' (to use another word Wilson favoured).

If that is the case, a number of explanations are possible of the stress in each paper on performance. First, in the absence of substantial policy disputes, politicians themselves would emerge as the locus of apparent conflict, and therefore of news interest: an explanation that especially fits the *Express*. Second, the papers would feel some obligation to dissociate themselves from the politicians' performances, to assert their own distinctive estate: if at the political level performance, not substance, was foremost, then we would expect the effort of dissociation to express itself in a counter-emphasis on the paper's own performance, as especially in the *Mirror*'s case, together with a qualifying scepticism towards the politicians, who in a certain sense would be the paper's rivals.

To those explanations, which do fit the analysis of the two papers, should be added a third factor, television. No longer the novelty it was in 1955, television may have effected (or been assumed by the papers to have effected) a profound alteration in popular attitudes towards politics and elections. To the voters, politicians were far more familiar as performers through television appearances than they ever could have been through pre-TV hustings. But the medium intrinsically favours a quite different style of performance from hustings oratory: a cool style, to use McLuhan's term. Furthermore, the experience of having a politician talk directly to you in your sitting-room tends to restructure political cognition, making it more private. Those two effects—cool persuasion, privatized judgements—take place among a network of other pressures on the voter, and will vary in their importance roughly in proportion to his initial degree of interest in politics; but there is much evidence in Blumler and

6 op. cit.

McQuail's study that for a majority of voters television was the principal channel of electoral participation, and for such voters the cool and privatized propensities could be described as altering electoral experience in the direction of 'consumer' politics, away from the collectivist experience encouraged by the hustings or other communal exchange. Whether or not that argument holds water, it seems that both papers accepted it; that they did is a sufficient explanation of their behaviour in the 1964 election.

It would preclude the *Express* from elevating another Laski, Churchill or Bevan figure: white heroes and black villains are incompatible with the cool realities of a television appearance. (The *Express*'s 'secrecy' image of Laski *et al.*, in 1945 could not have survived their being interviewed on TV.) In the 1964 *Express* Jill Butterfield, we have seen, thought that women

> will not be very impressed by the platform orator who is not prepared to listen afterwards, in private perhaps, to the kind of question that cowardice, self-consciousness, or incoherence prevents us asking publicly.

'In private, perhaps'—as in the privacy of the sitting-room.

The *Express* was pressed by its consensual assumptions about the parties and the electorate to seek its news in politicians' performances; but such 'platform orators' must, in a cool TV age, be regarded sceptically, as performers, symptomatic actors-out of the election rivalry. Even if any substantial policy were argued in such performances, it would have been pre-empted by last night's TV news, television's more obvious effect on the papers. The election process itself, the background of human-interest stories and organizational gossip, is more prominent in the 1964 *Express* than before for the same reason that show-business columns have always been popular: to give us the feel of the 'real' human life—the 'personal touch', the 'human drama', in the *Express*'s own words—that goes on behind all the role-playing and entertaining when the spotlights are turned off. It is, in a way, another response to television, which, especially during an election, can seldom show us politicians other than in their spotlit roles.

Amid the cool scepticism and neutral gossip, however, the *Express*'s Opinion column sought to reassert the part the press in general had historically played in pre-TV elections, and its own traditional identity. The vehemence with which it did so might be attributable to the *Express*'s conviction that 'far too much time, far too many words, are being spent on trivial issues'; alternatively, it might be a neurotic resentment of the assumed fact that most voters were now in the pocket of television, and less amenable to newspaper rhetoric. 'Neurotic', in its clinical sense, is not an unreasonable description of the striking disparity between the self-conscious assertiveness of the Opinion column and the cool audience assumed everywhere else in the *Express*'s tone for reporting the election. A resentment of television's cool privatization would also help to explain the prominence given to hecklers in the reporting. The *Express*'s picture of them was a little ambiguous Though sometimes shocked by their importunacy, the paper could, perhaps rightly, have sensed in them a reaction against the new, cool style of elections, and felt a sneaking affection for such as went on behaving as on the old hustings.

The *Mirror*'s response to the new, cool scene concentrated much more intensely on its own identity. Whereas the *Express*'s Opinion column occupied only some 6 per cent of its total election coverage, the *Mirror* spent more than half its coverage (52 per cent) on splash features and its bout with Hogg, in both of which the main function was self-assertion by the paper. Where the *Express* dwelt sceptically on politicians' performances, the *Mirror* was, rather, intent on rivalling those performances with its own. Its modes of address, comparable to those of commercial advertizing, treat the reader-voter as a private consumer, an object of persuasion by emotional manipulation, not by reasoned argument. The product offered for consumption is the *Mirror* itself: inside dope in a package of mythology about its own history. Only secondarily was that assumption of political authority converted into seeking support for Labour. The *Mirror* was as aware as the *Express* of television—'those rude and crude fellows who ask the awkward questions'; 'the Tory Blood-and-Thunder Brigade (they're the same, confused, weary Cabinet Ministers you've seen on TV)'—but, perhaps because of its clearer party preference, was much less passive in accepting that the cool mode would prevail among its readers.

Conspicuously absent from either paper was the reader's voice. The voter has vanished, except for the unruly heckling fringe (who were often too young to vote, anyway). It is not simply that readers' letters and stories played scarcely any part in the *Mirror*—that loss had occurred by 1955—or in the *Express*, where they never had, but that compared with previous elections there was notably little 'missionary' reporting, of the sort that tells us what 'the ordinary man' or the 'average voter' is thinking, in 'typical' or 'marginal' constituencies. Both papers have an ivory-tower remoteness from the actuality of their readers' daily lives or mood.

Instead of a voter hearing a candidate on the hustings, we have arrived at a public opinion poll addressed by party spokesmen on television. Instead of newspapers seeking, in various ways, to mediate between politicians and public, we have one paper that seeks to rival the power of the new medium by appropriating to itself the rhetoric of consumer persuasion, and another that mostly stands outside the whole argument and comments on it, like Apemantus, as a 'dog-fight'.

The controlling assumptions about politics as a mode of social action, about readers as voters, are those of atomization, privatization, and alienation. The shift, continuing that between 1945 and 1955, is still deeper into a view of political choice as a matter removed from community and reciprocal argument; now it is to be engineered by competing, one-way appeals beamed directly into the private, family-sized consumer group. Whether prosperity or television was more responsible for the picture of a consensual politics in the 1960s, it is certainly over that picture that both papers sketch their appeals.

6

WILLIAM HICKEY:
THE CHARMED SPECTACLE

The mass of the English people . . . defer to what we may call
the *theatrical show* of society. A certain state passes before them;
a certain pomp of great men; a certain spectacle of beautiful
women; a wonderful scene of wealth and enjoyment is displayed, and they are coerced by it. Their imagination is bowed
down; they feel they are not equal to the life which is revealed
to them . . . Courtiers can do what others cannot. A common
man may as well try to rival the actors on the stage in their
acting, as the aristocracy in *their* acting. The higher world, as
it looks from without, is a stage on which the actors walk their
parts much better than the spectators can. The play is played
in every district. Every rustic feels that his house is not like
my lord's house; his life like my lord's life; his wife like my
lady. The climax of the play is the Queen: nobody supposes
that their house is like the court; their life like her life; her
orders like their orders. There is in England a certain charmed
spectacle which imposes on the many, and guides their fancies
as it will.

—Bagehot, *The English Constitution*

UNDISCIPLINED by news, a gossip column is free to articulate
an informed but informal personality. It allows the paper to
suggest the company it keeps, its reference group, 'a selective microcosm of the newspaper's social universe'.[1] Its function is beautifully
described in Bagehot's 'charmed spectacle'. It may offer the reader a
'theatrical show', a style of life to contrast with his own and 'guide
his fancies'.

At the height of 'never had it so good', especially just after the
1959 election, the *Express*'s gossip column, William Hickey, offered
a 'charmed spectacle' so homogeneous in its characters, and constant in its concerns, that it serves as a valuable microcosm of how
the paper at large regarded social change. The *Mirror*'s gossip was
far more contingent upon the daily news, and to that extent less
free in its choice of actors, less 'pure' gossip. There remains, of course,

1 Stuart Hall, 'The World of the Gossip Column', in *Your Sunday
Paper*, ed. Hoggart, University of London Press, 1967.

a degree of selectivity in which news-actors the *Mirror* will choose to gossip about—the chummy, classless world of entertainment is predominant—but, in comparison with Hickey, no 'play' is consistently acted out, nor is there an enduring, named 'author'.

Why does the *Express*, but not the *Mirror*, offer a daily 'charmed spectacle' quite separate from anything happening in the news world? An examination of the Hickey column in late 1959, and some comparisons with the column a few years earlier and later, will help to answer the question.

A regular reader of the Hickey column in 1959 is soon caught up in a web of interacting people and families who populate the column and whose links, surroundings and activities accumulate in the mind. Sometimes Hickey himself makes the connection: 'One family affair follows another in the Elwes chronicle ...', 'As I said the other day, Lady Pamela Mountbatten...', but more usually he reports the latest story in isolation and leaves the rest to the reader. Some stories seem so insubstantial as to be meaningless unless they form parts of series. For instance, there is a sequence of snippets about the Duke of Norfolk's new house which, though intelligible by themselves, are scarcely of interest unless a story about the duke giving up residence in his castle, which appeared a few days previously, stirs in the reader's memory. Most series of stories involve more than one person; whole genealogies are constructed over a period of time, and even within single stories Hickey often mentions other members of the family, or social connections, who spread and place the main character's status and enhance the sensation that the Hickey world is indeed small. Closed, too; except for subsidiary characters in a service relationship to the main actor, the links are always with people of a 'higher' social status, or at least equally exalted. The subsidiary characters are often tenuously connected, and occur only as a name, or list of names. Sometimes the names add little more than their titles, since the people are completely unknown except as links in the column's network.

The Lady Pamela Mountbatten engagement story is a good example of the type of chain reaction that Hickey uses to people his column:

> On Sunday morning, Mr. Hicks went to the service with the party from Broadlands at Romsey Abbey. In the Broadlands pew were David and Lady Pamela, Countess Mountbatten, the Queen of Sweden, who is Lady Pamela's only surviving godparent, and the Duke and Duchess of Mecklenburg.
>
> After the service they were all taken on a tour of the abbey.

Although no decision has been announced, it is possible that Lady Pamela will want to marry in Romsey Abbey. Her elder sister, Lady Patricia, was married there to Lord Brabourne in 1946.
The Queen, then Princess Elizabeth, and Lady Pamela were bridesmaids.

The list effect is increased by the practice of printing names in bold type when they are first mentioned.

Hickey draws on few groups. Some also inhabit the remainder of the paper—royalty, Cabinet ministers, Miss World competitors. There are others whose ordinary activities would not normally be news, who are national public figures only by virtue of the daily jottings and speculations of such as Hickey (and they may have no public existence in other gossip columns, since each paper has its own gossip population). There is no evidence that gossip confers news status outside the column on, for instance, Viscount Emlyn, '27-year-old heir of Earl Cawdor', or 'diplomat's daughter Caroline Nicholls'. Even allowing for people who may be well known in a specialized sphere, like music or racing, in the first fortnight of November 1959 there were 48 stories in a total of 109 about people whose names would be unknown to the general public.

Both well-known and unknown people recur with Archer-like regularity, as subsidiary characters where they add lustre and emphasize the column's village ethos, and in stories of their own. During the fortnight the following people and their families cropped up more than once: five stories, Duke of Norfolk, Duke of Bedford, Churchill; four stories, Princess Margaret; three stories, Princess Anne; two stories, Mr. and Mrs. Jeremy Sandford, The Gaekwar of Baroda, Mountbattens, Stravinsky, Vladimir Nabokov, Mr. Huntingdon Hartford, Mr. Howard Samuel. Within the web of links and recurrence, Hickey's closed milieu admits the aristocracy and aristocratic connections, wealth inherited or earned, the arts, government and diplomacy, and entertainment. Royalty from anywhere, reigning, deposed or defunct, is Hickey's most natural topic, but otherwise money and aristocracy have the greatest pull.

Apart from their names, Hickey admires in aristocrats a certain freedom and smooth control that, despite his entrée into 'Society', he does not share:

> Lady Munnings is delighted that her difficulties with the transport authorities are resolved.

They have a variety of places to live in or to visit, and as soon as their education has been completed in a recognized manner, at public

school or Oxbridge, they appear to control their own time and
environment on a large scale, to move around effortlessly:

> This week-end Mr. and Mrs. Sandford have left their Battersea
> home for some fresh air in the country . . .

> James Meyer was much fêted at his 21st birthday party in the
> Savoy last night. He has become an important young man in
> the past year. When he had completed his education at the
> age of 20, his father, Mr. 'Leo' Meyer, Britain's biggest
> private house builder, gave him £50,000 and said 'Go to work'
> . . . Young James did. He is now the chairman of four com-
> panies and the managing director of eight.

Inherited wealth may permit the luxury of choosing an untypical,
even eccentric career:

> Police constable Benjamin Colman was back on duty last
> night after playing host at a rather expensive 21st birthday
> party in Salisbury, Rhodesia. Vintage champagne was flown
> in from Paris, foie gras from Strasbourg, salmon from Scot-
> land, and caviar from the Baltic . . . The party cost him £1,000.
> But Benjamin is no ordinary policeman. He is a distant cousin
> of Sir Jeremiah Colman . . . and on his birthday inherited a
> sizeable portion of Colman's mustard millions . . .

No ordinary policeman could presume to enter Hickey's world,
although that world is conjured up daily for the benefit of an
audience that is overwhelmingly ordinary in Hickey's terms. The
column could be seen as representing a shadow society, discrete
from the Welfare State, where inheritances survive death duty,
country houses and servants are not impeached by the humdrum
egalitarianism of tax, and snobbery is not levelled. In short, Hickey
people, at work and play, enjoy a power over their own style of life
undreamed of by other classes. The column's latent function is to
assert, and celebrate, the persistence of such power in the form of a
daily serial.

The power depends, of course, on Hickey's other main interest,
wealth. His occasions for dealing with wealth, property and luxury
are legion. Even if characters are not introduced as wealthy (they
are seldom plain rich), their ease of possession evokes a gilded world.
Money creeps into many stories. Apart from scandal, the arts, for
example, seem impressive mostly when large sums of money are
involved:

Artist Raoul Millais, who gets 2,000 guineas for his pictures, is negotiating with Lord Rhidian Crichton-Stuart to buy his estate in Spain for more than £10,000. Lord Rhidian, uncle of the Marquis of Bute, has moved to a house in Scotland . . .

> Mr. Millais tells me he intends to spend six months of the year there.

That example combines aristocracy and its family links, money, property, the free nobility that can suddenly take off for Spain or Scotland, and the establishment arts.

Wealth, aristocracy or achievement are not, alone, qualifications for entry to Hickey's world; they must give rise to a style of life to which no ordinary reader may attain.

Hickey's preoccupation with aristocratic behaviour is noticeable when he mentions dependent characters by category, or collectively, without names. They usually stand in a service relationship to the main character, whose essential aristocracy they confirm:

> The Duchess of Bedford's move from Woburn Abbey to Burrow Hill Farm, in Surrey, has been delayed for three weeks. She has come upon unsuspected difficulties with the builders.
>
> Because of a shortage of plasterers, work on the cottage by the gate, that will be the home of the duchess's housekeeper-companion and her husband, has been delayed. And obviously she cannot move without her staff.

In that, there is a second stratum of dependent and faceless people, because the builders need the services of the plasterers and the duchess's housekeeper's husband has to follow her to Surrey. Hickey uses such people to prolong the point of the story, inflating an ordinary activity like moving house, but has no interest in their own human lives. They are another indication of a closed world: while the ordinary *Express* reader will have had experience of 'difficulties' with people in a position of authority, such as bureaucrats, traffic wardens, head teachers or the boss, having 'difficulties' with servants and plasterers is an alien concept for most. Like the 'four-poster bed of which she is particularly fond', 'her staff' are another indication of the duchess's privilege and wealth, almost another possession. The naming of parts recurs in many stories: 'her solicitors'; 'the leader of her pack'; 'the railwaymen'; 'the ticket collectors at Liverpool Street station'; 'his stable boys and other tenants'; 'the one manservant at the house'; 'the rest of the servants'; 'the miners'; 'the Customs Officers at London Airport'; 'Mr. Godsal's staff'; 'a nurse was employed'; 'his secretary'; 'his advisers'; 'the estate

H*

bailiff'; 'one of our chauffeurs'; 'with its nanny'; 'the horse, jockey and trainer'; 'the 20 workmen on the site', 'the local police'; 'two champion cyclists'; 'one of the men'. Like the Chelsea pensioners 'standing awkwardly to attention' in the 1945 *Express*, such characters remind us, in their two-dimensionality, of a pack of Happy Families.

The few people in a service relationship to the main character who are named are either themselves professionally eminent, or serve employers so high in Hickey's hierarchy that on anybody associated with them is reflected enough charisma to merit a mention in his or her own right:

> One of his legal advisers, Mr. Billy Rees-Davies, the MP and barrister . . . (John Aspinall)
>
> Governess Katherine Peebles went with her . . . (Princess Anne)
>
> His agent, Mr. Trevor G. C. Evans said last night . . . (Duke of Norfolk)
>
> Colonel John Talbot-Ponsonby, who trains the British team is employed by the Duchess to run her stables . . . (Duchess of Norfolk)
>
> Mr. Peter Stainer, the duke's secretary told me . . . (Duke of Bedford)

Thus, as well as Hickey's absolute scale, each story carries its own hierarchical ranking around the main character. Named subsidiary characters range from very important ones who, as relations or aristocratic connections, provide the reason for the main character's appearance and people the web, to those who simply provide a service. The unnamed groups silently give evidence of the distance which separates them from the other characters, and underpin Hickey's status quo.

Occasionally the main actor in a story is presented without explanation, plain 'Mr. Aristotle Onassis', 'Mr. Noel Coward', 'Princess Margaret', 'The Duchess of Argyll'; a certain acquaintance with the social scene, or with aristocratic titles, is taken for granted, and so reinforced. More usually, Hickey fits the main characters neatly into his cast with brief placing phrases, a shorthand version of readers' expectations, in the same way that by simplification and exaggeration a cartoon cuts out subsidiary points and provides a visual short-cut to quite complex non-visual concepts. Those first few words set the climate of Hickey's world powerfully:

> Impresario Peter Saunders . . .
> Property man Howard Samuel . . .

Artist John Merton . . .
Labour MP Woodrow Wyatt . . .
Author E. M. Forster . . .
Composer Igor Stravinsky . . .
Australian heiress Beth Campbell . . .

The cursory classification into social types, modelled on *Time* magazine, is part of a general tightening-up of the column in the later 1950s; it did not occur in the leisured world that Hickey inhabited in 1954. The lack of 'Mr.' and definite or indefinite articles introduces a hot-off-the-presses, factual urgency that assures us the story will be important. Alternatively, there is a very definite article:

Sir Philip Dunn, the wealthy industrialist . . .
Mr. Hartingdon Hartford, the American chain store tycoon
. . .
Lord Lilford, the 28-year-old South African baron . . .
Mr. Howard Samuel, the Socialist property millionaire . . .
Mr. Gerry Albertini, the 26-year-old wealthy racehorse owner
. . .
Mr. Francis T. Williams, the wealthy racehorse owner . . .

During the fortnight, the only person mentioned with an indefinite article, which Hickey was not ashamed to apply to very important people in 1954, is 'Mr. Stanley Tomkins, a 62-year-old Bournemouth business man', who would not have appeared at all had he not complained about the fishing he leased from the Duke of Bedford.

By introducing his moneyed scene-setters with implied superlatives ('magnate', 'the distinguished journalist', 'the wealthy racehorse owner', 'celebrated author', 'eminent social scientist', 'wealthy industrialist'), Hickey offers us stereotypes of these people and their lives. The 'charmed spectacle' is reinforced.

Hickey's microcosm is closed tighter still by the range of activities. that are permitted, some of which recur again and again. Family occasions—birth, christening, birthdays, engagement, marriage, divorce—occur once a day on average; equally frequent are the occasions of cultured leisure, exhibitions, first nights, and a mystique of publishing ('has decided to hold up publication of his memoirs', 'has completed his second book'). Easily the most prominent activity however, preoccupying 36 of a total of 109 stories, was property transaction: the buying and selling of houses, land, paintings, movement from one house to another, movement of capital by inheritance.

Although wealth may be spreading, and traditional denizens of the column move house, the process is seen not to go too far. The Duke of Norfolk, 'a father of four daughters', is 'worried about running costs' at 'the vast castle at Arundel'. 'Since the duke has an estimated fortune of £5,000,000, these items might seem trivial. But obviously he has decided life would be more comfortable in a modern house.' Any homeliness in the last phrase is dissipated by the revelation that the 'modern house' is, in fact, a

> mysterious dower house which he was building so painstakingly in the parkland half a mile from the castle . . .
> For though it is a lot smaller than his present home, it is sumptuously appointed.

A photograph of the duke sumptuously appointed in Ascot dress is further reassurance to the reader that the old order is not crumbling away.

As royalty is still 'the climax of the play', its every gesture is of potential interest.

> Princess Anne takes a road safety walk for a Brownie test; builds a guy for a bonfire;
> Princess Margaret visits the West Country, lunches with a bishop, and may stay somewhere overnight; is enthusiastic about a film, and the Queen has asked to see it;
> Prince Philip tests a Mini, and sends it back;

Princess Alexandra attends a service for actors.
The reflection of royal glory lights up subsidiary characters:

> Esmond Butler, palace press secretary, writes to the Queen about an engagement; a schoolmaster who taught the Duke of Edinburgh and Prince Charles has gone over to a rival school; the house to which the former nanny of Prince Charles and Princess Anne retired has been sold for a nursing home.

Things do not just happen to Hickey people. The world is planned or can always be manipulated.

> When she first took her mews cottage as her London home, she found the small twin beds inside were not to her liking.
> To the neighbours' astonishment, the four-poster bed, almost half the size of the front of the house, arrived one day from Woburn Abbey. Naturally, it would not go through the door.
> The duchess had the frames removed from the bedroom window.

The bed was hoisted with great difficulty into the room.

Now the duchess has decided she needs the bed at Burrow
Hill Farm, her new home in Surrey. The windows of the mews
house were taken out again, the bed lowered to the street.

The duchess is seen merely to wave a wand, and others will toil
for her. Although there is some sense of tut-tutting over an autocratic
whim, one is left with the feeling that it is a fine thing to be able to
waft an ancestral bed around at will.

People with money, too, are able to have expensive hobbies and
caprices:

> Having bought an idyllic island in the Aegean off the coast of
> Greece, Mr. Stavros Niarchos set about populating it at con-
> siderable expense with a variety of exotic birds and game.

Hickey permits himself a little laugh, because Niarchos had omitted
to check whether the birds were migratory, and many of them
headed off south. That is treated as a rich man's whim, but in a
similar situation on the same day, involving business, Hickey remains
serious:

> Mr. Huntingdon Hartford, the American store magnate, has
> been telling me about his plans for Hogg Island, the beautiful
> place he has bought in the Bahamas. He proposes to turn it
> into the Riviera of the Caribbean.

The feeling of deliberated action, sometimes in respect of quite
trivial ends, is emphasized by the language: 'he proposes', 'set about
populating it', 'Lady Munnings is delighted that . . .', 'But the
duchess has said that she will now be unable to make her move for
at least three weeks.' As well as to the characters' behaviour, this
kind of emphasis adds weight to Hickey himself. It is a genuflection
to the Lords described by C. Wright Mills in his essay on 'Celebrities':

> In Switzerland are those who never know winter except as the
> chosen occasion for sport, on southern islands those who never
> sweat in the sun except at their February leisure. All over the
> world, like the Lords of Creation, are those who, by travel,
> command the seasons and, by many houses, the very land-
> scape they will see each morning or afternoon they are
> awakened.[2]

Hickey's praise is often given to a location. Cannes, the Bahamas,
a stately home or a flat in Chelsea—by the legendary milieu our

2 C. Wright Mills, *The Power Elite*, Oxford, 1956.

'imagination is bowed down'. Hickey environments connote mobility, freedom and play, but also property and status.

The latter is evoked by possessive pronouns, by 'at' instead of 'in', by elaborations of 'house' into 'home' or 'place', and knowing place names: 'Hogg Island, the beautiful place he has bought in the Bahamas'; 'at Eye Manor, her home near Leominster, Hereford-shire'; 'Dunecht, his place in Aberdeenshire'; 'her villa in Capri'; 'The Knightsbridge home of Lord Mountbatten'; 'gone down to Broadlands, the Mountbattens' country home in Essex'; 'their vast family home at Bankhall in Lancashire'; 'his 23-room mansion at Chislehurst, Kent'.

Nobody (except, as we shall see, the renegade Sandfords) lives in a street or road, or an ordinary house. If it is too small to be a home, it is a cottage or mews. Exotic playgrounds are in the minority. Most Hickey stories are firmly set within the British Isles and largely in the Home Counties. The international jet-set alone would not sufficiently feed that sense of tradition, British and hierarchical, which is so permanent in the *Express*. An international financier in white tie and tails cannot command the deference due to a duke in a sports jacket.

A character must be landed, in a shire, square, or legendary coast, must have a milieu that is immediately identifiable, whatever the story is about. The message of 'Inverary Castle—his Scottish home', or 'the new house he is having built above Lake Geneva', is not one of wealth and status only, but of a romantic style of life to 'coerce' us, a mystique of the unattainable 'higher world'. The people who have their being in it are not simply degrees above us in the hier-archy, they are different in kind. That is why a different kind of language from the everyday news columns is necessary to appre-hend them.

To read Hickey regularly is to enter a daily transaction with a 'theatrical show' whose cast, though varying in its names, is as constant and predictable in mythic role-structure as any saga by Galsworthy, any fictitious village like Ambridge. Only in the most parochial sense can the contents of such a column be called news.

The extent to which an activity is 'news'-worthy varies according to the status of the character. For Hickey 'naturals', like royalty, almost anything will serve as a trigger; lesser people must compete for inclusion by behaviour which is relatively more arresting, or by fame elsewhere. The Duchess of Bedford, for instance, is doing some-thing quite ordinary, moving house, but this bland event must be read against a network of previous speculation about her separation from the Duke.

Lacking the impact of news, Hickey has to make the most mundane activity arresting. His technique is generally to twitch our mild surprise at a discrepancy between what we might expect of a character and what Hickey can actually tell us. Thousands of little girls take Brownie tests without benefit of gossip. When Hickey reports that Princess Anne is taking hers it may shake up the reader's deposited sense of how princesses used to behave, and how things have changed. It brings a homely aura to the princess, makes her seem lovely and suburban; but even as we pleasurably exclaim 'Well I never' our sense of her distance from us, her royalty, is reinforced by the very fact that so commonplace an activity has won our attention. Hickey goes on to make it clear that princesses live in a protected environment and do not normally have much opportunity to practise being careful pedestrians. Thus, by emphasizing the adventurousness of taking a Brownie road test, he is feeding the traditional exclusive image of royalty back to the reader. At the same time, a perfectly ordinary event is turned into an occasion.

Few stories have no twitch of surprise. In the fortnight examined there were only four: Stravinsky and Cocteau collaborating over *Oedipus Rex*; two birthdays—Hannen Swaffer and A. E. Matthews; and E. M. Forster leaving for a lecture tour of Italy. It could be that ageing fame commands a kind of respect for the elders.

A story can consist of a succession of twitches. In a story about Lord Cowdray, the point that one of the richest men in the country has received £30,000 in improvement grants from a local authority is repeated four times in slightly different ways. Hickey arouses a feeling of incongruity by the headline, 'The rich Lord Cowdray claims £30,000 to help keep up his estates'. He does not openly criticize Cowdray (a rival newspaper proprietor) but piles on sentences which emphasize his wealth and privilege, and imply discredit on a bureaucracy which allows such a situation to occur. Each succeeding sentence contrasts wealth with grant:

> Some people have been surprised by the revelation that the Duke of Norfolk, a pretty wealthy man, has received Local Government grants of £1,203 to help him make habitable some cottages for his stable boys and other tenants. But the duke's claims are very modest compared with Viscount Cowdray's.
>
> Lord Cowdray is one of the richest men in Britain. He has enormous business interests and vast estates. But he has had more than £30,000 from the Midhurst Rural District Council to help him improve his properties.
>
> As Lord Cowdray said yesterday; 'The great advantage of

these grants is they are outright. There is no question of paying
it back, or of paying interest.'

Surprised

He had just come in from shooting—'about 200; most hens,' he
told me—when I phoned him at Dunecht, his place in
Aberdeenshire.

'I'm surprised I've had as much as £30,000 but we have had
a lot of work to do in the past years putting our cottages and
houses into good repair.

'We're just beginning to see the end of it now', he said.

These grants are made so that house-owners can bring
properties up to modern standards by installing baths, running
water and so on.

Sizeable

Lord Cowdray, chairman of six big City companies and a
director of Lazards, the bankers, owns about 18,000 acres in
Sussex, including a sizeable part of Midhurst itself.

He pays the Council about £4,000 a year in rates.

Such phrases as 'a pretty wealthy man' ('wealthy' is OK; 'rich'
invites disapproval), or 'a sizeable part' have a leisured effect, which
can sometimes seem patronizing; in his use of qualifying words,
like 'quite', 'rather', and 'not altogether', Hickey affects a tone of
upperclass understatement:

> Though it was not so sensationally successful as Mr. Merton's
> portrait of Lady Dalkeith the year before, the picture of Sarah
> aroused considerable comment at this year's Royal Academy
> where it was on show.

> Since the Princess has rather less chance than most girls of her
> age to study roadcraft, the leaders of her pack feared that she
> might find this test tricky.
> But in fact I understand that she has mastered roadcraft
> remarkably quickly.

> But this time, I suspect, there will be no ructions. In fact, I
> wonder whether Mr. Hunter's new work may not pass
> altogether unnoticed.

> One cannot help but be sorry. Only once did I see them not
> quite happy. (Marquis 'has ended his friendship' with a
> model)

It bears, according to Palace gossip, a distinct resemblance to
someone on the staff; but exactly who I am not permitted to
know. (Princess Anne's guy)

In those passages, Hickey creates an air of speculation around trivial
events, lending them the intrigue of a sanctum to which the general
public is not admitted. The air is thickened by Hickey's own intervening presence, the measured insertion of 'I understand', 'I sus-
pect' or 'One cannot help', coming between us and the mysteries of
which Hickey is privileged to show us something (only something).
He remains at a certain formal distance from the people he is
discussing, with a languid precision, rather like a snobbish butler,
to whom it is all familiar but yet who has to remain outside, reporting
on the guests to his minions. He is intrigued by the external symbols
of privilege, knows them and their genealogies, and assumes what is
widely supposed to be their language.

To be able to drawl 'not so sensationally successful as' is one way
of confirming your position with regard to both readers and subject;
another, equally common, is Hickey's use of implied superlatives.
These phrases put him in the position of judging and approving
certain kinds of people, their possessions, ('enormous business
interests and vast estates') and their behaviour, and set him up as an
authority. They also emphasize the point of the story, or a character's
deviation from the expected line, by building up status from a golden
array of its symptoms:

The most luxurious hotel in the town . . .
one of the world's greatest living composers . . .
the most elegant nun in the world . . .
a splendid political career . . .
a person of great discrimination . . .
uncharted expanse of parkland . . .
one of the most expensive belts of Hampshire . . .
the finest costumier, the finest hairdresser, and the finest
cameraman . . .
the vast castle at Arundel . . .

In such phrases there is the flavour of an estate agent's exaggerated
jargon, but the controlling tone is slightly ponderous and precise in
a dated, copperplate way, redolent of old leather and still older
port.

One story about moving house peculiarly reveals Hickey's
assumptions. The main headline is 'Heiress takes job in a sweet
factory at £3 a week', followed by 'She moves with her husband to

£700 house'. These activities twitch more surprise than most, and
are twice given the main story, occupying thirty-four column inches
the first time, and forty-five the following one, out of a possible
eighty-two column inches each day. Between them, the two stories
merit six photographs.

The actors are 'Surrealist writer Mr. Jeremy Sandford, 28, and
his wife, Nell, the 22-year-old daughter of Sir Philip Dunn, the
wealthy industrialist.' (It should not pass altogether unnoticed, as
Hickey would say, that Lord Beaverbrook had a very close friendship with an older generation of the Dunn family.) Both are good
gossip material, for 'At Oxford, Mr. Sandford was the leader of the
smart set'; and in 1959, writers, painters and other artists figure
more prominently on the Hickey scene than more recently. Still, an
heiress is obviously a finer trigger. The Sandfords . . .

> have moved from their fashionable, bow-windowed flat in
> Cheyne-walk, Chelsea, to a block of condemned houses in
> Battersea.

Small photographs of both places illustrate the violation of expected
behaviour, which is emphasized by the descriptive detail of the
Chelsea flat, and the contrasting generality of 'a block of condemned
houses'. A block is where ordinary people live together, undiffer-
entiated.

> Mr. Sandford, whose wife is an heiress and who has hitherto
> lived in impeccable style in one of the most enviable districts of
> London, is now anxious to experience life 'with real people'—
> so he tells his friends.
> His wife, carrying his philosophy to the extreme, has taken a
> job in a local chocolate factory at a wage of £2 14s. a week.
> She works from 1 p.m. to 6 p.m. putting the silver wrappers
> on liqueur chocolates.

The ordinariness of 'a job in a local chocolate factory' stabs a shock
into the otherwise elaborately languid tone: it is written with slightly
raised eyebrows, like a television news reader. There is a questioning
of the Sandfords' motives in 'is now anxious to experience life with
real people—so he tells his friends'; and 'carrying his philosophy to
the extreme' implies condescendingly that they have gone too
far.

At the back of the bland scepticism may be felt a fiercer mockery.
In part it is defensive—if the 'real people' are in Battersea, Chelsea
people are fakes; but perhaps it is still more a Mephistophelian
mockery of anyone who naïvely presumes that he can alter his own

reality even by extreme rearrangements of his way of life. One is
what one is: class will out, no matter what 'philosophy' (in context
the word is disparaging) you fill your head with. On that reading,
Hickey's basic stance is a conservative anti-intellectualism. Phrases
like 'leader of the smart set' and 'fashionable' now take on a pejora-
tive ring: like 'rich' as opposed to 'wealthy', they suggest a lack of
traditional substance. The 'shock area' of plain words is rounded off
by the elaborate precision of innuendo: 'putting the silver wrappers
on liqueur chocolates' is deriding one who goes to such solemn
lengths in the name of an obsessive philosophy.

Hickey goes on to describe and destroy the Sandfords' efforts to
remain incognito, telling us the house number and that

> This weekend, Mr. and Mrs. Sandford have left their Battersea
> home for some fresh air in the country.

As well as providing information of use to, say, burglars, Hickey
characterizes the Sandfords as people who need to escape from
Battersea in search of fresh air, and who are still the kind of mobile,
moneyed people who are able to take a short holiday when they feel
like it. The irony is enhanced by Hickey's po-faced treatment of
'their Battersea home', as though it were a perfectly normal gossip-
column location.

The next sentence illustrates the distance and incomprehension
created between Chelsea and Battersea, and also intrudes Hickey's
own acceptability in Chelsea:

> A friend tells me: 'Nell has not said much to us about her new
> life but it looks as though she is writing a book about the
> working people of London'.

The introduction of subsidiary characters removes Chelsea even
further from Battersea. The comments of a neighbour, Mrs. Violet
Ellway, 'she loves the kiddies. They are never out of her house', are
juxtaposed with those of the Sandford parents, 'I have been to the
house. But I would prefer to say nothing about it.' The cosy willingness of one to talk is thrown into relief by the other's formal refusal;
and while Hickey hardly bothers to introduce Mrs. Violet Ellway he
takes his usual care to set the Sandford parental scene, with 'At Eye
Manor, her home near Leominster, Herefordshire, Mrs. Christopher
Sandford, Jeremy's mother, said . . .' He begins their no-comments
by asking: 'But what do the Sandfords' parents think of all this?',
which prepares us to expect disapproval.

In the last paragraphs Hickey's homework shows us that the Sandfords are theoretically unfit for life in Battersea:

The Sandfords married in 1957. Since Nell's family is immensely rich—her grandfather, Sir James Dunn left a £25,000,000 Canadian steel fortune—it was a suitably smart wedding with a reception at the Ritz.

At Oxford, Mr. Sandford was the leader of the smart set. His rooms were papered in scarlet and gold and his bed, an Oriental affair, was perched four feet above the bath.

But in Battersea he has had to abandon extravaganzas of this sort. His furnishings are very little different from the house next door.

Here again, we find words and phrases corresponding to the earlier 'impeccable style' and 'most enviable districts' which are reserved for the typical behaviour of the gossip-column population. Stretched and qualified phrases evoke a languid privilege until, at the end, Hickey switches from 'an Oriental affair' to a sharp coda: 'But in Battersea he has had to abandon extravaganzas of this sort.' The tone invites us to bark a laugh with Hickey at the deviant Sandfords, who ought to know better.

The main story eight days later was headed 'William Hickey ON THE STREET WHERE THE HEIRESS LIVES' (*My Fair Lady* was 1958–9): 'The Sandfords get their first real taste of low life . . . BURGLARS!' Now Hickey is crowing. Look what happens when people imagine they can move out of their niches in the social scale.

Mr. Jeremy Sandford, 28, the young writer who with his wealthy wife moved recently into a terraced house in Battersea to study how the other half lives, has learned his first lesson. It has not been a pleasant one. His £700 house has been broken into and robbed.

Mr. and Mrs. Sandford were told of this uncharitable example of low life when they returned yesterday from a week's holiday in the country.

Obviously the thieves had heard who the new neighbours were and thought their haul would be a rich one—for 22-year-old Mrs. Nell Sandford is the daughter of Sir Philip Dunn, the immensely wealthy industrialist.

In this 'serve you right' passage, Hickey assumes that the thieves were neighbours, and is inexplicably applying phrases like 'the other half' and 'this uncharitable example of low life' to two-thirds of the *Express* readership. Equally pointed is the formality of 'moved recently into a terraced house in Battersea', which, in the context of 'low life', is loaded with sarcastic class overtones.

Missing were Mrs. Sandford's jewellery, including her engagement ring, her best dress, and the television and radio set in the parlour.

Luckily, acting with commendable caution, the Sandfords had little of their property in the house. The estimated value of the goods stolen amounts to less than £150.

A strange mixture of Battersea and Belgravia! 'Her engagement ring, her best dress' bring the Sandfords down to an ordinary level, her best dress implying that she only has one such. 'In the parlour' condescendingly evokes net curtains and antimacassars.

The next sentence returns us to Hickey-land, with 'commendable caution', 'little of their property'. Clearly, in spite of all, the Sandfords possess the material basis of privilege still, and the ponderous tone is one of approval that they have not forgotten it. For 'Luckily, acting with commendable caution . . .' we should perhaps read 'Really, they have not left Chelsea in spirit'. Mrs. Sandford's alleged comment on the burglary is also the stereotype of a slumming debutante tripping over reality:

'I am terribly unhappy. We had just moved into this area, which we love, to get away from it all and live a simple life . . . and now this.'

As often in the rhythm of a Hickey story, a new twist is introduced right at the end:

They are particularly upset because the new pink bath which they have had specially installed—theirs is the only bathroom in the street as most of the houses are condemned—has been badly scratched.

The idea of a shiny new pink bath where 'most of the houses are condemned' allows us a luxurious frisson, particularly as it had been 'specially installed', leaving the rest of the street to stay condemned and dirty, and envious of the strange new neighbours.

Hickey's stress at this time on people moving house could be a symbolic, unconscious response to a feeling that society was shifting all its traditional structures. When he tells us about someone in 'his place in Aberdeenshire' or 'the beautiful place he has bought in the Bahamas', the effect is to put us in *our* place. The class hierarchy has, till now, been safe as houses. Perhaps affluence is going to enable the new rich to buy their own place? What are the terms of hierarchy then? Faced with that threat, Hickey must assume that there are still things affluence (short of millions) cannot buy: tradition and breeding. These will be the upper class's defence against confusing infiltration by the merely fashionable, the smart set. The Duke of Norfolk may have to move out of his castle, but he still lives unequivocally in his grounds. For the time being, while the situation is delicate, the gravest heresy is not aspiration to upward mobility but voluntary abdication by the upper class. A storm of cruel derision breaks round the Sandfords' heads, especially Mrs. Sandford's—her husband, once 'leader of the smart set', perhaps does not know any better.

It is not simply a question of Hickey commenting on the social scene, however; the key dimension is that he is interpreting that scene to an audience. The point of Hickey's column is not, in the end, his subjects or his remarks, but the postures he invites us to adopt towards them. He is the intermediary between the 'charmed spectacle' and us, the explanatory critic, full of knowingness, whose tone is a ventriloquism not, as in the *Mirror*, of the readers but of the characters. His knowing language pretends to adopt an informed pose of appreciation of the 'higher world'. He lives in that world without being essentially of it, as a critic lives in the theatre; we, the readers, live in a different world altogether. As long as we are content to acknowledge our separateness, the fact of hierarchy, we can enjoy and perhaps even emulate Hickey's poise, model our manners on the upper class; but as much woe betide us as the Sandfords, in their different sin, if we presume to upset the higher world, by seeking entry or, more dangerously, asking *why* our house 'is not like my lord's house'. Gossip is matter for play—the small change of transaction in the global village, permitting us to try on new roles, but essentially confirming status and the status quo, and our acceptance of it.

* * *

There has been a long succession of William Hickeys since Tom Driberg began the column in 1934. For comparison with the main sample, of 1959, the corresponding first fortnight in November 1954 —a likely transition period in the incipient mood of prosperity— and in 1967 were examined, with a briefer look at Hickey still earlier, in November 1949. The table shows the breakdown of main characters by status or occupation in the three later samples.

	1954	1959	1967
Aristocracy	3	38	26
Arts	3	13	3
Diplomatic	5	6	9

	1954	1959	1967
Entertainment	12	7	5
Fashion	–	3	1
Film	4	–	3
Government and Parliament	8	2	13
Heads of State	1	6	4
Military	1	3	1
Money and big business	4	18	14
Oxbridge	1	2	2
Public schools	–	1	3
Religion	–	–	2
Royal Family	5	9	10
Secret Service	1	–	2
Science and medicine	3	–	–
Sport	2	–	–

The most striking feature of the table is the prominence of characters in 1959 and 1967 who are included because of their wealth or aristocratic connections: it suggests a definite need to reaffirm traditional privilege in the full-blown period of 'affluence'.

Newsprint rationing restricted the 1949 column to a weekly appearance, on Fridays. In form it was anecdotal, a collection of some half-dozen stories each complete in itself, quite different from the epic seriality of 1959. The subjects were equally different from the Hickeyarchy of 10 years later: sometimes no titled person at all was mentioned, and when a title did crop up it was because its bearer had earned attention in some public role—Lady Meynell, for instance, was the author of a book on economics. Entertainers and artists were the chief public figures, and Labour Ministers, nearly always disparaged; but often a story would mention no public figure and simply retail an amusing story from, for instance, the law courts. Perhaps a third of the space was filled with Hickey's own reflections on the social scene, as distinct from reporting other people's doings: he visited a crank offering to cure smoking, he discussed the organization of street betting, or argued about who endowed the nightly sounding of the Last Post at the Menin Gate. Of the fierce or fulsome tones of 1959 there was almost no trace; Hickey's voice varied from the mildly ironic to the sniffy, but remained quiet. Apart from his dislike of Labour politicians, it is hard to detect in the 1949 Hickey any strong feelings about the social structure, fear of threats to it or satisfaction with privileges in it.

By 1954, what was retrospectively defined as 'affluence' had made a beginning. Whatever the degree of actual social change, or of changed perception of the class structure, no such change was reflected in Hickey's world; although in his piece on May Day six months later, it has already been seen that he swallowed the affluence thesis, perhaps under pressure for electoral purposes. Mostly he was interested in gadding about town (and Greece and Italy in this fortnight), having a good time, 'champagne corks popping in the background', and telling us about it to brighten our more mundane lives.

> I am glad I did not miss Lord Mayor's Night—his banquet at newly-restored Guildhall. What a genial, fantastic, splendid time we had!

Some of the names in his columns are titled, but many come from entertainment (though none from television; Beaverbrook had not yet bought shares in commercial television, and the *Express* was antagonistic to the rival advertising medium). Considering that it was the year after the coronation, there are surprisingly few mentions of royalty compared with the later years; Hickey's emphasis is on occasions he visited, not gossip he overheard.

The resemblance is to Godfrey Winn, 'dashing' about in the 1937 *Mirror*. Hickey's yardstick in 1954 is not the recent austerity, but before the war, when things British were thought to be universally admired. His mood is not post-war but post-imperial. For instance, in Athens:

> Incidentally, most of the tramway system in this city is owned by Whitehall Securities, one of the interests of Lord Cowdray. It is said that they are painted yellow because that is one of his racing colours. A rather magnificent gesture for 1954!

At home and abroad, he was seeking out the faded remnants of a gracious, established way of life, not as in 1959, preoccupied with change, transactions, 'difficulties with the builders'.

> It was only natural, I suppose, that Lord Jowitt, a former Lord Chancellor, should be travelling down in the same plane as myself. I think the Greeks would be a little disappointed if a plane did not arrive from London with a lord or two.
> It is all a bit old world and crazy. But rather comforting in a Europe where most English people have got used to being treated as poverty stricken.

The mood is often elegiac.

You notice how all these decorations have to be begged and borrowed. The old days when British Ambassadors were rich have gone for good.

Still, in these days of currency restriction, anything that makes you feel an English milord is a good thing.

The English colony that lived here has disappeared with the war and the currency regulations.

No longer are the charming hills along the Arno dotted with pleasant villas where one's maiden aunt lived—talking excellent Italian, painting agreeable water colours, sometimes, alas, falling in love with handsome Italian gardeners—but also, bless their hearts, inviting impecunious young nephews out for a holiday in their Florentine Kensington.

But even if the British Ambassador had to borrow the gold plate from Lord Halifax—'I cannot afford a man to keep it clean'—it is still gold plate and 'it makes a tremendous impression on the Greeks'.

. . . the English are wonderful in treating splendour as an everyday business. Lady Peake's knitting was on one of the sofas.

Americans may be richer, but they do not know how to handle their colonial role with the easy grace, humour and gifted amateurism of the British ruling caste:

It was then I noticed that the whole evening the doctor had not laughed. And then I tried to remember an American abroad who had laughed. Precious few.

Greatness has been thrust upon them. We achieved it. We have taken it as a matter of course.

I think in my heart of hearts I am sorry for the Americans.

Hickey's stance before Americans is a familiar ambiguity in the *Express*. Giles constantly sees them in his cartoons as brash, lacking the ancient (if comic) stability of British tradition, ultra-modern beyond the point of vulgarity; but that push-and-go character is, we find elsewhere in the *Express*, exactly what has enabled Americans to reach a standard of living and self-confident exercise of power that we, with all our tradition and dignity, no longer have.

At home, too, Hickey admires privilege in mufti—laying a foundation stone, 'The Duke strolled in, wearing a casual suit and a blue pullover'.

Often, dashing around his appointments, Hickey has time to give us a friendly nudge. Engaged, for example, in the 'civilized business' of having tea at the Dorchester:

> The waiter asks 'India or China, sir?' I never know which to ask for. It's a far cry from the old days of 'char and wads' in the Naafi.

At a fashion show, the hats are 'delightful—on the models. I wonder what they would like on Mrs. Bloggs?' At other times, he flatters his readers' knowledge of Milton or Gladstone, Spanish ironwork, Ionic columns, or mazarine gowns. He leads us into educated fantasies:

> I have dreamed of the Parthenon, the temple of the grey-eyed Athene, goddess of wisdom, since I was a boy stumbling over my Greek.

Or again:

> It was a day for a long fire, an old-fashioned armchair, magazines, muffins, and dreams . . .
> The things one thinks about, half asleep, while it grows dark and the magazine slips to the carpet.
> I always dream on these occasions of a long, low white house in the country . . .

He goes on to describe the dreamed house in detail. Five years later he was no longer dreaming houses for himself, but celebrating other people's possession of them. Now,

> I could almost see my Salukis being gracious in that garden. But I saw the price instead—nearly £8,000.
> In that one moment I understood the fascination of the football pools.

When people are named in 1954, it is because Hickey has observed them at the occasions he has chosen to write about. No social web is required yet to hold the shifting houses together.

*　　*　　*

According to Christiansen,[3] in the middle of the 1950s Beaverbrook decreed that the anecdotal formula had lost its verve and bite, and that the Hickey column should change:

> When Donald Edgar . . . was hard up for a subject he could make up a dream-sequence of startling imagery. He could

3 Arthur Christiansen, *Headlines All My Life*, Heinemann, 1961.

make the buildings in his beloved Kings Road, Chelsea, talk to him. But one day, Lord Beaverbrook thought that Edgar was stringing it out and that the Hickey column should consist of short sharp paragraphs about important, glamorous people in the news. Edgar and the Daily Express parted; and now I understand at least six people do a composite Hickey column.

It was Hickey thus revamped in 1959, and it lasted throughout the 1960s. By 1967 the column has more pictures and a slicker lay-out, but similar, often identical, characters appear regularly, promoted not by 'the news' but by the quality of their social connections and effortless control of their lives. Big businessmen and captains of industry are more prominent than they were; usually 'rich' rather than 'wealthy', they serve the general *Express* theme of successful enterprise more than Hickey's web. Etonians can become 'jobbing gardeners' and remain only moistened by the scorn that Hickey had poured over the Sandfords' heads. But two changes in the cast are significant.

The first is that fashion and pop have crept in; combined with plenty of photographs of young people they give the column a more youthful look on first sight, though the actual number of stories about young people (apart from brief captions) has not much increased. Hickey is interested in pop partly because of the cash involved and, consequently, the apparent emancipation of pop stars into the effortless 'charmed spectacle'. He also acknowledges them as 'style-setters', which is the *Express*'s usual reason for interest in the young (unlike the *Mirror*'s vague sense of them as representing a political pressure). It cannot be said that Hickey finds it easy to comment on 'export booster Twiggy' or 'that million pound business, the Beatles' in any but his most conventional terms. Their family webs are at once as important as Lord Cowdray's. Paul McCartney's brother, a member of the Scaffold group, qualifies for a story to himself, as does 'Twiggy's Dad'. One of four prominent stories about the Beatles, concerning the cartoon film *Yellow Submarine*, is almost wholly about money, but ends by picturing the Beatles as 'enjoying the whole thing enormously'. All the other Beatle stories deal with Paul McCartney. One, in which he has set out for Nice without a passport but 'talked himself past the police', shows him to possess the ability to go where he likes at any time. Casually, 'he plans to spend a couple of days in the South of France shooting scenes for a television film.' With his tongue in his cheek, Hickey cooks up an anecdotal, old family retainer feeling in the Twiggy story.

Now let me present Twiggy's bodyguard.

I call up Tokyo to speak to Ted, the flower seller from Knightsbridge.

Between the frail figure of export booster Twiggy, 18, and the milling hordes of admiring Japanese this month has been the protective arm of wiry Ted 'Monk' Adams, 37, the ultimate in flower-power bodyguards.

Ted, a burly former boxer, is well-known to thousands of London shoppers as the man who usually sells them flowers outside Knightsbridge Underground station.

Hickey talks about 'the family flower and newspaper pitch' in the same voice as 'the family estate'. The mock-heroic effect is to re-assure us that Twiggy and her manager, despite commercial success, are still just as ordinary as when they were 'working down the Portobello Road'.

Interestingly, the other significant new category in 1967 is members of the Labour Government, featured more prominently than Macmillan's were in 1959, though in a special context: Hickey takes up the eternal *Express* theme of having a crack at 'Socialism'. Labour MPs are easily caught on the favourite hook of untypical behaviour. In Hickey's obdurate structures of wealth and position, the Labour MP who is becoming the master of a hunt is untypical. Even Nureyev is considered to have Socialist associations sufficient to make it seem remarkable that he occupies a £45,000 house.

The whole column was given to George Brown after a much-publicized outburst. Headed 'The George Brown Show after the reviews, resuming normal service', Hickey goes out of his way to show us an ordinary man who is plainly unsuited to the official splendour in which he finds himself.

Grey, dreary and unencouraging. Those were the conditions outside when George Brown woke in his bedroom at the Foreign Secretary's elegant official residence, No. 2, Carlton Gardens, yesterday. It was soon after 7 o'clock on the morning after the night of his outburst at Lord Thomson's Savoy dinner.

His wife Sophie was there as her husband read through the morning newspapers and breakfasted before one of his four private secretaries came in with his itinerary.

Mr. Brown has great powers of early morning recovery. He can get stuck into work however late and testing the previous night has been.

'The Foreign Secretary's elegant official residence . . . breakfasted . . . one of his four private secretaries . . . itinerary . . . testing'—they are all words which convey the dignity of the office in traditional Hickey terms, the conditions readers might expect for an important minister. But do important and dignified Foreign Secretaries 'get stuck into work'? And should they need to recover on a 'morning after the night'? Even though Hickey gives all the details of an arduous day, the tone minimizes Brown's own part and work:

> There was an hour of sorting through State papers until 10.15 a.m. Then George went down to the St. James' Park door of the Foreign Office building to meet King Hussein of Jordan. He good-humouredly went out into the rain to pose for pictures with the king.
>
> Then George explained he was off to meet President Cevdet Sunay of Turkey on No. 2 platform at Victoria station. It was noon.
>
> He was still in a lounge suit to greet the President with the Queen, and Prince Philip in field-marshal's uniform. There was time for a sombre Harold Wilson in morning coat to talk to George on the red felt carpet.
>
> It was one of those rare days when he didn't have an official political or private lunch to put the temptation of talking too much in his way. He went off on his own.
>
> Back to his gilded ornate office for more paper-signing and seeing minor officials.
>
> At 4.15 he had a courtesy call from Argentine's Minister for Economic Affairs, Dr. Krieger.
>
> George had to absorb a lot of facts and figures. The doctor left—and it was back to writing his signature again.
>
> Then he had to get home to change for the Queen's State banquet at Buckingham Palace for President Sunay.

A host of belittling phrases and innuendo ('the temptation of talking too much'—i.e. drinking) contrast with 'his gilded ornate office', 'minor officials' and 'Prince Philip in field-marshal's uniform'. Wilson is in 'morning coat', but poor old George, 'still in a lounge suit', cannot ever wear the right clothes for the occasion. He was, the hint is, on the carpet in more senses than one, before 'sombre' Wilson. 'Then George', 'Then George explained', 'he went off on his own', 'more paper-signing', 'George had to absorb a lot of facts and figures', 'it was back to writing his signature again', 'Then he had to get home to change'—it all sounds like a small boy pretending to do these things but doing them not very well, making a bit of a mess of them, and wanting to be naughty: a children's story told deliberately slowly, and toned down for the part. The repetitions of 'Then' suggest a random series of actions, not properly controlled. 'Writing his signature' could be a game.

The column implies quite plainly that the only people sure to be fit for positions of high responsibility are those who are born and bred to it. There will be exceptions—we remember the *Express*'s qualified admiration for Wilson in the 1964 election—but that familiar *Express* hero, the man who through free enterprise makes a spectacular career or fortune (such as the pop world's meteors) will, it seems, reach the top of his curve only to find himself overcurved by qualities he can never attain. Enterprise is specialized: Foreign Secretaries should be diplomatic with visiting VIPs, pop stars concerned with their fans, and millionaires with their business enterprises. They may all share the luxury of wealth, but their talents can seldom be transplanted, and the high responsibility of government is safely entrusted only to those who have been raised in the atmosphere of power, who know and respect its traditional controls.

*   *   *

Over the years Hickey can be seen changing his view of what is happening in the top layer of society. In 1954 his wistful, personal reflections evoked a static society gently pipe-dreaming about a lost imperious purpose. No dynamic of change is at work. By 1959 things were changing at a confusing rate, symbolized in his characters' changes of address and property transactions. Hickey responded as a defender of the faith, of the 'traditional emotions': the abstract qualities of royalty and aristocracy, rather than their visible trappings, were unchanging icons in a doctrinaire allegory of the traditional social structure of Britain. He was the Holinshed of the new Elizabethans. Eight years later, one change has been accepted: the style is now being set by the meteors of pop rather than by hunt-ball heroes. The other change has not been accepted, simply registered: Labour politicians are in the seats of government, but are liable to wear the wrong kind of suit at formal occasions. Over their highest secular aspirations still curves the impenetrable sky of traditional privilege and breeding; one day, it must reassert itself and receive again the deference due to it.

It is impossible to discuss Hickey without using vertical imagery. Hierarchy is the condition of the 'charmed spectacle'. Although Paul McCartney, with the power of his money and style, may step across from the news columns to a high position in Hickey's visible world; although at all periods Hickey, not being part of that world himself, can very occasionally give us a wink at some excessive caprice of the rich and fashionable; yet his world is always 'the higher world, as it looks from without'. The legions of unnamed characters, the plasterers and officials, are of course us, the readers, just as the journalists who compositely write Hickey are us also; but it is us seen from so unfamiliar an angle, as no more than the base of a duchess's pyramid of privilege, that we do not recognize ourselves at all.

7

CONCLUSIONS

WITHIN the altering personalities of the *Mirror* and the *Express* during the post-war decades, there can be perceived in each paper a persistent core of assumptions about its readers. The first objective of this concluding chapter is to describe those cores, to offer a thumb-nail sketch of each paper, answering the question 'who do they think we are?' The second level of conclusion will summarize the altering relationship of each paper to the political and social changes of the period. The theoretical case that can then be made about the social role that a newspaper performs will indicate what further questions need to be asked, and what other methods of analysis could be brought to bear.

To characterize the core attitudes to their readers which have persisted unalterably in the *Express* since before the war, and little altered in the *Mirror* since 1950, it is useful first to consider the format of each paper. Although it cannot be changed from day to day, a newspaper does express a choice in its format, since change is possible: both the *Daily Mail* and the *Sun* have chosen to shrink to tabloid size in recent years.

The broadsheet *Express*, in 22-inch columns, presents itself as a more linear medium than the 13½-inch columns of the tabloid *Mirror*. When allowance has been made for the *Express*'s layout, pioneered by Christiansen in the 1930s, opposing linear column depth with powerful horizontals (headlines, photos, panels), and using short paragraphs, often of only one sentence, a crucial distinction can still be made between the impact of each paper. It is governed by the size of headline type (consistently larger in the *Mirror*, both relative to page-size and absolutely), the length of story (typically shorter in the *Mirror*), and the number of items on each page (much fewer in the *Mirror*). The total effect is that a *Mirror* page presents its items as a simultaneous whole, often dominated by one photo, the *Express* invites the reader to make a number of different starts on each page. The ideal reader of the first would be McLuhan's instant-mosaic, intuitive man, and of the second a more linear, logical man.

The contrast can be overemphasized (as McLuhan overemphasizes the exclusiveness of his general categories), but should not be overlooked, or rationalized on utilitarian grounds into a preference among *Mirror* readers for a paper that will conveniently stuff into the pocket of overalls, and that can be read in brief intervals between manual work, and among *Express* readers, where manual workers are fewer, for a more leisurely reading style. The occupation-profiles of the two readerships are not different enough to account for the contrasting formats so simply. Some further explanation is required; and it may be found in the different social, and political, self-definitions that each paper offers its readers. The *Mirror* reader is invited to see himself as, in his private life and thought, more exposed to unforeseen events, both good and bad, less able to understand their origin and implications, less able to control them or keep them in cool, logical proportion, more emotional in his response to them. The *Express* reader in this comparison, is the reverse on each count, assumed to see himself as a man who can take a fairly long view, who appreciates the arrival of events in an explicable, linear order, and who thereby feels himself to have some degree of control over his response. Behind the sketches lie palimpsests of traditional working-class life, all huddled together and emotional, and traditional middle-class life, more calm and detached. It could be added that the broadsheet format (with more 'serious' news, and some classified advertising) has, in itself, an affiliation to the traditional shape of a newspaper, whereas a tabloid declares itself to be definitively modern.

Such a contrast is congruent with the trajectories of the *Mirror* and the *Express* since the 1930s. A simultaneous-mosaic paper is likely to prove more volatile than one which favours a more linear presentation, for the latter must at least maintain the pretence of a rational development of policy, consideration of past and future, but such obligations are less binding on a paper that habitually stresses the newness, *nowness*, of its material.

The *Mirror*'s picture of its readers as more vulnerable to events can also be recognized in the greater space it gives to news of accidents, and to what are known as 'human-interest' stories. Consistently, events are seen to happen *to* people; their lives are fortuitous, subject to authority or hazard. Where the *Express*'s puritan ethic celebrates the social climber, the self-making buccaneer, or—ultimately—the magical wands of Hickey people, in the *Mirror*, where gossip is retailed as much in 'news' stories as in formal gossip columns, success more typically arrives as a surprise, an unexpected jackpot. Working-class morality is interpreted not as a struggle to ensure a fair share for everyone but as each man privately hoping for a change of luck, within a system that yields jackpots for a few, and is made tolerable for the unlucky many by the cheerful note on which most human-interest stories close (whereas the *Express*'s fewer human-interest stories tend to end bluntly).

Within the perspective of surprise, nowness, the tone of Live-letters can be read as the *Mirror*'s own folk-memory, cheerfully resigned to the unchanging routine of days. Its pugnacity, like much else in the *Mirror*, was turned bland by 'affluence'. The Old Codgers' column is much more than a way of publishing readers' letters. It is a daily rehearsal of a particular humour, the humour of everyday life, of Us, neighbours, always ready with a cup of tea and a laugh when things aren't going too well, the laugh that compensates for the impossibility of actually changing the real situation, out there. Yet we are not, in fact, leaning over the garden wall or eaves-dropping at the local, but reading half a page in one of the most commercially successful newspapers in the world. We are being asked to forget that a way of speaking about our experience, formed in a particular social history, is being deliberately transferred from one cultural area to another, ventriloquised by professional journal-ists, and that in the process of transfer something is going to happen to that speech. A way of talking that grew up in the working class, and was a cultural defence against the different articulacy of the dominant class, is being imitated now in a newspaper which else-where is closely related to that dominant culture.

Other columns come and go in the *Mirror*. The Inside Page may rise to chatting about James Joyce's 'stream of consciousness', and Mirrorscope focus in depth on public issues (although it is freely acknowledged, in the *Mirror* building, that few readers actually read it). But the Old Codgers go on from year to year, new codgers succeeding dead ones, and 'posers' are still answered by consulting the 'Little Black Book', which is in fact a wall of filing cabinets in a large modern office.

If Live-letters is a sort of folk-tale, perhaps the nearest functional equivalent in the *Express* is the column called Action Line, in which victims of bureaucracy and dishonest trading are rescued by knight-errant journalists on a vaguely consumerist steed. Problems are tersely explained, action initiated, and outcomes seldom delayed or disappointing. Once the dragon has written its note of apology, replaced the faulty goods or scissored the red tape, those who have been rescued are briefly quoted in tribute:

> 'It's incredible,' said 30-year-old Tony Palfrey. 'Everything seems to be happening since we called in Action Line.'

Apart from the fairy-tale pleasure of seeing problems magically resolved, it is hard to decide whether the column's chief effect is that of a parable—we too should set about cutting our own knots with equal gusto—or a fable, teaching us that we stumble in the mire unless we acknowledge the higher wisdoms and powers of those set above us.

Set highest of all are Hickey's people, who need no Action Line:

> Quietly, the younger Princes of the Royal Family are emerging as talented characters in their chosen pursuits.

Draping velvet curtains of discretion around his subjects with 'quietly', Hickey identifies them in words that might belong to one of Shakespeare's Chorus figures. Compare the *Mirror*'s Inside Page:

> All the Royals enjoy a jolly splash-about in the pool.

Spanning the spectrum of English society, the contrasted tones are not the result of the respective journalists' savoir-faire, but of their contrasted assumptions about us, the readers. Again, compare the Talking Point at the foot of an *Express* leader:

> The optimist proclaims the world we live in to be the best of all possible worlds. The pessimist fears this is true.
> —Branch Cabell

with Today's Thought in the *Mirror* on the same day:

> When loving woman wants her way
> God hesitates to say her nay.

Urbane, literary, wit over the port, or proverbial, sententious, old-fashioned like a pokerwork motto, each summons up an absolutely different world of discourse. Yet these two best-selling national papers are published within half a mile of each other, and are read by broadly similar people, as defined by occupational profiles, up and down the land.

*   *   *

The most famous examples of *Mirror* ventriloquism are to be found on its front page. 'Watch It, Harold,' it advised Wilson; or, earlier, 'Mr. K. (if you will pardon an olde English phrase) don't be so bloody rude! PS: Who do you think you are? Stalin?' The technique is described by Hugh Cudlipp as 'a friendly shout from the crowd', and other journalists concur: the remark to Krushchev came 'from the British people, really', according to the editor of *The Sunday Times*,[1] and was 'catching the mood'. An alternative view, expressed by Raymond Williams,[2] is that when the *Mirror* uses 'naughty' words or 'plain' speech to those in power the self-conscious

1 Hugh Cudlipp and Harold Evans speaking on 'Cudlipp and Be Damned', BBC–1, November 27, 1973.
2 Article in *The Observer*, April 29, 1962.

tone invites us to find the paper 'intoxicatingly radical'; but, by failing to ask really critical questions about power, the *Mirror* in fact preserves only a façade of radicalism. Just as it is only a façade of going posh that char-ladies or delivery boys enjoy at one of the stunts, ball or banquet, that the *Mirror* stages. The paper's reports of such occasions suggest that a snook was cocked at the stuffy nobs who usually enjoy the hallowed halls: anything they can do we can do too, and have a lot more fun about it. But the quoted remarks of the revellers are awed, or defensively cocky: it's all just a giggle, really, and when Cinderella has gone back, with relief, to her humble home things will resume their natural course, the nobs will return to the hallowed halls, and the *Mirror*'s editorial heads will go on enjoying their daily working lunches in a private room at the Ivy. The structures have not been threatened. Once, they were; once, the *Mirror* not only identified the rich and powerful Them; it also offered some (if only some) explanation of the social mechanism of riches and power, and allowed some readers to demand its demolition, or expropriation. But that was thirty years ago. Now, it is the reader's voice that has been expropriated.

In 1945 the *Mirror* was a responsible newspaper in a literal sense: it responded to its readers' voices, which carried into the political domain some of the dense texture of working-class feeling. While the *Express* speaks of 'the nation', the *Mirror* spoke of 'the people': 'Forward with the People' was its post-war banner. In the 1950s, however, in Hugh Cudlipp's view, 'The people had gone forward. The question was, how to keep them there.'[3] The people, that is, were no longer the paper's subject, but its object. 'The popular press ... has taught ordinary people to question and to make up their own minds. They are still not very good at it,' according to Cecil King.[4] Increasingly, the *Mirror* took decisions for its readers. There is inside testimony that reports of social deprivation were suppressed because they 'might be considered offensive to the political power that now lurked behind the paper.'[5] Increasingly, too, the *Mirror* began to speak, day after day, of the people's need of 'leadership', a theme that had not been prominent in the paper since the early days of the war (though it recurs throughout King's various books of memoirs). The search for a leader reached a climax during the Wilson administration. King's first signed article in over 30 years with the *Mirror* (a service that was about to be ruptured) led the front page on May 10, 1968 with the theme 'we have suffered from a

3 Hugh Cudlipp, *At Your Peril*, Weidenfeld & Nicolson, 1962.
4 Article in *Twentieth Century*, Spring, 1963.
5 Claud Morris, *I Bought a Newspaper*, Arthur Barker, 1963.

lack of leadership.'[6] No goal was specified towards which the leader might lead the people, other than 'economic progress'. A single example from 1971 will illustrate that paternalism and incoherence did not leave the *Mirror* with King. It had been disclosed that lavatory attendants were earning £30 a week; in defence of them, the Industrial Editor wrote, deep inside the paper:

> The poor are still with us, in large numbers . . . the real difference between the lower paid manual workers and the higher paid has not varied by more than a fraction since 1886.

That fact would have been central to the *Mirror*'s rhetoric in 1945; but in 1971 there was a front-page splash the next day calling the £30 wage 'crazy', and ending:

> The nation is waiting for the voice of authentic leadership from No. 10 Downing Street.

The facts have been dissolved in opinion.

Through paternalism, the *Mirror* has promoted itself to be the people's tribune. It justifies that position by its mythology of itself (most blatant in 1964) as a political warrior, and by presenting itself as a repository of the popular memory: of the bad old days, the post-war struggle, and folksy neighbourliness. But, bemused by affluence, it has no clear idea of those for whom it has appointed itself tribune, or of the opposed Them. In spite of evidence[7] that working-class Labour voters 'overwhelmingly' define their politics in terms of class, there is not much of that in the *Mirror*. A classless society was, after all, a prospect it had looked forward to in 1945. Now, dependent on capitalism for its existence, the *Mirror* hesitates to inflame its readers' class-consciousness, except in times of election, when the rhetoric of manipulated images and shock disclosures briefly, but discontinuously, lends it a self-conscious air of class allegiance, and purpose. Nor can it admit radical alternatives to class-structured politics, such as those expressed in student protest or youth culture. Young people—their youth seen as more significant than their class—may be the bearers of lively styles and ideas, but only so long as they can be contained within the cheerfulness, the 'buoyant, racy' brightness, that is the *Mirror*'s predominant gift to its readers. For 'this cheeky pup of a paper', as Cudlipp calls it, the

6 For further description of King's article, and of the *Mirror*'s theme of leadership, see A. C. H. Smith, 'Enough is a Bit Much', *New Society*, May 16, 1968.

7 R. McKenzie and A. Silver, *Angels in Marble: Working Class Conservatism in Urban England*, Heinemann, 1968.

everyday heroes are entertainers, the fun-makers of television: and the *Mirror* itself.

Of the papers of the Left, it was not the old *Herald*'s plain speaking, or the *Worker*'s commitment to class conflict, that captured the largest daily audience in the country, but the paper which, starting from an authentic populism in 1945, has stylized working-class language into parody. Doing so has enabled it to go on addressing a mainly working-class readership with enormous success in terms of sales, yet without, from the 1950s onward, ever unbridling the radical conscience that, once, had helped its readers to recognize and accept their own political responsibility.

*   *   *

From the perennial rhetoric of the *Express* it is possible to deduce an identikit of its ideal reader. He has a Darwinian passion for 'the competitive life of nature'. The freedom he fought for was translated, after the war, as freedom to compete for 'more sugar in his tea' than the next man, for whom he feels none of the *Mirror*'s neighbourliness. His success is enjoyed with his family, inside his fenced-off house with a garage. As well as bringing material rewards, competition staves off the dullness of life in Derby or Rhyl. He is thrilled, too, by belonging to a competitive nation. Since his individual ambition can be seen as contributing to national progress, he is absolved from remorse about it. In his unquestioning belief that Britain's traditions have been proved the best, he is suspicious of fainthearts, intellectuals, trouble-makers and aliens. At the top of society, a pyramid that neither war nor prosperity has altered, the nation is embodied by the elect, not the elected. He votes for the Tories because they are 'the party of the whole nation',[8] and bred to 'govern the people wisely'; or, increasingly since 1951, because he calculates that they will serve his own interests. He may live to scorn any elected politicians, but never the elect, feeling himself their moral, if not their social, equal because 'all who properly fulfil their stations in life' (as 'Chelsea pensioners stood awkwardly to attention') 'contribute worthily to the common good'.[9] Consequently, he disapproves of those whose behaviour is dissonant with their station: the 'monstrous, flashy' tastes of a new-rich knacker, or the slumming of the well-bred Sandfords. He can laugh at people of all classes—the Littlehamptons, the Gambols, the Giles family (all matriarchal)— because between his individual struggle and the national effort no

8 Ibid. McKenzie and Silver make the distinction between 'deferential' and 'secular' working-class Conservatives.
9 Ibid.

collective strength in class intervenes. He is never working-class; at worst, a 'lower paid worker' who, like everyone else, can designate himself middle-class by pre-war standards of living.

'Class warfare' is 'wholly foreign to the nature of the British people,' wrote Beaverbrook[10] (in 1926!), arguing that 'Socialist-Communists' were seeking the 'class domination of a minority.' In 1947 William Barkley held that 'it is wicked to regard the rich with envy'; and another twenty years later the *Express* was complaining of a 'stupid, mean-spirited prejudice in Britain against the big-salary man—that is the man of exceptional quality.' 'Wealth and position and prestige are not ignoble ambitions. They are rough-and-ready but fairly accurate tests of the merits of individuals' said Beaverbrook,[11] the ennobled millionaire from New Brunswick.

The paper he created is a daily reading in the Protestant ethic, specifically in Calvinism. As for Calvin, it behoves us all to work for salvation, in the hope of joining the elect (Hickey people), yet the hardest work is no guarantee. The company of that charmed spectacle is an inexplicable gift, apparently arbitrary, unquestionable and unquestioned. The function of the spectacle is to keep us to the straight and narrow path, but not in the vanity that we shall be invited to join the elect, nor even, most of us, to meet them; their charm, like heaven's, relies on the fact that we can never test it.

It seems evident that many of the *Express*'s readers, uniquely spread throughout the social classes, have often disregarded their paper's party-political arguments. The transaction they value, apparently, is not with its views of passing governments, but with its daily reassurance of a fixed order in the nation. To give them all that reassurance, the *Express* characteristically speaks with a voice of authority, unqualified by the accents of time or class. It is a voice that, symbolically, removes the paper outside the hierarchic pyramid which, in its view, is the structure of society: it is, then, an abstract public address rather than a discourse, legislative rather than representative. The *Express*'s voice of authority is not that of the elect or the greatly wise, to whom alone it defers. So whose authority, what authority, does it have? Are the Old Testament cadences, Protestant pulpit imperatives and magisterial oratory to be explained as a lasting echo of Beaverbrook's voice? Immigrant and self-made millionaire, he was certainly at a remove from the social pyramid; and also typical of Beaverbrook is the optimism which Christiansen sought, and which, like the *Mirror*'s cheerfulness, creates a mood

10 Lord Beaverbrook, *Politicians and the Press*, Hutchinson, 1926.
11 Quoted by Tom Driberg, *Beaverbroook*, Weidenfeld & Nicolson, 1956.

that advertisers welcome. But a further explanation is suggested by a passage from T. W. Adorno:[12]

> While the cultural industry speculates blatantly on the level of consciousness or unconsciousness of the millions to which it turns, the masses are not the primary element, but secondary, calculated into the process, an appendix of the machinery. The customer is not king, whatever the cultural industry would have one believe, he is not subject, but object. The term 'mass media', which has asserted itself as designation for the cultural industry, shifts the emphasis toward harmlessness. The dominating factor is not the masses, nor the techniques of communication as such, but the spirit that inspires them, their master's voice.

Adorno has spoken of a 'jargon of authority': the habit of using certain key words out of their context (for example, the *Express*'s variations on 'free'), but keeping their aura, creates the impression that the speaker has recourse to a higher authority. It avoids the trouble of thought, says Adorno, by implicity gesturing towards 'true' human values and, especially, yearning for the good old days. By such forced, disintegrating language the press can hide contradictions in society.

A more pertinent phrase than 'voice of authority' might be 'the authorities': bureaucracy, persistently attacked by the *Express* as an authoritarian voice issuing from nowhere. Echo quarrels with echo in a void.

*   *   *

The relationship of the *Express* and the *Mirror* to the politics of the post-war decades can now be summarized.[13]

The *Express* entered and emerged from the experience of the war years unchanged. Before and after the war its rhetoric of leaders and the led was based on the same core set of meanings. Its collective personality seemed set, and this personality generated an 'inferential structure'[14] which foreclosed its chances of responding to the real

12 T. W. Adorno, 'Summary on Cultural Industry', *Parva Aesthetica*, Surkamp; translated for the Centre for Contemporary Cultural Studies by Brian Trench.

13 The closing sections of this chapter are based on a summary by Stuart Hall of the findings in the research report published by the University of Birmingham, 1970.

14 See K. and G. Lang, 'The Inferential Structure of Political Communications—Unwitting Bias', in *Public Opinion Quarterly*, vol. 19, Summer, 1965.

changes of mood and opinion that gathered slowly during the war, and fuelled the Labour victory. The point is not that the *Express* backed a loser in 1945—it was bound to support the Conservatives— but that its arguments were inappropriate to the political conscious- ness.

The *Mirror*, by contrast, emerged from the war a quite different newspaper from what it had been in 1940. It had learned to handle the news in terms of a demotic radicalism, at a historical moment when official politics was to be crucially restructured by that mood in the society. The *Mirror* did not 'decide' to support Labour, what- ever happened, once the war ended: it learned to speak to its readers in a certain way, and in doing so it placed itself in a position to hear, and then to articulate (in what must be counted one of the most sustained instances of journalistic ventriloquism ever practised), what its readers were feeling and thinking. Thus, in a sense, it *found itself* supporting Labour when the election came.

In later elections, 1955 and 1964, the *Mirror*'s demotic rhetoric was just as capable of hardening into a formula as the *Express*. Nothing coheres: everywhere there is a lack of conviction, of drive, in the political coverage. Already mesmerized by its own myth as the maker and breaker of the fortunes of political parties, the *Mirror* wants to be as right about 1955 as it was about 1945; but it is no longer in a position to be. When it needs a political rhetoric, only the obsolescent tones of 1945 are available to it. Its political coverage therefore looks strikingly out of date. The paper settles, on election day, for a slogan—'Keep the Tories Tame'—that fully reveals its defensive posture. In 1955, the *Mirror* is still a 'blunt', 'fighting', 'populist' paper of 'the underdog', but its deployment of the Us/ Them contrast, that had stood it in such good stead in 1945, no longer serves to interpret the new social mood.

In its effort to make political sense of the social experience of 'affluence', the *Mirror* in the mid-1950s is preoccupied with the question of 'Youth'. In the 1955 election it tries to harness this theme to politics. But whereas in 1945 the war theme of the underdog *versus* the old order had played straight into its imagery of Labour *versus* the Tories, the theme of youth, in 1955, critically interrupts the paper's political themes. Youth *versus* Age, as the *Express* was quick to see, worked as neatly *against* Labour. Further, Youth *versus* Age is a way of structuring the electorate that runs counter to the more familiar, class-based structure of political allegiances. In the early stages of affluence, youth culture was treated as part of its froth, unrelated to the basic social and political structure. Through the 1960s, youth culture generated its own form of politics, in the student

I*

and psychedelic movements, and we have come to understand that, though the relationship between youth culture and politics is often hidden and indirect, what we were seeing in the early 1950s was the beginning of a change in the structure of politics, and in the political culture itself, not a surface phenomenon. We have to turn to the *Express* to place this emerging theme fully, and to see how it can be politically orchestrated. 'Youth' was, in both papers, and, perhaps, in the whole press of the period (continuing right into the 1970s), a powerful but concealed *metaphor* for social change: the compressed image of a society which had crucially changed in terms of basic life-styles and values—changed in ways calculated to upset the official political framework, but ways *not yet calculable in traditional political terms* (the story of the political 'encashment' is *the* emergent theme in the politics of the late 1960s—a story not yet complete). The Labour Party, too, knew in the depths of its divided soul that politics would never be quite as it had been before; the political literature of the period is full of questioning, within and without the Party, about how Labour should adapt to and incorporate the 'affluent society'. The Party failed either to adapt to or to transcend the myth of affluence. Only in the early 1960s, when large holes had been drilled in the myth of affluence, substantial inequalities of income, privilege and reward, and major enclaves of real poverty 'rediscovered', was the stage set for a social-democratic political victory *in* an 'affluent' society.[15] The way the *Mirror* toys with the theme of Youth is a counterpart to the soul-searching in Labour's ranks about affluence. It is the Tories, in the mid-50s, who convert affluence into the fuel for political victory: Macmillan's 'Never Had It So Good' had the same gnomic force, the same idiomatic power, as the *Mirror*'s 'Vote For Him' at an earlier period, and derived from the same source.

One might expect, then, that the *Express* would be, *par excellence*, the paper which managed to harness the appeal to Youth to its political soul. That is not quite the case. On the strictly material side, the *Express* comes into its own as affluence begins to make its impact. Material prosperity, the glamour and gloss, the cornucopia of consumer goods—common coin of the affluent experience—become

15 Just as we can attribute Labour's indecisiveness—and the *Mirror's* loss of conviction—in the mid-1950s only to the impact of the 'affluence' myth, so the break-up of the Macmillan consensus is heralded most dramatically by the apparently 'un-political' fiasco of the Profumo affair. See Wayland Young, *The Profumo Affair: Aspects of Conservatism*, Penguin Special, 1963. It was in his speech to the Commons during the Profumo debate on June 17, 1963 that Macmillan passed the comment, as telling in its form as in content, 'I do not live among young people fairly widely.'

in the *Express* a positive celebration. But here is the central point. Affluence does not function in the *Express* simply as a new and convenient political slogan. It connects with deeper meanings written into the paper's whole social history. The *Express* becomes the paper of affluence, it inhabits the idiom of consumer riches, but *in a special way*: along the grain of its previous convictions. The complex social realities which lie behind the idea of affluence are hymned in the *Express* with telling success, because they lent themselves to powerful orchestration in terms of the paper's core structure of values.

Thus, there is contrasting evidence of the way underlying meaning-structures have functioned in the lives of the two newspapers. In the 1940–45 period, the *Mirror discovers* a theme, a tone of voice, which enables it to 'make sense' of changes in popular political consciousness. In the mid-1950s, the *Express*'s voice does not change —though it is enlarged and up-dated. This is the reverse of the paradigm, where the social themes *play into an existing structure of feeling*, and the coincidence of interests give its treatment a rare coherence. The affluent society meant something in the scheme of values of the *Express* because it could be presented as 'Booming Britain' and a 'prosperous nation'—and in these metaphors 'Britain' and 'nation' carry overtones for the *Express* older and more traditional in their resonance than 'affluence' itself. It would not be too fanciful to see the *Express*'s success in this period as a close parallel to the career of Macmillan, who steered the ship of state into and through affluent waters. There is some evidence to suggest that Macmillan's legitimation of affluence—a magnificent piece of political management—was accomplished, not by any inner concession to the prevailing 'American mood', but by adapting a strikingly caricatured Edwardian *insouciance* to the sudden flush of prosperity. Whether or not this was true of Macmillan as a man, it was certainly the *persona* which he consistently projected. It was a sustained performance— and Vicky seems to have been the only man in the *Mirror* office (at that very moment in the throes of abandoning its 'Forward With the People' masthead and searching for another political identity) to have penetrated to its core.

In the *Express*'s handling of the theme of affluence, there is the same confident *brio*, the same calculated vulgarity, the same sense of enacting a performance. There are, too, the same Edwardian undertones. These qualities give affluence in the pages of the *Express* a context and a meaning different from the mediations of the myth elsewhere. Thus, prosperity is valued, not—as in the typical affluent scheme of values—instrumentally, for what it brings in terms of classlessness, creature comforts and consumer durables, but for its spiritual essence: as witnessing to initiative, to individualism, to that competitive cut-and-thrust which accompanies the freedom from constraints. In the *Express* the affluent bonanza is the reward, here on earth, of that perpetual struggle which the paper has always enjoined its readers to wage, and which is positively Hobbesian in conception. Whereas some central part of the affluence myth included the notion of classlessness, the merging and blending of the lower and upper ends of the social scale, and the insertion of the working class into an 'embourgeoised' future, the concept of 'the nation', which continues to resound in the pages of the *Express*, is a corporate image of society—which includes and is founded on, rather than transcending, the hierarchies of social class. At the same time, the paper is sufficiently on top of the whole social experience to smother it in the glossiest and most vigorously pop forms.

The *Express* selected, triumphantly, those elements in the affluence myth which fitted in with older, more traditional structures of feeling. It situated itself within the social experience of affluence by finding a tone which most concisely expressed the new fruits of competitiveness in terms of *enduring* competitiveness. It identified the affluent society as only the latest, most glittering and heady, manifestation of that endless striving which makes any nation 'great'—especially *Britain*. The *Express* of the 1950s, then, brought off a feat of interpretation as significant in its own way as—though characteristically different from—that of the *Mirror* in 1945. Naturally, affluence was a less compact and collective, more diffused, social process than that which united the aspirations of the war with the demand for political change a decade earlier: but, within those limits, the parallel is striking. In the *Express* of the 1950s, the new social manifestations of an affluent society founded on private ownership and production were harnessed to a persisting, indeed eternal, view of the world and of human nature. Paradoxically, the paper both relishes the fizz and glitter of the new society, generates a breezy show-biz rhetoric to go with it, and, at the same time, infuses the idea of affluence with such apparently contradictory notions as patriotism, class and the puritan ethic. Clive Irving ascribed the paper's success in these years to Christiansen's awareness of the need for a new style of pop culture, and his success in discovering an appropriate idiom located firmly in those 'bijou houses on the Watford bypass'. Not only is this characteristic style everywhere in evidence—it is powerful at election times only because it is already so powerful an energy elsewhere—but it was maintained by the most rigorous exercise in processing copy into a formula that we have witnessed in the recent history of popular journalism. The *Express* was known, in this period, as the paper, *par excellence*, of the sub-editors. Its rhetoric, therefore, was not minted, as was the *Mirror*'s in the '40s, from 'below', but from 'above'. But the essential trajectory of that style would be missed if it were not seen as the coalition of Christiansen's show-biz flair *and* Beaverbrook's rigorous fundamentalism.

What comes through, in the mediation of affluence in the *Express*, is not classlessness, but rather a retained, refurbished, highly nuanced sensitivity to the persistence of class, the fluid penetration of money, into a changing class structure. The *Express* is a compendium of those perpetual slight shifts between classes which, in later years, has come to seem more essentially what affluence was really about than the current images of massive 'embourgeoisement' suggested. But this highly sensitive, retained sense of class is expressed, not—as in, say, the *Telegraph*—from a point of view within the establishments of power and authority in the society, but rather from a vantage point just below or outside the real levels of power. The readership of the *Express* is certainly not confined to the lower middle class—indeed, at the lower end of the spectrum, it overlaps a good deal with that of the *Mirror*. But its essential tone is *arriviste*. In class terms, it is a corporate, not a hegemonic, paper.[16] It is the paper of the social climber, at whatever position in the class structure he happens to be.

The *Express* of the 1950s is not—as the usual formulations would have it—'reflecting' social change: it is giving social change a particular meaning. The *Express* did not create affluence, any more than the *Mirror* made a Labour victory in 1945. But both papers made sense of those experiences in distinct ways, offered terms, images, ideas, sentiments, within which the experience of war and political change, or the experience of the spread of a certain measure of prosperity, could be 'made meaningful' to their respective readers. This is not reflection, but mediation. When the traditional rhetoric of a newspaper flows in the same direction as the emergent experience of social change, the convergence—in terms of confidence, coherence, mastery of language and presentation, inner assurance—is striking. When such convergence does not take place, the newspaper seems to go to pieces: the central organizing core is not there.

* * *

What readers get when they pick up their newspaper—and miss when newspapers do not arrive—is a particular way of structuring

16 The distinction is Gramsci's. cf. Gwynn Williams, 'The Concept of 'Egemonia' in the Thought of Antonio Gramsci', *Journal of the History of Ideas*, vol. XXI, No. 4, October–December 1960.

events, of producing 'the news' as a coherent entity. Within that broadly shared perspective, readers choose what topics are of immediate interest to them; and on occasion the newspaper may explicitly try to make us see things in certain ways, and may have influence. But the daily exchange is framed by a more inclusive 'inferential structure' of assumptions about the audience. That structure, which, persisting through time, constitutes the heart of the newspaper, seems a more useful critical concept than the traditional one of intentional bias.

Digging even a little below the notion of bias will unearth more interesting things. There are, for example, definitions and constraints common to most national newspapers, whatever their political bias: definitions of what constitutes the news, and the terms within which it is to be debated—the agenda. A study of the unstated but shared constraints upon which the free, commercial press is organized, the working compromises struck every day, from the 'quality' to the 'popular' ends of the spectrum, would tell us much about the limits of the political consensus upon which our society rests, and which the press must honour, and operate, in order to survive. The consensus runs from the respect which all newspapers pay to official off-the-record briefings, the informal ranking of who constitutes a prestige or expert source, and who does not, to where the fine distinction falls between the right of minorities to express unpopular views and the exercise of political or civil violence.

The level which this study has aimed to penetrate lies below such informally negotiated compromises. There are powerful ways in which a newspaper typically defines situations for its readers.[17] These are ingrained frames of reference, collective structures, which have a life and continuity of their own. From that matrix, certain broad themes, dispositions and motifs emerge. A great deal of the daily news, events and personalities are 'made sense of' within such existing schemes of interpretation. Once a news story has crystallized in a particular form, the 'frame of reference tends to overshadow subsequent information to the point at which even specific new

17 Beyond the transaction of definitions and interpretations through the reporter-editor-reader complex, which is the point made here, a further problem in deciding what constitutes an event, or fact, is that pseudo-events are manufactured in order to seek the attention of the media; or the actors in the event may be influenced by what they perceive the media to expect of them—teenagers as 'mods and rockers' rioted, as 'hippies' threw flowers, as 'revolutionaries' chanted and charged, for the cameras.

information is ignored':[18] it generates its own momentum, and subsequent events take their meaning from it.

Deep structures come into being—they cohere and form themselves—at crucial historical junctures, or at specific moments in the inner organization of a newspaper's collective life; and, once formed, they exert a persistent influence on the contents and make-up of any single day's newspaper. They are held in place, partly, by the very pressure of production, which requires a paper, in the heat of swiftly-moving events, to appear to be the same paper from one day to the next. The available structures and routines serve to orient the variety of personnel hastening to produce the edition. No doubt such routines are influenced by the powerful figures within the office; a strong editor, a powerful sub-editorial desk, a successful columnist, learn to inhabit the structures in a personal and characteristic way, and to bend them to their own interests. But, essentially, these are not the creations of single men, a Beaverbrook or a Cudlipp, a King or a Christiansen. Journalists of very different backgrounds and political opinions, as they move from one paper to another through their careers, learn the informal system of each and can adapt to it. The collective identities of newspapers, though difficult to pin down, are wider than can be accounted for in terms of individual personalities. They must continually refer themselves to their readers' experience and, more broadly, to the experience of the society on which they report and comment. It is a question of reciprocal structures: the images newspapers form of their readers, the imprecise notions they have, as rules of thumb, for figuring out what is happening in the society for which they write. Some information is available to them in the statistical analyses of their readerships, their class and educational character, as well as, more broadly, in reports, surveys, investigations and studies of how the society is changing. But, in the end, most working journalists will come back to 'flair', just as all good editors will come back to 'news sense', by way of professional working rationalizations of their own daily practice. What is meant by news sense is something like an intuitive ability to judge, from a host of varied and differently-weighted news items, how things are shifting, opinion is moving, new interests are emerging, in what direction society is evolving. What is meant by 'flair' is the ability to capture, within the noose of 'news', the unformed and kaleidoscopic flow of events, to present disconnected items within something that looks like an informed, coherent perspective. The retrospective-prospective process by which a newspaper formulates its unstated assumptions about its readers and

18 K. and G. Lang, op. cit.

society, and from which it consistently speaks, is just as much the real process of constructing newspapers as the daily tasks of briefing journalists, cutting copy, choosing illustrations, re-writing reports and setting up pages.

This study has identified some of the structures of assumption in the *Express* and the *Mirror*, and shown how they influence, in turn, the handling of new social experiences. But what have the findings to do with the news-making and news-selecting process? With the form of social production by which newspapers are made? Are the 'inferential structures' related to the professional ideologies of journalists? Who, in any particular paper, is the informal 'gate-keeper' of such structures? Are they ever formally codified, and, if not, how are they transmitted from one generation to the next? What is the relation of unwitting bias to intentional bias? And to the overt political opinions and commitments of owners and managers?

The answers to those questions require analysis of a different order from this study. What we hope to have established as a principle is that such questions should not be answered, as they usually have been, simply by reference to the biography of a newspaper, the manifest influences exerted by changes in personnel, technology or economics. All such changes take place within a modifying system of meanings, transmitted among the paper's staff and down through generations. What the discipline of cultural studies has to offer is the project of understanding and describing those meanings, as they are embodied in the language a newspaper uses to address its readers.

BIBLIOGRAPHY

THE PRESS

Abrams M.   *The Newspaper Reading Public of Tomorrow*, Odhams, 1964.
Beaverbrook   *Politicians and the Press*, Hutchinson, 1926.
Boston R. (ed.) *The Press We Deserve*, Routledge & Kegan Paul, 1970.
Boyle P.   *Cassandra at his Finest and Funniest*, Paul Hamlyn, 1967.
Cassandra   *Reflections in a Mirror*, Cassell, 1969.
Christiansen A. *Headlines All My Life*, Heinemann, 1961.
Cudlipp H.   *Publish and Be Damned*, Dakers, 1953.
                 At Your Peril, Weidenfeld & Nicolson, 1962.
Driberg T.   *Beaverbrook*, Weidenfeld & Nicolson, 1956.
Edelman M.   *The Mirror: A Political History*, Hamish Hamilton, 1966.
Hall S. and
  Whannel P.   *The Popular Arts*, Hutchinson, 1964.
Hoggart R. (ed.) *The Uses of Literacy*, Chatto & Windus, 1957.
                 Your Sunday Paper, University of London Press, 1967.
Kimble P.   *Newspaper Reading in the Third Year of the War*, Allen & Unwin, 1942.
King C.   *The Future of the Press*, MacGibbon & Kee, 1967.
                 Strictly Personal, Weidenfeld & Nicolson, 1969.
Matthews T. S.   *The Sugar Pill*, Gollancz, 1958.
McLuhan M.   *The Gutenberg Galaxy*, Routledge & Kegan Paul, 1962.
                 Royal Commission on the Press, Report, HMSO, 1948, 1949.
Seymour-Ure C.   *The Press, Politics and the Public*, Methuen, 1968.
Taylor A. J. P. *Beaverbrook*, Hamish Hamilton, 1972.
Thompson D.   *Between the Lines*, Muller, 1939.
Williams F.   *Dangerous Estate*, Longmans, Green, 1957.
Williams R.   *The Long Revolution*, Chatto & Windus, 1961.
                 Communications, Chatto & Windus, 1966.

POLITICAL AND SOCIAL HISTORY

Abrams M. and
  Rose R.   *Must Labour Lose?*, Penguin, 1960.
Anderson P. (ed.)   *Towards Socialism*, Fontana, 1965.
Avon   *The Reckoning*, Cassell, 1965.
Beveridge Report   *Social Insurance and Allied Services*, HMSO,
                        1942.
Booth A. H.   *British Hustings 1924–1950*, Muller, 1956.
Bottomore T. B.   *Classes in Modern Society*, Allen & Unwin, 1965.
Butler D. E.   *The British General Election of 1955*, Macmillan,
                        1955.
                      The British General Election of 1959, Macmillan,
                        1960.
  and King A.   *The British General Election of 1964*, Macmillan,
                        1965.
Calder A.   *The People's War*, Cape, 1969.
Churchill Sir W.   *Triumph and Tragedy*, Cassell, 1954.
Cole G. D. H.   *The Post-War Condition of Britain*, Routledge &
                        Kegan Paul, 1956.
Crosland A.   *The Future of Socialism*, Cape, 1956.
Daily Express   *The Laski Libel Action*, Daily Express, 1947.
Directorate of
  Army Education   *The British Way and Purpose*, HMSO, 1944.
Foot M.   *Aneurin Bevan*, vol. 1, MacGibbon & Kee,
                        1962; vol. 2, Davis-Poynter, 1973.
Galbraith J. K.   *The Affluent Society*, Hamish Hamilton, 1958.
Goldthorpe J. et al. *The Affluent Worker: Political Attitudes and
                        Behaviour*, Cambridge University Press,
                        1968.
Hamblett C. and
  Deverson J.   *Generation X*, Tandem Books, 1964.
Hopkins H.   *The New Look*, Secker & Warburg, 1963.
Jackson B. and
  Marsden D.   *Education and the Working Class*, Routledge &
                        Kegan Paul, 1962.
Laski H.   *Reflections on the Revolution of Our Time*, Allen &
                        Unwin, 1944.
Lewis R.
  and Maude A.   *The English Middle Classes*, Phoenix House,
                        1949.
                      Professional People, Phoenix House, 1952.
Low D.   *Years of Wrath*, Gollancz, 1949.

Macmillan H.
Tides of Fortune 1945–1955, Macmillan, 1969.
Riding the Storm 1956–1959, Macmillan, 1971.
Pointing the Way 1959–1961, Macmillan, 1972.
At the End of the Day 1961–1963, Macmillan, 1973.

Madge C. and
Harrison T.
Britain by Mass Observation, Penguin, 1939.

Martin K.
Father Figures, Hutchinson, 1966.

Marwick A.
Britain in the Century of Total War, Bodley Head, 1968.

McCallum R. and
Readman A.
The British General Election of 1945, Oxford University Press, 1947.

McKenzie R. and
Silver A.
Angels in Marble: Working Class Conservatives in Urban England, Heinemann, 1968.

Miliband R.
Parliamentary Socialism, Merlin Press, 1964.

Milne R. S. and
Mackenzie H. C.
Marginal Seat 1955, Hansard Society for Parliamentary Reform, London, 1958.

Mitchell J.
Crisis in Britain 1951, Secker & Warburg, 1963.

Montgomery J.
The Fifties, Allen & Unwin, 1965.

Moran
Churchill: The Struggle for Survival 1940–1965, Constable, 1966.

Mowat C. L.
Britain Between the Wars 1918–1940, Methuen, 1955.

Nicholas H. G. and
Butler D. E.
The British General Election of 1951, Macmillan, 1952.

Nicolson Sir H.
Diaries and Letters 1939–1945, Collins, 1967.

Orwell G.
England Your England, Secker & Warburg, 1953.
The Collected Essays, Journalism and Letters, 4 vols., Secker & Warburg, 1968.

Rose R.
Studies in British Politics, Macmillan, 1966.

Runciman W. G.
Relative Deprivation and Social Justice, Routledge & Kegan Paul, 1966.

Sampson A.
Anatomy of Britain Today, Hodder & Stoughton, 1965.

Seaman L. C. B.
Post-Victorian Britain, Methuen, 1966.

Sissons M. and
French P. (eds.)
The Age of Austerity, Hodder & Stoughton, 1963.

Taylor A. J. P.	*English History 1914–1945*, Oxford University Press, 1965.
Titmuss R.	*Problems of Social Policy*, HMSO, 1950.
	Essays on the Welfare State, Allen & Unwin, 1963.
Waugh E.	*Men at Arms*, Chapman & Hall, 1952.
	Officers and Gentlemen, Chapman & Hall, 1955.
	Unconditional Surrender, Chapman & Hall, 1961.
Young K.	*Churchill and Beaverbrook*, Eyre & Spottiswoode, 1966.
Zweig F.	*The Worker in an Affluent Society*, Heinemann, 1961.

CULTURAL STUDIES OF COMMUNICATION

Altick R. D.	*The English Common Reader*, Chicago University, 1957.
Barthes R.	*Elements of Semiology*, Cape, 1967.
Boorstin D.	*The Image*, Weidenfeld & Nicolson, 1962.
Dalziel M.	*Popular Fiction 100 Years Ago*, Cohen & West, 1957.
Ford B. (ed.)	*The Modern Age*, Pelican Guide to English Literature vol. 7, Penguin, 1961.
Hoggart R.	*Contemporary Cultural Studies*, University of Birmingham, 1969.
	Speaking to Each Other, vol. 1 About Society, vol. 2 About Literature, Chatto & Windus, 1970.
Holbrook D.	*The Secret Places*, Methuen, 1964.
Leavis F. R. and Thompson D.	*Culture and Environment*, Chatto & Windus, 1933.
Leavis F. R.	*Education and the University*, Chatto & Windus, 1943.
Leavis Q. D.	*Fiction and the Reading Public*, Chatto & Windus, 1932.
Lowenthal L.	*Literature, Popular Culture and Society*, Prentice-Hall, 1961.
Marcus S.	*The Other Victorians*, Weidenfeld & Nicolson, 1966.
Martin H. C. (ed.)	*Style in Prose Fiction*, University of Columbia Press, 1959.
McLuhan M.	*Understanding Media*, Routledge & Kegan Paul, 1964.

Morin E.   *New Trends in the Study of Mass Communications,* University of Birmingham, 1968.

Rickman H. P.   *Understanding and the Human Studies,* Heinemann, 1967.

Sartre J.-P.   *The Problem of Method,* Methuen, 1963.

Shuttleworth A.   *Two Working Papers in Cultural Studies,* University of Birmingham, 1966.

Thompson D. (ed.)   *Discrimination and Popular Culture,* Pelican, 1964.

Williams R.   *Culture and Society,* Chatto & Windus, 1958.

Wolfe T.   *The Kandy-Kolored Tangerine-Flake Streamlined Baby,* Cape, 1966.

SOCIAL-SCIENTIFIC STUDIES OF COMMUNICATION

Bateson G. and Ruesch J.   *Communication: The Social Matrix of Psychiatry,* Norton & Co., 1968.

Berelson B. and Janowitz M. (eds.)   *Reader in Public Opinion and Communications,* The Free Press, New York City, 1966.

Berelson B.   *Content Analysis in Communications Research,* Free Press, Glencoe, 1952.

Berger P. and Luckmann T.   *The Social Construction of Reality,* Doubleday, 1966.

Blumler J. G. and McQuail D.   *Television in Politics: Its Uses and Influence,* Faber & Faber, 1968.

Cicourel A.   *Method and Measurement in Sociology,* Free Press, Glencoe, 1966.

Dexter L. and White D. (eds.)   *People, Society and Mass Communications,* Free Press, Glencoe, 1964.

Festinger L. and Katz D. (eds.)   *Research Methods in the Behavioural Sciences,* Holt, Reinhart & Winston, 1953.

Halloran J. D.   *Attitude Formation and Change,* University of Leicester, 1967.

Hyman H. and Singer E. (eds.)   *Readings in Reference Group Theory and Research,* Free Press, Glencoe, 1968.

Katz E. and Lazarsfeld P.   *Personal Influence,* Free Press, Glencoe, 1955.

Klapper J. T.   *The Effects of Mass Communication*, Free
                       Press, Glencoe, 1960.
Lindzey G. (ed.)   *Handbook of Social Psychology*, 5 vols., Addi-
                       son-Wesley, 1954.
Pool I. de S. (ed.)   *Trends in Content Analysis*, University of
                       Illinois, 1959.
Rose A. (ed.)   *Human Behaviour and Social Processes*, Rout-
                       ledge & Kegan Paul, 1962.
Rosenberg B. and
  White D. (eds.)   *Mass Culture*, Free Press, Glencoe, 1957.
Schramm W. (ed.)   *The Process and Effects of Mass Communication*,
                       University of Illinois, 1954.
Schutz A.   *Collected Papers*, vol. 2, Nijhoff, 1964.
Stone P. (ed.)   *The General Enquirer*, Massachusetts Inst. of
                       Technology, 1966.

INDEX

Entries in italics denote that the subject is quoted

Beaverbrook—*cont.*
testant ethic, 53, *239*, 245;
Mirror's attitude to, 96–7, 128,
134
Bedford, Duchess of, 209, 212–3,
214
Bedford, Duke of, 207, 210, 211,
214
Beethoven, 84
Belgium, 87, 106
Berelson, Bernard, *14*, 16
Berger, P. (and Luckmann, T.), 19
Bevan, Aneurin, on postwar mood,
25, *60*, *137*; on Tories, *61*;
supports *Mirror*, *65*, 82; and
National Health Service, 144;
treatment in 1955 *Express*, 150–1,
157, 202
Beveridge Report, 33, 112, 139,
142, 145–6
Bevin, Ernest, 26, 27, 33, 43–5, 57,
57, 74
Bible, 108
Birch, A. H. (*et al.*), 160
Birmingham, 54, 169
Blackheath, 133
Blackman, Honor, 182–3
Blakenham, Lord, *173*, 197
Blumler, Jay G. (and McQuail, D.),
201, 202
Bond, James, 182–3, 186
Bonham-Carter, Charles, *69*
Booth, A. H., 29
Bournemouth, 211
Brabourne, Lord, 207
Bracken, Brendan, 27, *28*, 38
Braddon, Russell, *151–2*
Braine, John, *166*
Brentford Football Club, 57
Bristol, 126–7
British Gazette, 30
British Institute of Public Opinion,
26

British Medical Association, 145,
147
Brooke, Henry, 184
Brown, George, 169, 172, 173,
193–5, 228–30
Brown, Sophie, 228
Buckham, Bernard, 99, *111–2*
Buckingham Palace, 229
Buckman, Philip, 102
Bulganin, Marshal, 151
Bute, Marquis of, 209
Butler, D. E. (and King, A.), 168,
179, 181
Butler, Esmond, 212
Butler, R. A., 30, 168, 184, 196
Butterfield, Jill, *170–1*, 191, *202*

Cabell, Branch, *235*
California, 167
Calvin, 239
Campbell, Beth, 211
Campbell, Jock, 190
Cannes, 213
Capri, 214
'Cassandra', 76, 99, 167; on war
effort, *69–70*, *94–5*, *95–6*, *96–7*,
106, 108; on social justice, *84*,
94, 103, *149*, 191; on Labour
Party, *95*; on 1964 election,
192–4, 197; tone of, 85, *93–7*,
101, *106–7*, 132, *154*, *192–4*;
position on *Mirror*, 64, 97–8, 173
Catterick, 100
Cevdet Sunay, President, 229
Challis, William Sidney, 94
Chamberlain, Neville, 33, 64, *94*,
96, 105, 106, 138
Charles, Prince, 156, 212
Chelsea, 213, 218–9, 221, 227
Chislehurst, 214
Christiansen, Arthur, *226–7*, 232,
247; attitude to Churchill, *25*,
52; treatment of 1945 election,